A MINER'S LIFE

John Brophy

An autobiography edited
and supplemented by John O. P. Hall

A
MINER'S
LIFE

JOHN
BROPHY

The University of Wisconsin Press
Madison and Milwaukee, 1964

Published by the University of Wisconsin Press
Madison and Milwaukee
Mailing address: P.O. Box 1379, Madison, Wisconsin 53701
Editorial offices: 430 Sterling Court, Madison

Printed in the United States of America
by American Book–Stratford Press, Inc., New York, New York

Library of Congress Catalog Card Number: 64–17770

II

During the early days of the CIO, when America's mass production workers were creating their own industrial revolution, the United Mine Workers were of invaluable assistance to those of us struggling to build our own unions.

While workers in our country's basic industries provided their own spirit and determination, it was—for the most part—the Mine Worker "porkchopper" who provided the organizational know-how.

These were the men who climbed out of the coal pits to become the missionaries of industrial unionism. Raised in the traditions of organized labor, bloodied and experienced by their own organizing battles, these men were both idealists and skilled tacticians. Unions were their life; the industrial unions of today are their monument.

One of these men was John Brophy. As the CIO's first—and only— full-time director, he was in the forefront of every organizing campaign that made national headlines during the last six years of the 1930's.

It was John Brophy who helped rally striking rubber workers in Akron after they discovered that they could "shut the machines down." It was John Brophy who climbed a barbed-wire fence in Flint to encourage sitdown strikers not to surrender. It was John Brophy who went to New Orleans and Jersey City despite publicized threats that if he addressed scheduled labor rallies, he would never leave either city alive. And, it was John Brophy who helped form the Steel Workers Organizing Committee.

What kind of man was John Brophy? Unlike so many of his fellow miners, he was slender in physical stature, quiet, dignified, and intellectual in nature. Although surrounded by industrial warfare for most of his life, he hated violence and was a stranger to it.

This book tells his story. In it, John traces his union roots back to the last years of the nineteenth century, when his father dug coal in an English industrial town for $2 a day. Describing his childhood environment, he wrote: "Everybody belonged to unions—it was taken for granted as a normal part of life."

From England, John came to the "land of opportunity" and the Pennsylvania coal mines. Instead of prosperity, his family found strikes, blacklists, and privation. Of eleven Brophy children, John was one of five who reached adulthood.

John's early years in America gave him the dedication to the cause of working people that was to last throughout his lifetime. He never forgot his childhood days when his family had difficulty paying $4 a month house rent for a renovated stable. Nor did he forget the bitter—and lost—strikes that destroyed the Knights of Labor in the coal fields and wiped out the miners' union.

Life for the Pennsylvania coal miner at the turn of the century was anything but easy. John's description of company towns with no doctor, no church, and a company-owned store that was always owed more money than the miner earned, serves as a reminder of the great strides our unions have made in the last three decades.

The struggle to build the United Mine Workers—and John Brophy's role in this historic battle—is part of our country's heritage. Only the most callous will fail to understand why the desperate need for organization compelled the miners to look upon unionism with a religious fervor.

The growth of the United Mine Workers, its strikes, its organizing efforts, and its determination to win a measure of human dignity for its members takes up a large part of this book. Through these chapters parade many of the famous names of early American unionism: Mother Jones, John Mitchell, John L. Lewis, Philip Murray, Bill Haywood, Clarence Darrow, and Eugene Debs.

As the UMW grew in stature, so did Brophy. His leadership in the fight for an eight-hour day, his election as a local union official, his winning of the union's District 2 presidency, and his disagreements with Lewis—strong-minded union leaders sometimes differ—are all detailed. So is John's unsuccessful 1926 campaign to become president of the UMW.

By 1933, on the eve of the birth of the CIO, John, again allied with Lewis, was serving as a UMW trouble shooter. Among his other duties, he was preaching industrial unionism to workers who wanted organization but opposed the craft structure advocated by the American Federation of Labor.

An active participant in the arguments between the craft and industrial unionists, he was an eye witness to many of the events that led to the split in American labor.

Following a meeting on November 9, 1935, it was John and Charles Howard, president of the International Typographical Union, who wrote a short press release announcing the formation of a Committee for Industrial Organization. What followed is, of course, history.

No one can adequately write of the excitement and rapid series of amazing successes enjoyed by the CIO in its earliest days. John was everywhere and his book describes the events he witnessed and the public figures he met. His recollections are filled with stories of individual courage, the strategy of industrial warfare, and the stubborn resistance of desperate corporate management.

Reading these pages will bring back memories to everyone involved in those days when democracy was being won in the workplace. For union members, the pages will re-awaken old memories and lead to hours of reminiscence. For those who sympathized, but did not participate in these early struggles, the pages will reaffirm their stand.

As CIO's director, John was one of those responsible for bringing industrial democracy to millions of American workers. He gave sorely needed advice to many of us who now lead the unions he helped to build.

John's service to the labor movement was far from over when the post of CIO director was eliminated in 1939. During the next twenty-two years, he carried out important assignments for the CIO, the government, and the Industrial Union Department, AFL–CIO. Among other tasks, he directed state and city councils when the CIO fought to eliminate Communist influence from within its ranks. Later, he played a key role in the CIO's affiliation with the anti-Communist International Confederation of Free Trade Unions.

From the beginning of 1956 until he officially retired in 1961, John continued to act as an advisor to large and small unions while heading the IUD's community services activities department. But "retirement" did not stop his participation in the labor movement. He was active until he died on February 19, 1963.

Those of us who knew John best loved this man who spent his entire life fighting injustice and working to build a better world for all of its inhabitants. In August, 1961, when the Industrial Union Department honored his departure from full-time service to trade unionism, we said: "John Brophy can never really retire from the American labor movement . . . he has become a symbol of industrial unionism—its dedication of purpose, its moral courage, and its deep convictions."

John died while the AFL–CIO Executive Council was holding its annual winter meeting. A statement issued by the Council pledged that "we shall never forget his kindliness and wisdom. He was a leader, a teacher, and a guide. We shall strive to carry on the work of the labor movement in the spirit of brotherhood that he personified."

Today, John's memory is still with us. Surely, as the labor movement goes forward we must remember our beginnings. We must also remember that dignity, self-respect, and economic justice do not come without struggle and sacrifice.

For almost three-quarters of a century, John Brophy helped lead labor's fight for mankind. This book, reminding us of our past, serves as an inspiration for our future.

Our industrial unions are living testimonials to the men like John Brophy who dedicated their lives to building a better world for working men and women everywhere.

> WALTER P. REUTHER, *President*
> *International Union, United Automobile,*
> *Aerospace and Agricultural Implement*
> *Workers of America, AFL–CIO*

> JAMES B. CAREY, *President*
> *International Union of Electrical, Radio*
> *and Machine Workers, AFL–CIO*

Washington, D.C.
February 10, 1964

CONTENTS

ILLUSTRATIONS

IIIIIIIIIIIIIIIIIIIIIIIIIIIIIIIIIIIIIIIII

xi

INTRODUCTION

Commenting on his first election to the presidency of District 2, United Mine Workers, John Brophy referred to himself (see Chapter 9) as an "habitual rank and filer." Though he intended the term to apply only to that situation, it also describes felicitously one of the most important aspects of his career. He never lost the habit of thinking about the problems of labor and the labor movement from the perspective of the rank-and-file worker. This is a virtue far from common among those who rise to the higher ranks of any movement.

Almost equally unusual was his automatic preference for talking about issues and principles rather than personalities and power struggles. His reluctance to discuss faults and errors of other people at times created difficulties in getting the full story of certain events. A way of circumventing this obstacle was to get the story from other sources, present it to him, and then count on his intellectual honesty to make him accept the distasteful task of passing judgment.

These two characteristics help explain the almost universal respect and affection for John Brophy throughout the labor movement. He never allowed himself to become a "big shot," nor was he diverted from what he liked to call "the larger program" in pursuit of lesser objectives. His strong dislike for John L. Lewis is here expressed in the course of discussions of policy, and the personality clash between the two men is subordinated to what Brophy considered more important matters. He had more opportunity—and occasion—than most to ponder the personality of Lewis; his judgment on that, as on other matters, is in this book.

All this is not to suggest that he was infallible. But he was as nearly selfless as a man could be in his devotion to what he considered the best ideals of trade unionism, to such an extent that concern for the movement crowded out of his mind the personal interests that tend to dominate most men's minds. This trait, in fact, created the primary weakness of the 265,000-word manuscript he wrote before my work with him began. There were entire chapters which did not contain a single use of the pronoun "I." Most of it was detailed history of the United Mine Workers and the CIO, with minimal references to his own role in either. His campaign against Lewis for the presidency of the Miners' Union was dismissed in a thousand words: a restatement of his platform and a summary account of the vote. Details of the conduct of his campaign, sources of his support, and his evidence for the charge that the vote was dishonestly reported I had to learn by questioning him and others, and from documents.

Nevertheless, most of the facts and all the opinions expressed in this book came from John Brophy himself: from his original manuscript, from the transcript of interviews conducted by a representative of the Columbia University Oral History Project, and from over fifty taped interviews and many conversations I had with him. Mrs. Brophy was invaluable in persuading him to talk about personal matters, and in adding her own point of view on some things. From other sources (described in the Note on Sources) I put together my own versions of events he had passed over. Chapters 14, 15, and 16 were constructed in this way, as well as parts of chapters 10, 11, 13, 18, 19, and 20. The first five chapters, on his childhood and youth, are almost exactly as he wrote them, with only minor details added. These chapters demonstrate that he could write well and vividly about his personal history.

He read the entire manuscript in preliminary and final versions, made corrections and suggestions, and approved in its entirety the version offered for publication.

I have retained as much of his phrasing as possible, because of its distinctive personal flavor. But the present version is a synthesis: I have edited and in part rewritten some sections from his manuscript, and have written several parts directly from interviews and other sources. If the account is partisan, it is because I believe he had a right to have his say, and that his views have historical value in themselves.

In the writing of American labor history, so much emphasis has been placed upon institutional history that it is often hard to find out what the movement has meant to its members. Personal history can help correct this imbalance; certainly the story of John Brophy's early years in the mines provides insight into special characteristics of coal mining and the coal miners' union, from which such men as John Mitchell, William B. Wilson, John Brophy, William Green, John L. Lewis, and Philip Murray have emerged to play large roles in the history of their country.

JOHN O. P. HALL

A MINER'S LIFE

1

III

CHILDHOOD IN ENGLAND

My first childhood memories are of an industrial town of 80,000, St. Helens, Lancashire, England, where I was born November 6, 1883. My father was a coal miner, and the men of my mother's family had been miners for several generations. St. Helens had been a coal-mining center since the early eighteenth century. Large numbers of Irishmen worked there, producing the coal that powered English industry.

One of my earliest memories is of my father returning from work, with the black of the mines upon him. My mother prepared his tea, and I listened as they talked about the news of the day and the work in the mysterious world underground. Sometimes my father returned early. The mines were gaseous: if too much gas seeped into a workplace during the night, it was closed off, and there was no work that day. I learned early that miners' work was dangerous. Miners were not allowed to take matches or pipes into the mine. Sometimes the men were frisked as they entered the mine, because men who lived with danger might get careless and forget to be on their guard.

Ordinarily my father left before I was out of bed, but occasionally I woke up and watched his preparations for work. He dressed in his pit clothes and ate his breakfast. My mother wrapped some sandwiches in a clean cloth, which he tucked inside his shirt; a large tin bottle filled with cold tea was slung across his back by a piece of rope. The mines

3

were a mile or two outside the town, so that he had a fair walk to and from work every day.

St. Helens was not a one-industry town: there were large glass and chemical factories and some cotton mills. The Irish had been a major part of the population since the famines of the 1840's. They assimilated easily, partly because English Catholics, with whom the Catholic Irish intermingled, were numerous in St. Helens.

My parents were an example of this intermingling. My grandfather Brophy left Dublin in the 1840's as a young man and settled near Liverpool, where he met my grandmother, Bessie Carroll. She was born in Dundalk, Ireland, but was brought to England as a child. My mother's people, on the other hand, were English Catholics. It was a matter of pride with them that they had maintained the faith despite persecution and the defection of many. Her father, James Dagnall, had been a miner all his life.

The Brophys were not miners until the English generation. Grandfather Brophy had some education, and learned the shoemaking craft in Dublin. He operated a shoemaking shop in Liverpool, with two or three journeymen, making shoes by hand to individual order. His children all went into the pits. Demand for hand-made shoes was declining but the mines were expanding.

There was a tradition in the family that one of my great-grandmothers on my mother's side had worked in the mines in her youth. I have read about the use of women harnessed like mules to pull the mine cars in early Victorian times, but I never heard that she did that kind of work. As the story was told in my hearing, she helped with shoveling, car pushing and such jobs, though she probably did not use the pick. She was a strong, healthy young woman, capable of doing a heavy day's work, and she was proud of her service in the mines. She lived to a great age, perhaps because female labor in the mines was outlawed while she still had her health. Much of her work was probably done in shallow pits, though I remember hearing tales of how she would slide down the rope in the pit when the hoisting engine was not working. Her pride in her youthful labor was part of the lore of the family.

Our home in St. Helens was one of a row of brick houses, built flush with the sidewalk. My grandfather Dagnall took his bride to that house, at 29 Barrow Street, when the row was new, and lived there until he died. Shortly after his death, we moved in. He had rented the house, and so did we, for four shillings a week, which was low for that time and place.

The house had five rooms and a large pantry, also used as a wash-room. There was cold running water in the pantry, and a big sink. In the back was a small paved yard, with a shed where we put our ashes and other refuse. Attached to the shed was a privy—no running water there, of course. Once a week the corporation, as the city government was called, sent big enclosed wagons through the alley, which picked up the tanks from the privies and the ashes and other refuse, so the backyard was clean and presented no problem of sanitation. Three houses shared the yard. Some cousins of ours lived in one of the other houses backing on our yard, so we children spent a lot of time playing out there.

The center of our life in the house was the kitchen, which also served as a living room. It was a large and cheerful room, very clean and tidy. The fireplace, a great square box with an oven on each side, filled most of one wall. The hearth was white-stoned, and the fender was kept polished and shining. The kitchen floor was paved with flags, over which tiles were laid later. The fireplace supplied our heat, and was used for cooking. We burned coal, which my father got free at the mine where he worked, paying only a small charge for hauling it. The fireplaces in the other rooms were rarely used. The house was so solidly and tightly built it was not too hard to keep warm. Besides, the climate was mild, with none of the extremes we found later in Pennsylvania.

The front room was rarely used. The most important thing I recall about it is a large grandfather's clock in one corner. My grandmother Dagnall, who lived with us for some time before we left for America, taught me to tell time by that clock.

When we left for America, my father was making about eight shillings a day (worth two dollars in American money) and working a five-day week. That was a good wage. With only about one-tenth of his pay going for rent and heat, there was plenty to take care of our needs, as long as work was regular. In fact, he was making a better living than we found for some time in America.

My father did better than average, for he was a good workman, and was in a part of the mine where conditions were favorable, so he could get out a good day's run of coal. The company he worked for had no trouble marketing its coal—"had a good contract," as miners say—

so work was regular, except for days lost because of gas in the mine. The English miners had a fairly strong union, to maintain working conditions and safety regulations, though there was still a high rate of accidents in the mines. One of the union's primary concerns was to see that the miner's output was weighed accurately, for he was paid by the ton. The unions were regional, because collective bargaining was conducted on a regional level. It is only in recent years that a national combination of the British miners' unions has finally been established.

The terrifying threat to our security was illness. My father had one long siege of pneumonia, brought on by bad working conditions. His pay stopped, of course, and as my mother nursed him through the long weeks, we got poorer and poorer. Our few belongings began to go into the pawn shop. I remember one bitter winter day when I was sent with our last shilling to buy bread and lost the shilling on the street. I returned home in tears to report the tragedy. My mother broke down and cried with me, exhausted by sleepless nights, worry about my father's slow recovery, and the poverty that was crushing us. The union gave us a small sum, but most of our help came from my grandmother and other relatives, though they had little to spare. It was months before we recovered from the effects of that illness. We could live decently when there was regular work, but we had no real security, nor was there any margin for savings.

My father went into the mines at the age of nine, as was common in those days, with practically no schooling. Though nine was a little young for a miner, there were jobs in which even so small a child could earn a few shillings. His first job was as a trapper, or door tender, opening and closing the doors which controlled ventilation, for the mine cars and for miners going to and from their work. In a few months, he was driving a pit pony, one of the tiny animals used to pull the mine cars. Then, as he advanced in years and strength, he became a drawer, helping load the pit "tubs" or cars and pushing them to a siding where they could be picked up to be hauled to the surface. Eventually he was set to any task not too heavy for his strength; where skill or judgment was required, as in timbering, the miners would supervise the boys.

By the time he was seventeen, he was doing the full work of a miner and being paid accordingly, but a notion of seeing the world and having some adventure led him to enlist in the British Army. After a few months of training in England, he was stationed for a year at posts in Ireland, which gave him his first chance to see the land of his forebears and to confirm his sentimental attachment to it. He was one of the 40,000 men sent by Gladstone to South Africa after the Boer victory at Majuba Hill in 1881. As peace was re-established shortly after the arrival of this force, its duty was confined to occupation. My father spent some time in Cape Town, but most of the year in Natal Colony. From South Africa he was sent with an army of occupation to Egypt, after the bombardment of Alexandria late in 1882. He also served in Malta, Cyprus, and Gibraltar during his six years in the Army. He was relayed home to England to convalesce after a long siege of illness, and there discharged. He learned to read in the Army, but he never learned to write much more than his own name. Back in St. Helens, he settled down, married, and returned to work in the mines.

He was very much interested in trade unionism. I remember many times when he would talk with my mother or with friends about better wages, hours, and working conditions, or the need for better safety regulations and mine inspection, and a check on the weighing of the miner's daily production.

Politically, he was a Gladstone Liberal, as were most of the Irish in England, because of Gladstone's support of home rule for Ireland. My father was much interested in the land question, because of the vicious system of rack-renting landlords in Ireland. This interest carried over to America, where he was attracted to Henry George's single-tax doctrine, though I'm sure he never mastered single-tax economic theory, any more than I did. Still, the social reform aspect of the doctrine appealed to him. He had no urge to go back to the land, but he found the general idea of freedom to live on your own land attractive.

My father also felt there was more hope of getting labor and social legislation from the Liberals than from the Tories. I don't recall any discussion of Socialism at that time. Whatever interest there was in Socialism was confined to groups of intellectuals in the cities, like Hyndman's Social Democratic Federation. British labor's interest in Socialism was a development of the nineties and later, after we had left England, and had no influence on my father's thinking.

All mothers are extraordinary, I've heard, but mine was even more extraordinary than most. She was a woman of the working class, who lived always with the grim necessities of working-class life. Her great concern was the welfare of her family, and devotion to it was her way of life. She accepted the perils and hardships that came to a miner's family, and did the best she could with the situation from day to day. She had the strength to meet all duties and demands of life, and a loyalty to her family that was inspired. She had had very little school-book education, but she had great good sense, and tenacity in holding to what she considered right. Unlike my father, she was very quiet, but she could be as firm as he when she had committed herself to a task or to a principle. She never whimpered or weakened before adversity.

My father was lively, humorous, and articulate. He loved to be with people, to sing, talk, tell stories of his experiences, and discuss issues of the day. Despite his limited formal education, he could read the newspapers with great discretion and judgment. When he read something he disapproved of, he would say, "I wish I could write. I'd tell them what for." That was one of his favorite phrases, "I'd tell them what for."

Naturally, with such a father there was much discussion of public affairs in our home. Father did most of the talking, and mother listened, but did not take much part. In public affairs, as in family relations, to her what we did was right because she counted on us to do the right thing. She might put in a word of caution here and there—not the caution of fear, but a caution to be sure we were right.

My parents were a remarkable combination, complementing each other in many ways. My father was always overflowing with good nature and friendliness. He often brought home acquaintances for a meal and a bed—frequently miners just passing through town looking for work—in the hospitable tradition of an earlier generation. My mother met his requirements as a matter of course, because hospitality was only what people should be able to expect.

When my mother spoke of the right, the meaning was plain, in relation to the life and labor of our family. The right thing was a good relationship to the family, the union, the community. The relation with the union was taken for granted, much like that with the church, because the commitments to both were ethical and social obligations toward other people.

There were three children in my family by the time we left for America. I was nine, the eldest, and there were two younger sisters,

Mary, six, and Beatrice, two. Between them, my parents provided us children with a secure, loving home, built firmly on just and friendly relations with others. The atmosphere of that home has stayed with me all my life.

We never felt any sense of separateness or of being in a minority in St. Helens because of our religion—that was an experience I encountered first in America. Actually, between the Irish immigrants and the native English Catholics—the two groups were very harmoniously integrated within the Church—we were a major element of the city's population. The people of the city came from all parts of the British Isles, but this did not set them apart in groups, because there was so much variety of occupation, religion, and other kinds of association. Even attendance at the parochial schools did not set us apart, because both Catholics and the Church of England had parochial schools, and there was a third system of what Americans might call public schools, attended by children of the "free" churches and the unaffiliated. In all three systems, a little later, the teachers' salaries were paid by the government. The churches built the buildings and supplemented the government allowance from their general funds. Parents did not pay tuition in the church-operated schools. The only government intervention took the form of visits by inspectors to see that the schools conformed to certain academic standards. Occasionally, examiners would come in at the end of the term to test the children.

Our parish church, Holy Cross, was near the school. On Sunday mornings at Mass I saw large numbers of adults I never saw at other times—working men, mostly Irish, who labored in the mills, factories, and pits of the community. I got my first sense of kinship with people as I watched these rough, hardworking people worshipping their God. I was moved by the divine mystery, the stately drama of the Mass, the momentary hush that falls upon a congregation at the moment of consecration. In this church I got my first feeling for the beauty of line and form, light and color. The statues, the paintings, the beauty of ritual, all combined to impress upon my mind an affection for this scene of my childhood which is one of my most persistent memories.

I started school early—I couldn't have been more than four—in the chart class, which we might call the kindergarten. One of the great thrills of my life was the day I first wrote my name, toward the end of the first year. I don't recall that I was an especially brilliant student, but I was once one of two students who received prize books. Mine was a simple story of an adventurous youth who returned to England for Victoria's jubilee from foreign parts, with a parrot. I was more interested in the description of strange lands than in the chatter of the parrot. My classmate's book contained more accounts of foreign lands. I envied him the possession of that book, borrowed it from him, and read it greedily.

There were three or four classes in our large schoolroom. A glass case called the museum stood in one part of the room, containing some minerals and plants, stuffed birds, and other specimens. Whenever I could, I would stand gazing at the exhibits and imagining the strange lands from which they had been brought.

There were both nuns and lay teachers in Holy Cross school. I remember the fresh rosy complexion of Sister Rose, a young Irish nun who had come to England to teach. One of my lay teachers, an English girl named Miss Appleton, had known my father when they were children. My last teacher in that school was a man, I think the only one in the school. I liked the studies and the school, and the wonderful way things were opening up before me. During these years I began to receive instruction in the catechism from the priest, and to gain some understanding of the faith of my parents.

We lived only a square from the town hall, so I saw many political gatherings. I understood very little, except that there were two parties, Liberal and Conservative, and my people were against the masters, represented by the Conservatives. Among the political leaders who came to speak were John Burns, Lloyd George, John Morley, Michael Davitt, a founder of the Irish Land League, and T. P. O'Connor, the Irish Nationalist M.P. from Liverpool. The best thing about the town hall was a public reading room, where I spent hours poring over the pictorial magazines. A large billboard occupied an open space in front of the town hall. Each day on my way to school I delighted in studying the posters advertising plays and operas at the Theatre Royal. I am afraid I was late more than once as a result of dawdling there. I had the equivalent of a third-grade education by the time we left England. I could read the St. Helens paper—called, I think, the *Echo*—and the Liverpool *Weekly Post,* and enjoyed knowing what was going on in the world, even the things I couldn't understand. When Cardinal Newman died, in 1890, one issue of the paper was devoted entirely to his life and work. Cardinal Manning, the other great leader of the

English Catholic Renaissance, died during the year that we left England. My father and the teachers at the school told me about Cardinal Manning's work on behalf of the London dock strikers in 1888. Not until much later did I make the acquaintance of Cardinal Newman's great literary and spiritual gifts.

The young cousins, children of my mother's sister, who lived in our block, were my favorite playmates. A couple of them who were older than I went to work in the "glass house," which was what we called the nearby glass factory. I would carry their lunches to them and seize the opportunity to stay around as long as I was permitted to, watching the exciting work of the factory. I liked the color of the flaming metal and the swift skillful motions of the men, who worked stripped to the waist. They worked the molten glass into a long cylinder, blown out by the glass blowers on the end of a long pipe. When it was worked to the right texture and size, the cylinder was broken off onto a cooling rack, then put into a kiln for tempering. The heating, cooling, and shaping of the glass required a series of operations, all exciting to watch.

I never went into a coal mine in England, but I saw the pitheads from the distance as I walked with my father and listened to his stories about the work underground. There were no open-pit operations there; the pit was a shaft into the earth, and the miners were called "pitmen." My father's tales of working in the hot depths of the mine, dressed only in short drawers, were made more vivid by watching him scrub the coal dust from his body when he returned home.

I often accompanied my grandmother Brophy to the market place, where she had a fruit and vegetable stall—the general greengrocery line, as it was called. She had kept her stall in the market ever since she was a young woman, to help support her family. Even in her old age her earnings were welcome, especially in times of slack work or illness. I enjoyed the color of the piles of fruits and vegetables, and, even more, the flow of people. I would go to buy something for our lunch, usually bread and cheese, from a neighboring stall. Customers joked with my grandmother about her young helper. When I returned home in the evening, I was exhausted but happy, overflowing with gossip and stories.

My father once took me to a Christmas pantomime in Liverpool, a glimpse of an enchanted fairyland. Even more exciting was the annual outing, or "demonstration," of the Lancashire and Chester Miners'

Association, held at Southport, a seaside resort near Liverpool. Thousands of miners gathered on the beach. Each delegation brought a band, and there was much martial music. Between numbers, speakers addressed the crowd around each bandstand on the problems of the union. There were no organized games, as at a comparable American outing, but people bathed in the surf and amused themselves on the sands. When they grew weary of that they would go to the nearby pubs to chat with friends over mugs of ale. Southport was only an hour by train from St. Helens, so whole families went early in the day and stayed until dark, both for a good time and to demonstrate the solidarity of the union.

Everybody belonged to unions—it was taken for granted as a normal part of life. Both for protection on the job and as a social group, the union was a permanent and necessary institution. I heard many discussions of pay scales and percentages, of the checkweighmen and why they were needed. I learned that the union was responsible for the small benefits paid when men were injured. Fortunately, my father suffered only minor injuries, but when he was kept from work long enough to get compensation, those payments were very welcome. Altogether, I got a solid indoctrination in the value of unionism.

Some of my relatives emigrated from England in the early eighties to the coal fields of central Pennsylvania. My mother's brother and my father's sister, who had settled in Philipsburg, Pennsylvania, shortly after their marriage, wrote to us about life in America. My father, as always, was intrigued by distant places, and by the idea of America as a country of growth and opportunity. My mother was more impressed by the fact that the relatives in Philipsburg had bought their own home, and had a cow, two pigs, chickens, and a garden. This sounded to her like a life of greater security and broader satisfactions than we were enjoying. Even more important, she thought America might provide better opportunities for her children.

Sometime in 1888, my father decided to go to America and see for himself what it was like. He went to Philipsburg, in the heart of one of the early bituminous fields, and got work at the Pardee mine. Unfortunately for him, the market for coal was not very good at the time, so throughout his year in Philipsburg work was slack. He managed to get by, but not much more than that. Nevertheless, he found American ways attractive, and came back to England convinced that although things had not gone too well during his first visit, there were opportunities in the New World and he would like to try his fortunes in an expanding country, whatever the risks.

With both parents interested in America, we began preparations to move the entire family across the ocean. My father's troubles in getting good and regular work were overshadowed by his optimism that he could do better in a land where there was room to move. In fact, the thing he talked most about had nothing to do with the question of emigrating. This was the great Johnstown flood in the spring of 1889. My father had gone there with a group of men from Philipsburg, after the flood, to help with rescue and clean-up work. He spent three weeks there, and his often gruesome experiences provided him with many stories to tell in later years. We had read about the disaster in England and were worried until we heard from him. We knew very little about the geography of Pennsylvania, or, for that matter, America, and assumed that since Philipsburg was in the same state, it must, of course, be directly involved in the flood.

It took us two years to make the final decision to emigrate, and to get our plans made. Disposal of our worldly effects was not a great problem. Most of our furniture we left behind with relatives and friends, including the grandfather clock. Another precious possession we had to sacrifice was a large picture of Gladstone's home, Hawarden Castle, which hung on our living-room wall. It was too bulky to take across the ocean, but it was also too precious a symbol of my father's hero to be discarded, or perhaps allowed to fall into the hands of a Tory. My father finally found a sound Liberal friend who could be trusted to cherish the picture as it deserved, and gave it to him.

Though my parents must have thought deeply about the risks involved in the move, for me, a nine-year-old, the prospect was exciting. Relatives and friends dropped in often to question my father about America, and especially about the chances of bettering themselves by going there. He did not paint a fanciful or over-optimistic picture. He said things were not bad over there; there was a good deal of freedom, but the ups and downs were greater. More opportunity meant also greater risks, without the protection of the long-established community of family and friends one would leave behind in England. Though I am sure he was realistic about the perils of the change, I believe it was the prospect of novelty and adventure that impelled him to emigrate. And my mother's insistence helped persuade him.

It was, on the whole, a pleasant life we were leaving behind in

England. As I have said, my father was earning a fair living; it was not poverty or oppression that made us decide to leave. Even in adversity, we had the help and comfort of family and friends to tide us through. Two of my mother's sisters lived on the same street and my father's people were not very far away. And my grandmother Brophy had her stall in the market place nearby. What we hoped for was something a little better than we already had: a home of our own, the chance to improve ourselves, and above all, opportunity for the children. As the poet MacLeish has put it, America was promises for us, though not all the promises were fulfilled.

!!

2

EMIGRATION TO AMERICA

In the early hours of a cold, foggy December morning I was awakened by my mother to take the early train to Liverpool, twelve miles away, where we would board ship. A few relatives came to the station to bid us farewell. We rode in silence to the great city. As we walked through the dark, deserted streets from the station to the dock, father tried to divert us by pointing out the sights—St. George's Hall, where public meetings and music festivals were held, and a statue of Queen Victoria. But the murk was so thick we could hardly see anything, and besides, I was still more than half asleep. Some hot tea at a little restaurant near the docks was comforting. But the docks themselves, with their clatter of trucks and trolleys shifting freight about, the bustle of people, the strangeness of the ships and the tugs hooting in the river, were bewildering to children already confused by too-early rising. As soon as we were assigned to a cabin, we three children were tucked into our berths for a nap, so we slept through the actual departure.

In the afternoon father woke me and took me on deck. We had sailed out of the estuary of the Mersey River and were heading southward through the Irish Sea. He pointed out to me the distant eastern coast of Ireland, shining in the bright winter afternoon, and told me that that was where my Brophy grandparents had come from. I felt the emotions stirred in him by that passing glimpse of our ancestral land. In later years I saw the coast of Ireland under other circumstances, and I once visited Dublin and the nearby countryside, but Ireland in my memory is still that shining coast I saw on a December day in 1892.

Our winter passage across the Atlantic was very rough and took two interminable weeks. Our steamer was old and slow, with far from luxurious accommodations. We had taken a cabin, so we were spared some of the discomforts of steerage—at least we had a stateroom of our own and a little privacy. Though the ship was small, it was clean. There were probably four or five hundred passengers on board. The greatest hardship was the rolling of the ship. I expect that we did better than the average of immigrants coming to this country at that time.

Both mother and children had more than a fair share of seasickness, but toward the last days of the voyage we were able to take some interest in the people and sights around us. We spent Christmas and New Year's Day at sea and derived some comfort from special parties put on for the children on those days. The cabin passengers included a number of people with some talent, who provided informal entertainment from time to time. My father was delighted to take part in all this. He had a fair tenor voice and loved to sing. He had enjoyed the Gilbert and Sullivan and light opera companies that alternated with dramatic troupes at the theatre in St. Helens, and he remembered many songs he had learned during his army service.

As I recall, most of the steerage passengers were non-English-speaking people from central Europe, many of whom, no doubt, had just passed through England on their way to America. Many were Jews, a people I knew very little about.

As we approached America, excitement increased. People talked of their plans and the places to which they were going. I heard strange names of states and cities, and hopeful speculations about how things would be. We were to land at Philadelphia. The suspense was almost unbearable as we sailed between the snow-covered banks of the Delaware River, through fields of floating ice. The sun was shining brightly on the wintry landscape of farms, occasional quiet hamlets, and groves of trees shrouded in snow.

We landed around noon, and got through the immigration formalities and the unloading of our luggage quickly. We didn't have a great deal with us—some clothes, bedding, and things of that sort, and some pieces of English china brought as presents for relatives. All of this was packed into a few boxes.

We walked from the river front to the station through downtown Philadelphia. Everything was spotless from the heavy fall of snow. I remember people shoveling their walks and children playing with their sleds. It was a very vivid and cheerful picture, with a magical charm for me, because I had never seen so much snow on the ground in England. The strangeness of the scene gave me a brief seizure of homesickness, but I took comfort in the knowledge that my parents and sisters were with me.

We had arranged, in England, for our passage all the way to Philipsburg. We waited in the Broad Street Station for an early evening train to Tyrone, 180 miles along the Pennsylvania main line, where we would change to a branch line to Philipsburg, high in the Allegheny Mountains.

We learned, after a while, that we were at the wrong station, so we walked from there to the North Philadelphia station through the snow, carrying some of our things, to meet the immigrant train from New York. When we finally got on the train, we found some of the people who had come over with us. Like us, they had bought lunches in Philadelphia, so we talked with them as we ate. Most of them were going farther west than we were. About midnight, after we had finished our shared supper, the children dropped off to sleep, sitting up in their seats. I doubt that my parents got any sleep at all through that long night journey.

We reached Tyrone early in the morning and waited several hours for the arrival of our American relatives. Part of the time we spent cleaning up in the station washrooms. Around noon, my aunt, who was my father's sister, arrived. There were only two trains a day over the ridges to Philipsburg, so we had still some time to wait. She took us for a walk down the main street of Tyrone, then a small railroad-junction town of about six thousand, and into a restaurant for our first American meal. The numerous side dishes in which vegetables were served were a novelty to us, helping make that a memorable meal, though the state of my appetite also had something to do with it.

Late that afternoon we boarded another train for the last stage of our journey, thirty-five miles over the ridges to Philipsburg. My uncle was at the station to welcome us. We walked about a mile to the Dagnall home, on the outskirts of town. I remember that one sight

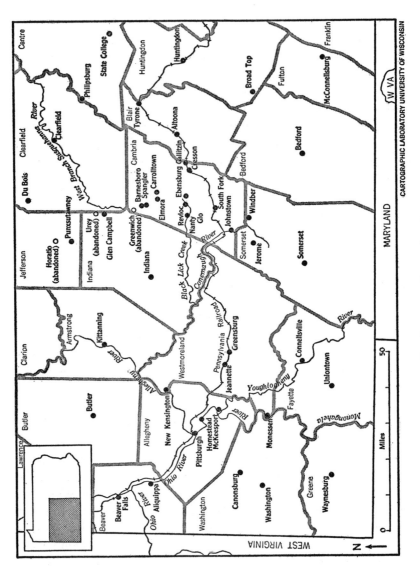

Southwestern Pennsylvania

along the way puzzled me—tombstone-like protuberances which turned out to be stumps of trees, covered with snow. I learned later that Clearfield and Centre counties had once been covered by a heavy growth of timber, mostly pine, which had been logged off before the mines were opened. Philipsburg had had some history before it became a mining town as a lumbering center and market town for neighboring farms. So it was not just an improvised collection of shacks, like many mining camps, but a fairly substantial place.

At my aunt's house we found a family of five children. The seven of them and our five crowded the little five-room frame house badly, yet we lived there until spring. It made for some congestion, but my aunt and uncle were cheerful, kindly people, so we got along.

We soon learned that all was not well in Philipsburg. The panic of the nineties had started. Work was slack and wages were being reduced. After a while, my father got a job in one of the mines, but earnings were low even when he worked, and there were far too many days when he had to loaf. Though my uncle and father clung to the hope of better times, it seemed impossible to get together the few dollars we needed to start housekeeping on our own.

I was sent to the Philipsburg public school with my cousins. My cousin Polly enjoyed showing me off as the newly arrived old-country greenhorn. I believe it was a good school of its kind; Philipsburg was proud of it. I only attended for part of a term, and I can't say that I got much out of it. I fitted in only slowly, and my recollection of my first weeks there is one of misery. Parents had to buy textbooks even in the public schools at that time, and I'm sure this created a problem for my parents.

One of my new experiences in that school was my first encounter with Negroes. They were the children of people who worked in a local tannery. After the first strangeness wore off, I played with some of the colored children who lived nearby and who were in my grade at school. Probably because my parents had no racial prejudice, it didn't occur to me to shut out the Negro children as some of the other white children did.

Of course, I myself was considered something of an oddity by the other children. Things I said, the way I formed some of the letters, little things like that were different. I don't mean that the children deliberately were unkind to me, but they sometimes teased me, which emphasized my feeling of strangeness. I was probably fortunate in the fact that the largest immigrant group in the town was British. A Lancashire miner named Barnes had become a mine operator, and had encouraged some Lancashiremen to settle there in the eighties. Slavic and other non-English-speaking immigrants were beginning to come in, but they settled out of town, for the most part, in neighboring mine patches. Besides the aunt and uncle we stayed with, there was a brother of my mother's living in Philipsburg, so we were well provided with connections to help us adjust. By the time I left the Philipsburg school, I was fairly well acclimated to the new country.

An English paper, the Liverpool *Weekly Post*, came for a year, keeping us in touch with the homeland. And some people who had come earlier from our part of England called on us, from time to time, to talk about the old country and its news. The British immigrant, with the advantages of a common language and a similar cultural and political background, usually fitted more easily than others into American life. Nevertheless, our poverty and suffering made adjustment to and acceptance of life in America slow.

Besides the shortage of jobs in general, my father suffered from being a new arrival, so that he had to take the poorest of what jobs there were. He would have to go to work in what was known as a "top drift," the miners' term for an opening into the poorer strata of a coal seam, where it was difficult to get out enough coal for a decent day's pay even with the hardest work. Our relatives were up against it, too, because they had barely enough to eat. The Dagnalls' cow had died, the pigs were eaten up, and only a few of the chickens were left. My uncle was a skillful gardener, who got the maximum return out of his small garden. There was, of course, no provision for public welfare aid or other help to the unemployed, and we were neither eligible for, nor receptive to, charity, as long as we could piece out an existence by occasional work and much penny-pinching.

After several months we finally found a place we could move into, a renovated stable in an alley about two blocks from my aunt's home. We got together essential furniture, some given to us and some bought out of our remaining savings—a couple of beds, a table, a few old chairs, and a small, battered coal stove. Fortunately, it was summer by then, so we did not have to worry about heating the place, and we got out by fall. Winter in that rickety old shack would have been unbearable. The rent of $4 per month was considered nominal, but that was about what we had paid for much better quarters in St.

Helens, and with work so poor we had trouble paying even that small sum. Instead of the improvement in conditions we had hoped for, the panic deepened; idleness became chronic and continued so for two years. How we kept body and soul together, I still do not understand. At times, my mother helped by doing washings and charwork in homes or offices of those who were better off than we. And in the midst of this dreadful poverty came a new baby, who lived only a few hours. I can still see the tiny white box that contained my baby sister on my father's knee as he and another man drove in a buggy to the Catholic graveyard in Osceola.

In the fall of 1894 we moved just outside the corporate limits of the town into Cold Stream Township. There I attended a one-room school with six grades under a single teacher, for a full term. The children were graded by the reader they were using. I was in the third reader, but I think I spent as much time following the recitations of the classes above me as I did on my own work. I took every chance that offered to pore over the other readers. We were too poor to own any books of our own, so those school books were my only reading matter at that time, and I would say they were pretty good. They contained some poetry, simple stories, usually illustrating a moral, and some history and description of this country. The latter I found especially interesting; my curiosity about America was boundless.

I remember two of my fellow pupils in the Philipsburg school. One was a girl who sat across from me, whose father ran a store. She often brought to school candy and cookies, which she shared with me and other children. I was very shy; perhaps that is why I was often a beneficiary of her kindness. I never saw her again after I left that school, but I have never forgotten her.

The other was a boy near my age, Bill Welsh. He had the same background as I: his people were Irish, and had come from England a few years before we did. He was active, full of fun, and a born leader. He took me under his wing and guarded me from other young-sters who might tend to pick on the little greenhorn. Though our families were separated for several years, he and I got together from time to time. About eighteen years later, he married my eldest sister, Mary. In our young manhood, we worked together very closely in the miners' union.

I probably learned as much, if not more, about America sitting out under the apple tree in my uncle's garden as I did in school. In the warm weather, people would gather there to talk about the old country and the new, and I was always there, taking in everything that was said. People would talk about conditions of work in the mines of central Pennsylvania. Talk of hard times and grievances led to discussion of the need for a union. These British miners had had a good union at home, and they saw the need for one in Pennsylvania, too. The Knights of Labor had had some following, but were declining. Local Assemblies of the miners in the Knights of Labor had been brought together into District Assembly 135, the nearest thing to a national union allowed by the structure of the Knights, and I heard many discussions of its ideals and purposes. The national leadership stressed co-operation and education—self-improvement, you might call it—as the solution to the workers' problem, and discouraged strikes and even boycotts against unfair employers. The high point of the movement had been reached in 1886, before our arrival in America, and I heard many discussions of the bomb explosion at Haymarket Square in Chicago in that year, which was blamed on the Knights and contributed to their downfall. Closer to us, in time and distance, was the Homestead steel strike of 1892. These tales of violence made it clear even to me that it would take more than talk to win decent conditions from the employers.

Uncle Charles, my mother's brother, was a member of the union's mine committee. Among other things, he had the responsibility of going to the company office in town on paydays to collect from the miners their contributions toward maintenance of a checkweighman.

In January, 1890, District 135 of the Knights of Labor and the National Progressive Union of Miners and Mine Laborers merged into the United Mine Workers of America, but the merger was largely on paper. The Pennsylvania locals kept alive their interest in the Knights of Labor. At best, the new union was not very strong, and the depression of the early nineties did it no good. All through 1892 and 1893, prices were falling, wages being cut, and miners being thrown out of work altogether, or kept on at part-time work only. Public appeals for help for the miners met with no response in the capitals of the mining states. The leaders of the union decided to follow the strategy used by the English miners a few years before—to call a suspension of work until the glut of coal on the market was eliminated, and then try to restore the wage rates prevailing in May, 1893. On April 1, 1894, the suspension began. Although the national union had barely 13,000 dues-paying members and less than $3,000 in the treasury at the time, 125,-000 miners in eight states answered the call. Eight weeks after the strike began, the union claimed that strikers numbered 180,000, but the effort failed to achieve its purpose. Prolonged depression, with coal consumption at a minimum, had created a terribly glutted market to begin with. And the stoppage had not had the desired effect in reducing surpluses, because of increased activity in the anthracite fields untouched by the strike, and in unorganized Virginia, Maryland, and West Virginia. By the end of July, the strike was lost. In most districts, including central Pennsylvania, the union disappeared completely.

Both my father and my uncle were active in the strike. They picketed mines which tried to operate with scabs. Most of the latter were native Americans from the back country, known as "buckwheaters," because their little patches of land would grow buckwheat, but not much else. A few recent immigrants from central Europe were brought in as strikebreakers. To help maintain morale, the miners would parade to other towns and hold mass meetings. There was no money for relief, of course, but the miners helped each other out as much as they could, which was not much, and some storekeepers donated flour and other food. In spite of efforts to divide the miners along lines of national origin, they held together very well.

During the strike, the press used the argument that the strike was a foreign conspiracy, because many leaders of the union were British immigrants. This gave the superpatriots a chance to fight the Revolutionary War all over again and drive the agents of British imperialism away from our shores. It is strange how often this kind of "patriotism" has been used successfully against just such agents of foreign imperialism as my father and uncle.

I understood much of what was going on, though of course with the partisanship of a child I made the problem simpler than it actually was. The name of John McBride, president of the UMW, became familiar, and I first heard of William B. Wilson of Tioga County, then a young man and an active leader of the Knights of Labor.

Wilson came to Philipsburg during the strike of 1894. He had no expense account, nor even a salary to pay his way as he bummed around the district. Miners took him into their homes overnight and shared what food they had with him. I remember some of the men saying he looked as though he had slept in his clothes, and he may very well have done that if nightfall caught him out on the road. The

Philipsburg miners took up a collection to buy him a pair of shoes because his soles were worn completely through—he was literally "on his uppers." Billy Wilson's later career was founded on years of self-sacrificing service to the miners. He had come to this country as a youngster from Scotland, so he had never worked in the old-country mines. Nevertheless, his ideas of unionism were of the British kind, learned from older British miners, especially some of the Scots who boasted of having sat at the feet of the great Sandy MacDonald. He made a successful mixture, in his own thinking, of the practical trade unionism and the idealism of the Knights of Labor. His speaking was not impassioned; he had a studied, orderly manner of presenting an argument which made his point always clear and impressive. He had no need of spread-eagle forensics to impress his audiences; they knew him and they understood what he was driving at, so he could be effective without putting on a show. On the other hand, he could put on a show of a kind: I remember at some of the district conventions in later years how he would take over the platform during a lull to recite from Scottish poets, mostly Bobby Burns, or to tell some story of the struggles of other years. Some years later (1899) he became president of District 2 of the UMW, and the following year he was appointed secretary-treasurer of the national union. He later served two terms in Congress and was the first Secretary of Labor, in the cabinet of President Woodrow Wilson. When he was in Philipsburg in 1894, his reports on the progress of the strike were quoted in my hearing until I came to feel that I knew him, though I never saw him until years later when, as a working miner, I attended a District 2 convention.

During the summer, I heard of other events marking that year of discontent: Coxey's march to Washington, dramatizing unemployment and hunger, and the Pullman strike with its injunction (I didn't know what an injunction was, but I knew it was a sinister and terrible thing) and use of troops against the workers. I first heard the name of Eugene V. Debs, the leader of the railroad workers. All these events were vividly real to me, both terrifying and challenging, as I heard my father and his friends discuss them.

Our lot was hard enough during the strike, though we had the consolation that we were suffering to improve things for the miners. But with the end of the strike, something close to despair descended upon us. Both my uncle and my father were blacklisted and denied work at their old places in the Pardee mine. This blow was made more crushing by the fact that after the strike the mine secured a railroad order and worked steadily for a couple of years, while slack work continued at other mines in the area. When my father finally did get a job, it was in a small mine operating in top veins where the coal was low and hard to get out. As the market fluctuated, such mines were the last to start up and the first to shut down.

Most of the decade of the nineties was a period of crisis and discontent. Conditions were only somewhat worse for the miners than for other workers and for the farmers. In addition to talk about trade unionism, there was much talk about Populism. This movement and its predecessor, the Greenback Party, had greatest appeal to farmers, who hoped that inflation would raise the prices of their products, but as a radical criticism of the way things were, Populism—especially in its agitation for unemployment relief, public works, and government ownership of certain key industries—had some appeal to wage workers, particularly to miners not far removed from the farms.

But political solutions were at best rather distant and visionary compared to problems—better jobs, higher pay, and elimination of unemployment—that could be dealt with by a union. Although a variety of reform ideas circulated, my father and his friends always returned to the fundamental need for a union to protect the worker on his job.

I had two experiences with the mines in Philipsburg. After the strike, my father took me with him into the Pardee mine, when he went to get his tools. This was only a brief visit, but a little later I spent a whole day with him and my uncle in the smaller mine where they found very unsatisfactory jobs. They were working in a "back heading" —a corridor paralleling the main course of the mine, intended to improve ventilation. The heading was wet, and under the arrangement they had made, my father would get to work at about five o'clock in the morning to bail out accumulated water, which he had to carry about one hundred feet in empty powder cans to a place where it would drain away. By the regular starting time, he could get the workplace dry enough so that they could clear up loose coal left over from the previous day's run. The two men soon got fed up and decided to quit. They took me along for their last day in that mine. I was eleven years old. I was fascinated by the strange darkness, broken by the flickering mine lamps, and by the work. Each time the mule which drew the mine car arrived, he caused a stir. Other miners talked to my father and uncle about their decision to quit. I got much attention from the men, including some good-natured joking. After a while, I fell asleep by the side of the workplace, and was covered by my father's and uncle's coats. I was glad when the work ended and we gathered our tools together to walk out to daylight. I had enjoyed the privilege of going along with my father to his work, but it was good to be released from the mine to the outside world again.

The impossibility of earning even a bare living drove my father to hunt beyond the mining region, in the fall of 1894, for a job. He headed for Pittsburgh, walking and bumming his way. He called on friends in glass-factory and mill towns. They could give him a meal or a place for the night, but no help in finding a job. Many were as hard pressed as he to find work. He canvassed the Westmoreland County coal fields, without success. His days of absence mounted up; for my mother, each day was an eternity of anguish.

I remember the quiet urgency in her voice when, one day, she sent me from our home, empty of food, fuel, and comfort, to get my aunt who lived a mile away. I ran that mile with terror driving at my heels lest I should fail to bring help to my mother before the crisis arrived. My aunt arrived in time, and in the midst of poverty and loneliness my brother Charles was born. When the crisis had been lived through with the help of almost equally destitute relatives and friends, the relief from strain was wonderful. Even more wonderful was the return of my father a few days later, though he brought no good news. He had walked and bummed from Pittsburgh in the bitter November cold. He had ridden freights in a blizzard. One night, the only place he could find to sleep in was an empty coke oven on a mountain top near Gallitzin. It was hard to rejoice as one should in the birth of a son, when there was no way of telling whether it would be possible to feed him.

Shortly afterward, we moved from Philipsburg. Though we lived for years within fifty miles of the town, my parents never saw it again. Life there had been too cold, hard, and bitter for them ever to want to see the place.

!!!

3

UREY, A COAL CAMP

We finally made our escape from Philipsburg with the help of the owner of a local hotel, Mr. Passmore. He was part owner of a small mine in Urey, Indiana County. My father went to talk to him about moving there, and got both the promise of a job and an advance of $5 for train fare.

He went to Urey in July, 1895, and "batched" with two other miners in a shanty until he had earned enough money to send for the family. For several months, life was comparatively easy for us, as steady work continued. With the help of better food and some long-overdue shoes and clothing, our family life was more cheerful than it had been since we left England. This is not to say that we had a bed of roses; my father's work was hard and his hours long, but at least he was making a living for us, and what pay there was came regularly.

Urey was a tiny hamlet. The mine never employed more than 70 or 80 men at most, often dropping to 25 or 30. There was nothing in town but the mine. When the mine was opened, around 1890, the company had had twenty or so frame houses put up by the lumber company that had logged the area. A few were doubles, with four or five rooms on a side, but some were singles, of different sizes. They were frame boxes, set on wooden foundation posts, with no porches, no running water, and no plaster. The walls were covered with wooden siding inside and out, sometimes lined on the inside with a thinner

27

finishing board. This did not provide such good insulation against cold as plaster, but it could have been worse, and in some mine camps it was worse. Rent for these shacks was four or five dollars a month, deducted from the pay along with the bill at the company store. The rent was low, but it gave the company a more than fair return on what little investment it had made.

Fortunately, coal was cheap, so we could keep warm. We got coal from the company for fifty cents a load, which supposedly covered only the cost of hauling it. Even cheaper was the coal the kids could pick out of the slate dump near the tipple. They would knock bits of coal loose from the slate, and bring it home in bags.

Our first house in Urey was a two-room shack, but as work slacked off some of the miners left and we were able to get a four-room house. Each house had an outdoor privy and coal shed behind it. Water was drawn from wells by a bucket on a windlass. Three to six houses shared the use of each well. We had a cookstove in the kitchen and a small stove for heat in the front room. The two rooms upstairs where we slept were unheated, lacking even registers to let warm air up from below. We didn't consider that a hardship, however, and I doubt that my parents would have thought it worth the cost to heat the whole house.

We used kerosene lamps for light, though they got relatively little use, except in the winter. The rule was early to bed and early to rise. Work began in the mines no later than seven o'clock in the morning, and sometimes earlier. If the men were to get a night's sleep, they had to get to bed soon after supper. The house was furnished with the few castoffs we brought from Philipsburg, to which we added very little for years. Besides the stoves, we had beds, a table, a cupboard, and some chairs. That was enough to get by with, and just about as much as we could afford.

The only public building was the company store, which also housed the post office and the only telephone in town. Although Urey lay at the end of a short railroad spur, running three or four miles from Glen Campbell, only freight came in and coal went out on those tracks. There was no passenger service at any time. Even the mail was brought in over the hills on horseback. The small pouch that arrived daily contained little but company mail.

The store stocked all the supplies available to the miners—food, dry goods, clothing, shoes, tools and other hardware, patent medicines, and a little candy for the children. The nearest doctor lived in Glen Campbell, a town of about five hundred people. Only difficult cases of childbirth or the approach of death brought him to Urey. People treated their ills with home remedies or patent medicines. We had no church, and even the school was a mile and a half away.

This was a one-room country school, supported by the county, with one teacher to cope with all the grades. It was not much of a school, and was open only for a very short term. I attended it for four or five weeks, but learned little or nothing. The children walked to school in a group, carrying their lunches. The best thing about the school was that it gave me an introduction to the other children.

Though there was no church for miles, from time to time some of the farmers nearby conducted a Sunday School for adults in the schoolhouse. It was the only public building around, so they just used it when it was idle on weekends—no need to ask permission or worry about separation of church and state. These farmers were Protestant Ulstermen, for the most part. Another boy and I were surprised to find, as we wandered around one autumn afternoon, that the schoolhouse was open, and we peeked in to see what was going on. Somebody invited us to come in, and we soon found ourselves in the Protestant Sunday School. I got considerable attention from the adults, as I drew on the catechism I had learned in England to keep up with the discussion. I was flattered by this interest, but never returned, in spite of hospitable invitations to do so. One reason for not returning was, of course, the religious difference, but another was the fact that the miners and farmers did not mingle. The Sunday School was a farmers' meeting; miners of all faiths left it alone. The two groups were separated by their work, but also by the fact that some of the miners came from non-English-speaking countries, and the difference of language and manners made them strange and unacceptable to the farmers. About thirty Slav miners lived in Urey at this time, crowded into a half-dozen houses. Most of them were unmarried, or had not brought their families with them. Few spoke English, and with rare exceptions they kept to themselves. Most of the other miners were English, Welsh, and Scotch. A very few native Americans had come in from the farm patches nearby.

In spite of differences of language, nationality, and religion, there was a good degree of mutual acceptance among the miners. We were so few and so bound together by the mine, that we got to know each other well and more or less had to get along. Ours was one of only two Catholic families in the town; the others were Protestant or Orthodox. But nobody paid much attention to differences of religion. There was no church to go to, anyway.

I learned far more from my highly miscellaneous reading than I did from the schools I attended in the mining towns. I cherished anything readable that came along. One of the greatest events of my childhood was the acquisition of a quantity of boys' magazines—three or four years of one called *The Golden Days,* and a couple of years of *Youth's Companion.* In one of the homes where my mother worked in Philipsburg, there was a boy a few years older than I, whose magazines were stacked in a pile in the cellar. My mother once remarked to the lady she was working for that she had a boy who was interested in reading. The magazines were doing nobody any good, so the lady said we could have them for carting them away. I borrowed a child's wagon, loaded it full, and dragged the treasure trove home with me.

I reveled in those magazines for a year or more. They were a source of pleasure through the bitter months, revealing in their articles and stories some of the wonder and excitement of America not visible in the mining camps. I read about New England, the South, the Far West—above all, the Far West—and learned about the opening up of the country by explorers and adventurers, and about the great men who had created the nation. Some of the most wonderful stories were about the Chicago World's Fair of 1893 and its marvelous exhibits.

Our little village of Urey was bereft of books. I never saw any in the neighbors' houses. However, a windfall came to me in an unexpected way. The storekeeper had a couple of books, shipped in by mistake, no doubt, which had been lying forgotten on a shelf gathering dust for a long time. One day he came across them and said to my father, who happened to be present, "Why don't you take these books for your boy Johnnie? He likes to read." My father looked them over, agreed to pay the nominal sum the storekeeper asked, and brought them home. One was the autobiography of Buffalo Bill, and the other a pictorial history of the Civil War. Buffalo Bill gave me a thrilling view of the West, and the other book gave me my first real introduction to the history of this country. I read both books to rags. One day a peddler drifted by and sold Father a book called *A Compendium of Useful Knowledge,* which was turned over to me. It was not exciting reading; actually, it was intended as a grab-bag reference book for farmers, but it did contain much information, useful and not, and I read it avidly.

Nobody in Urey got a regular daily newspaper, but on occasion a salesman passing through town would leave a Pittsburgh or Philadelphia paper behind, which would be picked up and read, sometimes going the rounds of several families before being discarded. The most widely read journal was a weekly called the *Pennsylvania Grit.* I understand a descendant of that paper is still published for small-town readers. It carried summaries of national and international news and features of a superficial nature. Novels were serialized in it over a period of half a dozen weeks. Its most popular feature, however, was local news from as many as thirty or forty towns. Miners moved frequently in search of work and they enjoyed reading about the events in towns where they had once lived. A correspondent who knew the mining region of central Pennsylvania well wrote a regular column for the *Grit,* with mining and labor news, and occasionally a letter from a miner about some problem of the industry. The miners found his comments extremely interesting, even though they might disagree with some of his rather conservative opinions.

A neighbor named Armstrong received a weekly called the *Irish World,* printed in Boston and devoted to advocacy of Irish nationalism. It had many articles about the troubles and injustices suffered by Ireland and the history of her struggle for freedom. My father fell heir to some copies of it which he liked to have me read aloud to him. After we left Philipsburg, we dropped the Liverpool *Weekly Post,* losing touch with our English home.

This reading provided me with the essentials of my education, much more than the few weeks of dreary study in school. I got my view of America from Buffalo Bill and the boys' magazines; a broader perspective of the coal-mining industry from the *Grit;* and impressions of England, Ireland, and the world from the Liverpool paper, the *Irish World,* and occasional copies of American dailies. It was not a systematic or well-balanced course of study, but I learned a lot, nevertheless.

We children did not play organized games, like baseball or football, perhaps because we couldn't afford the equipment. We played tag and similar games, or spent our time wandering in the woods nearby. In the fall, we collected chestnuts. The men and older boys went hunting for rabbits or other game, and we younger ones would pretend that we were hunting too. The streets were unpaved, so in wet weather it was muddy and in dry it was dusty. Usually we had to walk in the grass along the edges. Most families had small gardens with vegetables and a few flowers, but there was no effort to maintain lawns. The mine was far enough from the houses so that the coal dust did not drift down to them, making it a fairly clean town for children's play. There were no distinctions among the children; even those whose parents spoke foreign languages learned English quickly, and the town was so small that we all knew each other.

The people of the town had to provide their own amusements, and these were few and limited, because the men had little energy to spare after the long hours in the mine. In the winter, when the mine was working, after the men had had their supper and washed up, some of them would walk over to the company store and sit on the floor with their backs against the counter, at a reasonable distance from the pot-bellied stove. There they discussed the day's work, news of the town, or any news that had filtered in from the outside world. Boys who had graduated to working in the mines, as I did in Urey, were privileged to sit in and listen.

When the weather was good, in the summertime, the discussions moved outdoors. Across the road from the store were several shade trees, one of which had been cut down and lay beside the road. "The log," as it was called, was worn smooth by the breeches of the miners who sat there for hours talking and resting from their labors. It was the nearest thing to a community center in town. It was a pleasant, relaxed setting, and talk was easy and casual. Men told stories, usually of experiences in the mines, here and in other countries. I heard many of these tales also in the mines, when the turn of the cars was slow or for some other reason the men could take a few minutes to chat with those in the next workplace. This was the special lore of the mines, in which great mine disasters of the past were prominent. Older miners told of the Hartley Colliery accident of 1862, in Newcastle, England, a horrifying tale. The pumping engine of this mine was set midway of the shaft. The beam supporting it broke and fell, filling the pit with debris and cutting off the air through the only entrance to the mine. About two hundred men were entombed, and in spite of heroic efforts to reach them, almost all were found dead, poisoned by the foul air. This horror roused public opinion to the need for more than one shaft to a mine, which Parliament later made compulsory.

A similar disaster still fresh in the memory of the miners of Urey was that at Avondale in the anthracite district of Pennsylvania, in 1869. There, the shaft caught fire from a furnace used to ventilate the single entrance and 109 men were suffocated underground. As in England, this brought belated legislation to require two entrances to a mine. Mine explosions and other accidents were—and still are—too frequent, often caused by shortsighted indifference to the safety of men underground, until some spectacular event rouses public interest. The slow development of mine regulation has been built on the sufferings of the miners and their families.*

My father was one of the liveliest conversationalists in these community talkfests. Not only had he traveled in foreign lands, which he loved to describe, but he had also developed opinions on a variety of subjects from his experiences and from his reading, for though he was never a rapid reader, he never forgot what he had read or heard read by others.

It was around the log in Urey that I heard him tell about his eldest brother, John, who was killed in a mine at the age of twenty-two. He and another brother, Tom, had secured jobs in a new pit. A few men were working around the bottom of the pit, preparing the shaft for installation of the hoisting cage. They traveled up and down the shaft in a large bucket suspended at the end of a rope. The two brothers had dulled their picks and were finished for the day at about noon. Each put a foot in the bucket, grasped the rope, and rang a bell as a signal to the engineer to pull them up. He began to hoist the bucket too rapidly, then suddenly stopped, which set the bucket swinging dangerously to and fro. Before the two men could steady the swinging bucket, the engineer began to hoist again, and the bucket caught

* I heard many tales from British miners, in my youth, about Sandy MacDonald. He was president of the Miners' National Association of Great Britain, and a legendary figure in the coal towns of America, as well as in his own country. He entered the mines of Lanarkshire as a child of eight, and in spite of the hard labor of his childhood, managed to educate himself, even putting himself through the University of Glasgow. During the 1850's and 1860's he emerged as the most important leader of the Scottish miners. He made several visits to America between 1867 and 1873, to carry the gospel of unionism to immigrants from Britain, campaigning in all the coal fields from Pennsylvania to Illinois. MacDonald was a colorful and stimulating orator, who made an unforgettable impression on his hearers. He was elected on the Liberal ticket to Parliament in 1874, one of the two first "labor" Liberals. In Parliament, he led the fight for employers' liability and mine safety legislation, for limitations on the hours of labor, and for the right of miners to have checkweighmen. Cf. C. K. Yearley, Jr., *Britons in American Labor* (Johns Hopkins Studies in Historical and Political Science, LXXV, no. 1. Baltimore, 1957), pp. 126–129, 133, 134, 136; R. Page Arnot, *The Miners* (London: Allen and Unwin, 1949), pp. 50, 55, 123–125, 274.

under a piece of timber on the side of the shaft and tipped over. John was thrown to the bottom. Tom managed to cling to the rope until he was pulled safely to the top of the pit. Crazed with grief, he ran to the engine house to take revenge on the engineer for the carelessness that had killed his brother, but the engineer, realizing what had happened, had fled.

Father also told how my mother's father, at the age of sixty, had collapsed at the pithead one morning, his picks falling from under his arm to the ground. He had labored for fifty years in the pits; his bones had been broken and his body crushed by falling rock and coal; he had breathed the foul air and gas of the mines; he was worn out. And the tale of my great-grandmother who had worked in the English mines three-quarters of a century before was also told.

Not all of the talk was of this somber character. There were many jokes and yarns, and much teasing and joking about local events and people. When the miners were feeling particularly good, which was not too often, they would sing, with my father taking the lead. The pit boss at this particular mine would often join the group and take part in the talk or in card games. The favorite game of the miners was Seven-Up, though they did not gamble on it to any great extent.

Especially when the work became slack the whole community drew close together. The boss was not so different from the rest of us; slack times were almost as hard on him as on the miners. And we were all the same breed of cats; we shared the burdens of the mine.

Though Indiana County was dry by action of the county judge, who refused to grant licenses to sell beer or liquor, some of the younger men managed to get stuff to drink. The two drugstores in the county, one in the town of Indiana and the other in Glen Campbell, sold raw alcohol surreptitiously, which the gay young blades mixed with equal parts of water. Also, the company store stocked patent medicines which contained a lot of alcohol. The popular brands were "Beef, Iron, and Wine" and "Wild Cherry Tonic." Nobody bothered about the taste, as long as the kick was there, which it certainly was. Older men usually abstained from these desperate measures, perhaps because they could not spare the money as readily as the youngsters. An occasional individual brewed his own beer, but this was definitely a luxury. There was no place to have a wild time except in somebody's home or outdoors. And since nobody could afford to give an alcoholic party, the young men had to howl off their wild spirits in the open air.

There was no need for either law or exhortation to keep us from squandering our time and money in riotous living. We never had enough of either to spare. The miners were given a statement twice a month, listing tonnage credited and pay due. From this total the company deducted the rent and the amount charged to each man's account at the company store. If there was any balance in the miner's favor, he got it in cash. It was much more common, however, for a balance to be due the company, in which case there would be a long black stroke at the foot of the statement, which the miners called a "snake": "What did you get this payday?" "Nothing but a snake!" If an adverse balance was carried over for too many weeks, you might be warned by the storekeeper to cut down on your purchases. But usually you were allowed the credit unless your scale of living was too far out of line with your earnings.

Prices at the company stores were much higher than in private stores. There was no other store in Urey, so we had no choice about where to buy, even if we had had any cash to spend. The company guarded its monopoly carefully, and if a miner got caught bringing in things he had bought out of town, he might get fired.

If a miner had to buy furniture or any other item too expensive to be covered by a single pay, he could arrange to have the cost deducted in installments. There was no credit charge for this; or, to be more accurate, the charge was concealed in the original price. In the depression years of the nineties, the miners believed that even if the company wasn't making money out of the mine, it was still doing all right from the company store. Everything the miners earned went right back to the company again, so it was hard to see how the company could fail to make money. Chances of saving were worse than slim; the miners lived from payday to payday, barely earning their keep and dreading the onset of slack work or of illness, either of which meant destitution.

The steady work that prevailed at Urey when we first went there ran out after a few months. The company lost its good contract and was reduced to dependence on spot sales here and there. For the miners, this meant a reduction to only one or two days of work a week. First the single men, who were more footloose, left to find better jobs. Then some of the men with families heard of prospects elsewhere and went to take advantage of them. Before long, there were very few families left, but even these could not get enough work to make ends meet, and winter was near.

I was to be twelve years old on November 6 of that year. Twelve was the legal age for working in a mine in 1895, so it was decided that I would have to enter the mine with my father, to help increase the family income. Father talked to the mine boss, who asked my age and was told I would reach the minimum age on the sixth.

He said, "Well, take him in along with you on the first of the month. It will be all right." So, on the eve of my twelfth birthday, I entered upon a man's job as a coal miner. I was childishly excited by the prospect, and pleased that I could do something to help the family through hard times.

The boss, a good-hearted man, gave me a new mine cap and an oil lamp. I got a dinner bucket with a short enough handle so it wouldn't trail on the ground, a small shovel which had been worn thin by the trackmen, a small pick, my first long pants, and I was equipped to go to work. I was small even for my age—I couldn't have weighed over seventy-five pounds—so for a while I was the subject of good-natured teasing by other miners.

Undercutting the face of the coal was done by hand with a pick; no machines or electricity at that mine in those days. My father had to do the harder and more skilled part of the work, while I tried to be useful at shoveling and the lighter parts of the job. Miners usually worked in pairs—referred to as "butties"—so I was officially rated for a full share of our output, though I could not do half the work.

As I walked into the mine with my father on my first day, I was reminded of a boy named Lindsay, a year or two older than I, who had been killed in the mine a few months before. He had tended the first trap door, about three hundred yards from the entrance to the mine. His job was to open the door to let the mine trips—mules pulling a train of cars—through, and to see that the door was closed behind them, because the door had an effect on the ventilation of the mine. When the last trip of the day was coming out, he decided to ride the front car out to the entrance. He jumped for the bumper of the front car, but his hand slipped on the edge of the car. He fell in front of the loaded car and was crushed to death beneath the wheels. I had known and liked the boy, and I never went through that door without a twinge of regret for his death, and a touch of fear.

My father led the way, each of us carrying flickering oil lamps that emphasized the shadows. He explained that the scurrying sounds we heard were made by mice in the gob, the edge on either side of the track where waste was thrown. Mice and rats came into the mine to live on oats spilled by the mine mules and on other refuse. They would rush to hide in the gob whenever people came through the mine tunnels. Though I had no fear of the mice, it gave me a strange feeling to think of the invisible eyes watching me.

There were two entrances to the mine. The main entry, from which work places were opened off, was paralleled by another for purposes of ventilation. There were cross cuts, sometimes called dog holes, between the two entries to allow circulation of air.

We took off our coats and put down our dinner pails, tools, and supplies. This drift was near the surface, so the temperature was low—about sixty degrees—unlike the heat of deeper mines. There is usually a slightly musty smell in the mine, depending, of course, on the efficiency of the ventilating system, which was not always very high in those days.

My father gave me a short lecture on the care and use of supplies—oil, powder, squibs—and on tools, and on proper behavior in the mines, especially matters having to do with safety; then he showed me how to undercut the face and to manage the other operations involved in breaking the coal loose from the seam. I knew much of this already, at least in theory, from listening to the talk of my elders, but I was now to become a practical miner under my father's tutelage, and there was much for me to learn.

4

IIIIIIIIIIIIIIIIIIIIIIIIIIIIIIIIIIIII

THE WORK OF A MINER

In the central Pennsylvania bituminous district, coal seams are flat and near the surface, some cropping out on the hillsides. A workable seam is three and a half to five feet thick, the thicker the better, of course. It may extend a great distance horizontally until it is cut off by a fault or outcropping of rock. The opening into such a mine is called a "drift." After the surface covering was cut away, the entry was advanced into the hillside, becoming a tunnel with the overburden supported by timbering. When the seam was reached, tunneling was easier because the overburden was partly supported by a layer of rock, usually slate, above the coal.

Capital costs of opening a mine, under these circumstances, were less than where seams were deep. Mineral rights could be bought, in the nineties, for as little as twenty-five dollars an acre, though sometimes the landowner was paid a royalty of eight or ten cents a ton. With a tipple built at the entrance, and a railroad siding run up to it, the operators were ready to ship out coal.

An opening parallel to the main drift, called a "monkey drift," was driven in to provide ventilation. Where level entry was not possible, a shaft had to be sunk to the seam. In the Urey mine where I started work, there was a short ventilating shaft with a grate of railroad iron at the bottom, on which a brisk coal fire was kept up. The shaft acted as a smokestack, and helped draw a current of air through the mine.

Such a primitive ventilating system was effective only for a small mine. An elaborate system of fans and blowers was "too costly," so the miner had to pay for bad ventilation by "miners' asthma" and other ailments caused by bad air, stagnant at best, and in many mines polluted by seepage of gas, which created the added danger of explosions set off by the miners' naked lights, by the blasting of coal, or even by an accidental spark.

Smoke from explosions of black powder, the reek of oil lamps, and the pervading coal dust made breathable air something of an obsession with the miner. Gaseous mines sometimes had to be abandoned until power-driven fans could be installed to force air in. Moreover, any impairment of ventilation was apt to ignite accumulated "fire damp," causing a terrific explosion which would send a roaring whirlwind of flaming air through the mine, wrecking the entire structure and suffocating any living thing.

The Urey mine was non-gaseous, but like others in Pennsylvania it was visited by state mine inspectors three or four times a year. The inspector measured the capacity of the ventilating system, tested the air for explosive gases, and then posted his report at the tipple. Such a superficial inspection was better than nothing, but it left a lot to be desired. The inspector could recommend improvements, if the circulating system was inadequate. Then the company might install a power-driven fan to push more air into the mine, which might or might not correct the defect. It took years of agitation by the union before state safety standards were really enforced.*

In gaseous mines, there was a "company man," called the fire boss, whose job was to inspect each workplace before the men came in to work. He had a safety lamp, whose flame grew larger in the presence of dangerous gas. He would hold the lamp near the roof, where gas would be thickest, and if he found a dangerous condition he might

---

* Even today, much more could be done. In fact, in one respect things are worse today; machine cutting makes the mines dustier than hand cutting did. Machines pulverize the coal to a fine dust almost impossible to deal with. It is disagreeable to work in this dust, which under certain conditions is explosive. The menace of lung troubles is if anything greater now than before the modern "improvements" in mining technology. Besides, the machines now set the pace of work. The miner has lost the freedom he had to set his own pace and to shift from one kind of work to another. There is a strain to mining which makes the shorter day a necessity. Miners still work too hard and too long for their good. This is just one of many illustrations of the fact that improvements in technology, conceived only as a way of increasing production, do not always mean a better life for people.

block off that entry or workplace, posting a wooden rail with "Danger" written on it in chalk. He would put the date in chalk on the roof of each workplace, and a miner coming to that point would know that he must go no farther. Both the company and the miners clamped down on a man who ignored the fire boss's warning. That part of the mine would remain closed until it became safe to work there. The fire bosses were usually conscientious men, partly because they had to live with the miners whose lives they were hired to safeguard.

Cave-ins were a different sort of problem from gas, because they usually happened as a result of the standard method of removing the coal. As the main entry was opened up, workplaces were turned off it like a series of steps. They would be advanced 350 to 500 feet, and were 25 to 30 feet wide. A "pillar," 18 to 20 feet thick, was left between workplaces to support the roof. When a man reached the limit of his workplace, he cut through the pillar into the next place and started working it back. This was called "retreating" or "robbing." If several pillars are pulled back between adjoining workplaces, a great area of roof is exposed, which eventually will weaken and fall. A thickness of 10 to 30 feet of the roof will begin to work loose from the overlying strata. The sign of this is visible in the weight on the timbers set up as props. The miner says, "The damn roof is getting heavy," and from then on he keeps one eye cocked for the signs that show he has gotten all the coal he is going to get out of that workplace. As the roof gets heavier, it "softens" the pillar, making the coal easier to cut out. This is another sign to watch, but it also tempts the miner to wait until the last minute and take advantage of the opportunity to get out a good run of coal.

After a while the timbers begin to splinter and you can hear the roof "working." This means that the strata of slate in the roof are beginning to break. It makes a sound like thunder, which can go on for as long as two or three days. An experienced miner can tell from the way the roof is "working" and from the splintering of the timbers just about when the roof is ready to fall. Then he gets his mine car and himself out of there, fast. It is a matter of pride to get as much coal out as possible, but nobody gets any credit for foolhardiness.

The roof breaks through with a tremendous roar. The miner then returns to his work, secure in the knowledge that the fall has reduced the weight on the coal he is digging. He might work for weeks before another fall of the roof occurs.

An experienced miner would often work calmly on under conditions that would terrify a novice. This was not because he liked taking chances, but because he had to work steadily, with as little lost time as possible, to get out a good day's production. He had to develop something like a sixth sense that would tell him when the chances were going against him, and never miss that warning, or his career in mining would be a short one.

The miner was subject to several kinds of discipline. I've already mentioned the discipline of state safety regulations. That did not amount to much.

Company discipline was another matter. The company's interest was to keep the mine producing. This was the reason for the fire boss's inspections in gaseous mines. In non-gaseous mines, the pit boss would go through the mine regularly, visiting each workplace once or twice a week. He could usually assume that the men knew their business, and just drop in to look around and chat a while. If he noticed some little slackness—maybe timber not as close to the face as it should be— he would say, "It seems to me you had better get a prop set up there; you've got them a little far back." And the miner would answer, "Yes, I was just about to do that; I'll get it up right away." This was considered a suggestion, not a reprimand, though one the miner always followed. The boss in Urey was friendly with my father and would often stop for a chat with him.

Probably most important to the miner was the discipline of the work and of his fellows. The flow of the mine cars was one form of discipline. A man's car should be filled and ready to go when it was his turn to get an empty. If he fell behind the pace set by the other miners, he would have to admit that they were better men than he. Loyalty to his fellow workers required a very alert awareness of danger every minute that he spent in the mine. Careless or selfish actions that endangered lives were unthinkable, and any miner who broke the safety rules was quickly made aware of the other men's disapproval. Nobody could work in this kind of situation, where every man had to depend on every other man, if he was not respected as a practical miner.

The discipline of the fellow worker was particularly important in maintaining what might be called good manners in the mine. A man was expected to so conduct himself that he would not make conditions worse for his neighbor. For instance, if he had need for a bowel movement he would take care of that need over in the gob, and cover the

waste with dirt and slack, to minimize contamination of the air. He
must not create unnecessary smoke, because it would bother his neighbors. At any sign of danger, he was obligated to warn others as well
as to take care of himself, and he must be ready to give aid whenever
it was needed. The men policed each other in respecting the fire boss's
danger signs. No man would enter a forbidden area, even if he knew
that the coal there would be easy to work, because he would be risking
destruction of the mine and everybody in it just to get himself a good
day's pay. The company would come down on him hard, probably
fire him from his job, and the workmen would refuse to have anything
to do with him, not just because of the one offense, but because it
was an indication that he was not a good miner, not a man with a
proper regard for his work and for his fellows.

In most respects having to do with the conduct of his work, the
miner was his own boss. His judgment was at work as well as his
muscles, and he made his own decisions—how deeply to undercut the
face, how much powder to use, how to pace himself in loading the car,
and many other things. The one factor outside his control was the
turn of the cars. The drivers who brought the empty cars back to the
workplaces were supposed to deliver them to each one in turn, because each miner was entitled to an equal chance to get out coal.
Passing up your turn for a car was just not done; it would lead to
loss of face. Others would say, "I guess he just isn't a good miner, or
there must be something wrong in his workplace." But it was equally
"not done" to take a car out of turn. If the driver was willing to play
favorites, the miner had to refuse such favors or be marked as a cheat
who sought special treatment, and probably needed it because he
could not compete fairly.

A terrible crime—perhaps because it was so rare—was stealing coal.
When a man finished loading a car, he put a small metal check on a
hook on the side of the car. The check bore his number, to which the
weight of the coal was credited at the tipple. During the long trip
from the workplaces to the outside, it was possible to change the check
on a car. But this was not an easy trick to get away with. The checkweighman and the weigh boss kept a record of the number of cars
and weight of coal to be credited to each miner, and, separately, a
tally of each car as it came out in order, with the check number and
the weight. If a miner complained about a "lost" car, it was easy to
identify any oddity in the order of cars coming out. Sometimes it

would be obviously impossible for the thief to have loaded all the cars credited to him.

A miner knew how many cars he had loaded, and if he found he was one short, he would complain to the weigh boss, "Look, I'm short a car. I should have six and there are only five, and they ought all to be out by now." Occasionally a check would get knocked off and lost, but the tally sheet would show an unmarked car, to be credited to the right man. If there were any dispute about ownership, the order of cars would usually provide good evidence as to the right claimant.

Similarly, if a man shifted a check from a partly loaded car to a full one, he was likely to be exposed. Miners usually filled their cars to about the same level, and if one was markedly short, the man would be suspicious. The cause might be a wreck, that is, a car jumping the track and spilling coal. Several cars behind the derailed one might also spill coal. Cars were pulled to the outside in "trips" of half a dozen or more at a time. A man called a "trip-rider" rode with each "trip," and in case of accident would chalk "wrecked" on the cars that had lost coal, and the miner would be credited with his average weight of coal for that particular car.

The actual work of a miner was very different then from what it is today. Machines have taken the place of hand tools, making the skills of the old-fashioned miner obsolete. The equipment used when I started work included picks, a shovel, an auger, a tamping bar, squibs, a needle, black powder in 25-pound kegs, and a can of oil for our lamps. Tools and supplies, when not in use, were carefully kept together in a spot well back from the work face. They represented too much of an investment to be dealt with carelessly, for each miner paid for his own.

The first operation was undercutting the face of the coal. At the bottom of the seam the miner would cut away with the pick, as deeply as he expected to be able to blast the coal loose—usually three or four feet. Most of this undercutting had to be done lying on your side and swinging the pick in a very confined space. There was always danger of coal falling from the face onto a miner while he was undercutting. A man had to know the condition of the coal he was working on and judge his safety accordingly.

When the undercutting was finished, a hole had to be driven into the coal with the auger, usually on the left, or "rib," side of the face.

The auger was at least five and a half feet long, with a breastboard at one end against which the miner braced himself as the auger bit into the coal. It was turned by a U-crank, like the common brace-and-bit. The hole was started a foot or so below the roof of the seam, to allow room for turning the crank, and was driven in at an angle calculated to bring the end of the auger to the level of the roof. If the miner judged his boring accurately, the explosion would not only break loose the coal below the hole, but it would also jolt the roof hard enough to dislodge any coal which might adhere to the roof—a prudent calculation, to get the most loose coal for the powder expended.

The powder was poured into a paper cartridge moulded around the pick-handle, about a foot of the cylinder filled with black powder, and the paper crimped at the ends. An iron needle, five or six feet long and about as thick as a lead pencil, was used to push the cartridge as far as it would go into the hole. The needle was left in the hole, resting on the lower surface, while dampened dirt was packed in tight with the tamper, a wooden stick of the same diameter as the hole cut by the auger. The tamper had a groove cut into the underside to fit over the needle. Thus it rode on the needle, packing the filling so that no loose dirt would fall into the channel. When the hole was filled, the needle was given a sharp push to puncture the cartridge, and then very gently withdrawn, being rotated all the way, to leave a small channel under the dirt from the entrance to the cartridge.

A squib—a thin roll of waxed paper about the size of the needle, with a little powder in its upper part—was then inserted into the entrance of the channel, to act as a fuse. The lower few inches of the squib contained no powder, because the time it took the paper to burn up to the powder was the time the miner gave himself to get to safety in the main entry. The miner lighted the end of the squib with his lamp and then ran to his refuge. When the powder in the squib ignited, it flashed a flame up the channel, the cartridge exploded and the coal was shattered away from the face, a ton or more by a single explosion.

If for any reason, loose dirt blocking the channel, a defective squib, or whatever, the squib failed to set off the explosion, the miner went home for the day. Nobody fooled around with a misfire, lest he be caught in a delayed explosion. The next day, the tamping could be dug out and the whole operation tried again, on the assumption that any lingering spark would by then be dead.

Usually, bituminous coal was shattered enough to be loaded into the waiting car, though sometimes larger lumps had to be broken up with the pick. The amount of powder used had to be judged correctly; there there was no profit in wasting powder, but also no profit in being niggardly and leaving coal adhering to the roof and sides.

Loading was a straightforward job of shoveling coal into the cars, though it was no simple matter to shovel coal in a tunnel rarely more than five feet high, and to throw it high enough to clear the sides of the car without hitting the roof or spilling over the far side. One of the most exhausting things about mine work was the necessity of spending a ten- or eleven-hour day without a single chance to stand erect and stretch. It was a great advantage to be short, as I was. My father didn't share this advantage; he was about 5 feet 10 inches tall.

To save labor in heaving the coal, the miner always tried to get the car as close to the face as he could, which might mean that he had to push the car himself for some distance. The cars were pulled to the entrance of the workplace, and, in some mines, also up to where the miners were working. In a badly managed mine, cars would be swung off the main line by a switch into the neck of the workplace and left there for the men to push the rest of the way themselves. Since these cars weighed from 1600 to 2000 pounds empty, it was hard work to push them up even a slight grade. The workplaces usually were opened out with a slight upgrade, to help with drainage and with rolling out the loaded car, though the main entry was kept as level as possible. A man sometimes had to get down on his hands and knees, with his left shoulder, well padded, against the car, bracing himself with his toes against the ties and the dirt of the floor. Another worker would take charge of the brakes, to keep the car from rolling back on the pusher if he slipped or grew tired. Car-pushing became a bitterly fought issue because it was so strenuous and caused so many injuries. Many men were crippled by back injuries in those days. It was particularly hard on the older men, because it was so easy to miscalculate, or lose your footing in the stuff underfoot.

Getting out the coal was not the whole job of the miner. He had to lay the track from the main entry into his workplace. He had to timber his own place, and he often was required in thin seams to "take up bottom," as it was called, to enable the cars to get to the work face. The roadway had to be high enough to let the mine cars through loaded; perhaps four or five feet. If the coal seam was not that thick, and it frequently was not, rock or dirt had to be cut away to lower the floor. This was "company work," for which the company gave no pay unless forced to do so by the union.

Not all workers in the miners were engaged in mining coal. There were some "company men": tracklayers, maintenance men, trip riders, and others, who were paid by the day. Track men laid the tracks in the main entry and the switches to the workplaces, and kept them in repair. These tracks were iron rails laid on crosspieces somewhat smaller than railroad ties. From the switches into the workplaces, the rails were wooden, resembling two-by-fours. The cars did not move as easily over the wooden rails as over iron ones, of course. Company men were also responsible for any timbering that might be needed in the main entry, the ventilating drift, and the cross cuts between them. About a fifth of the help in a mine were company men. They were not called "company men" because they were any more attached to the company than anybody else, but because they did what was considered to be the company's work, as distinguished from the miner's own work on the coal. The miners resented being required to do work they believed the company should take care of. A miner's job was to get out coal, and as a tonnage worker, that was what he was paid for. He didn't mind timbering so much, because that was clearly related to his own safety, and he preferred to make sure himself that it was done right, but car-pushing and taking up bottom were definitely oppressive.

For this arduous and hazardous labor, the miner was paid at the rate of forty to fifty cents a ton. We got forty cents in Urey. In a good seam of coal, a competent miner could get out four or five tons of coal in a ten-hour shift. Therefore, he earned about two dollars a day when he was working, barring complications, such as short time or time wasted on company work. If the miner could be sure of six days of work a week the year round, he could make a living, not a good one, but a living. But work was never that steady, nor could the average man have endured the strain if it had been.

He had to get out his four or five tons a day by hand labor. Undercutting, drilling, blasting, loading, all were hand jobs, to say nothing of timbering, tracklaying, taking up bottom, and car-pushing, which made heavy demands on his strength and stamina without putting a penny in his pocket.

The miner's pay was not free and clear. As I have said, he had to provide his own tools and supplies. A 25-pound metal keg of black powder cost him $1.50 to $1.75, and lasted about two weeks. We paid fifty cents a gallon for lard oil to use in our lamps. Picks and augers had to be sharpened regularly, which meant a blacksmithing charge of fifty cents or so each payday. If there was a checkweighman in the mine, his pay was the same as an average miner's, costing each man a ton of coal semi-monthly, as a rule. If there were a doctor in the town, he worked for the company, which deducted a flat fee for his services: seventy-five cents a month for a single man, a dollar for a family. This did not provide for much service, but where it was available it indicated a superior mining town. A miner got his pay twice a month, twenty or thirty dollars, less the deductions mentioned above and his rent and store bill. It is hardly remarkable that the "snake" showed up so often, the miner typically ending each period with a small debt carried from pay period to pay period, and sometimes inherited from father to son. The company was willing to carry such a debt indefinitely, provided it did not grow too large. It had its value in keeping a man from trying to better himself by leaving town or agitating against the company. A troublemaker could be fired, kicked out of town, and his few possessions seized to satisfy his debt. The company owned the town, the police, if any, the county government and courts. It was a perfectly secure system—for the owners. Only my mother's rigidly economical management of what income we received saved us from ever getting into debt slavery.

The margin between costs and selling price for the company in a mine like that in Urey was not large, though it was adequate to enable a concern to make a fair profit as long as its contract kept the mine operating steadily. The Urey mine was getting out coal for seventy-five to eighty-five cents a ton. This included: eight to ten cents a ton royalty to the landowner; hauling and dumping, seven to ten cents; payments for company work, three to five cents; supervision—one boss —two to three cents; office costs, three cents; maintenance and improvements, five cents; forty cents to the miner; and other costs of operating the business, such as charges for capital. The coal sold at the tipple for $1.00 or $1.10 a ton, if of good quality, as the Urey coal was. Poorer grades, at other mines, might bring as little as seventy-five cents a ton. It cost twice as much or more to freight the coal to market as to mine it. The company had to manage carefully to guard its margin of profit. However, as long as the demand for coal was good, the companies could, and did, make good profits on their total business operation. Overproduction in a declining market reduced the industry to desperate straits later on.

This, then, was the kind of work to which my father had to introduce his young son. I was healthy, but small, and certainly no more than average in strength for my age. He was kind, and considerate of my inexperience and frailty. He would explain to me patiently how things were done and why, but it took some time and added strength before I could apply the knowledge as a fully competent miner. I shoveled coal from the far ends of the workplace over nearer the track, and helped as best I could with loading the cars. I brought him his tools and supplies, filled his lamp with oil, and did such other jobs as came my way. I had to be busy doing something to keep warm.

One of my jobs was to fill father's pipe for him—no miner could afford cigars or would be caught smoking a cigarette. Many comforted themselves with chewing tobacco, which had the advantages of not requiring a light and of not pouring smoke into the limited supply of fresh air. Very often a miner would put a small piece of coal in his mouth to suck on as a substitute for tobacco.

This custom illustrates one thing about work in the mines which is not usually understood by non-miners. One of the first things that strikes the observer is that the miner comes out of the mine covered with coal dust: his clothes, his hands, his face, his hair, filled with it. He looks dirty, and it is true that he badly needs a wash. But to the miner the coal itself is not dirty. Other things might be—grease, for example—but there is no harm in good black coal dust.

I remember that once I dropped a piece of bread butter-side-down on the floor. I picked it up and showed it sadly to my father. He said, "Brush off the lumps. It's all right. Just good clean dirt; and anyway, you've got to eat a peck before you die and you might as well start now."

Even so, the wash-up after work was a necessary and elaborate ritual. There were no company-provided wash-houses at the pithead then. The miner trudged home with the black of the mine on him, to find a washtub ready on the kitchen floor and the kettle hot on the stove. He would strip to the waist and scrub himself thoroughly, while his wife worked around him, preparing the evening meal. Boys always had trouble getting the coal dust washed out from around their eyes. It stuck stubbornly to the eyelashes, and beginners were reluctant to scrub too hard for fear of getting soap in their eyes. But the art had to be learned, because if you went out with a little ring of black around your eyes, people would say, "That lad's not a miner yet, and he'll not be a miner until he knows how to wash his eyes clean."

My father had arranged for us to start in a new place, so he and I had our full two turns with the cars, just as though we were two men. To keep up with our turn he had to work much harder, because I could not do my full share. He had to do all the pick work, under-cutting and such, for both of us, and much more than half of all the other work, though I tried my best, to the limit of my strength. He was much more concerned lest I do too much than too little. He went to work early, and often went in on days when the mine was idle, to loosen coal for us to get out when we had a working day.

Fortunately for me, and for him, in a sense, work was slack during the beginning of my apprenticeship. Some of the men had left so that there were plenty of cars available to give me my turn, and nobody was pressing to get the coal out fast. After a few months, or a year, as I gained strength, weight, and experience, I began to try under-cutting. I could get the cut started in a few inches, working standing up or squatting; then my father had to take over the harder part of the job, which he had to do lying on his side. It was a long time before I could manage that work. To spare me, my father would sometimes go in for a half-day without me. Our house was so near the mine that I would take his lunch to him, sometimes finding that he was the only one in the mine. Actually he was working overtime, I suppose, though miners would often loosen coal for themselves on slack days. Then they could get the most out of the time when the mine was officially operating, loading steadily without interruptions for cutting and blast-ing.

On a regular day we entered the mine not later than seven o'clock, and by ten we were ready for the first of our two meals out of the lunch bucket, sandwiches and cold tea. Even though these lunch breaks were never long, perhaps fifteen minutes, we would join others in a nearby workplace or call to them to come visit with us while we had our bite. There was a good deal of visiting back and forth if work was a little slow. I had to take a lot of good-natured kidding, and the men would put on tall talk for my benefit, watching to see if I took it seriously. And the driver usually had something to say about the "new buttie" when he brought us a car. My father would tell them about my efforts at undercutting and the men would say, "Well, get this boy broken in right and he might make a good miner yet." I could get no higher compliment than the prediction that I might become a "good miner." After a long ten-hour day in the mine (eleven hours, including time out for lunch), I would go home a thoroughly tired child, with the task of washing up still facing me. It was a rigorous routine for a youngster, but I had the comfort of my father's unfailing kindness and of pride that I was learning to do a man's work. It was not an education I would recommend for all youngsters, by any means, but my experience was not so exceptional in that time and place that I felt particularly sorry for myself. If I was exhausted after a day's work, that was just what a day's work did to one, boy or man. That was the way it always had been for people like us, and barring miracles, the way it probably always would be. The union, by breaking that pattern of resignation, has performed something very near a miracle in the coal camps.

!!

5

ON THE MOVE

Miners of those days had to lead a gypsy life.
Regular employment was rare; there were too many hazards of the
market for any mine to operate steadily. In a town dependent on a
single mine, people were constantly moving in and out. If a company
had a good contract, both company and workers rejoiced while it
lasted. But buyers were always looking for a better bargain and when
the market deteriorated, the best contracts were the first to be lost.
As time went on, through the first decades of this century, more and
more mines were opened, to compete for a shrinking market, so that
part-time work became the rule everywhere. Men working on short
time, or laid off altogether for an unpredictable period, were constantly on the alert for news of better conditions. Sometimes a rumor,
sometimes just a hunch or a hope, would move a man to try getting
a job in another town. Rarely did such moves lead to any great improvement, but it was impossible to sit around and make no effort to
do better. Even if the grass turned out to be no greener in the other
yard, a man felt he at least had to take a hopeful look.

We left Urey in 1896, and for a decade thereafter we were on the
move every few months in search of steady work or better conditions.
Our frequent moves cannot be blamed on my father's restlessness. He
was too good and steady a man to jeopardize his family's welfare for
a whim. On the other hand, he believed that a man had no right to

make his family suffer hard times because he lacked the courage to speak up against oppression. He had his opinions and standards, and considerable independence, manifest in his speech and bearing; this did not endear him to the bosses in non-union mines.

An excellent illustration of his independence and outspokenness occurred in Urey. My father was on very good terms with the foreman, who had worked in the mines of northern Wales and had secured a foreman's certificate after coming to this country. He was a sound practical miner, and, as foremen went, a good one from the point of view of the men. He was friendly and helpful, and made no attempt to put on a big front of authority. His wife was a good, hard-working woman, who boarded some of the bachelor miners. She did all her own work and was always ready with help or advice in time of sickness or other trouble, not as a Lady Bountiful, but as one who had experienced all the trials and tribulations of a miner's wife. The foreman, Tom Bellis, had a half-interest in the company store and put his son in charge of it. One of Tom's daughters was a clerk, and his younger brother made deliveries and brought supplies in his wagon from wholesalers in Glen Campbell and elsewhere. It was a tight family operation, unusual even then, but it worked, because the Urey operation was small. The store was operated according to the prevailing customs, but because of Tom Bellis's friendly ways there was less friction with the men than in other towns.

At the time of the incident to which I refer, we were getting forty cents a ton, but working very short time, because the company had lost its principal contract. We were down to a couple of half-days a week. The foreman called in some of the men and explained the situation. The company was getting as little as ninety or eighty-five cents a ton at the tipple. Other mines were paying as low as thirty-five cents to their men, and the Urey mine would have to cut costs to operate, even on short time. He proposed a direct cut to thirty-five cents a ton.

One of the men suggested, "Why not let it stand at forty cents and add three hundred pounds to the tare of the car?" The tare was the average weight of the empty car. I suppose his idea was to save face by keeping the official rate the same, though the actual cut in earnings would be more than the foreman had proposed. When we had loaded the standard long ton of 2240 pounds, we would be credited with only 1940 pounds.

We had had a couple of days of work, and my father, tired out by keeping up with the turn of cars for both of us, had gone to bed early. While the conference at the foreman's office was going on one of the men came to our house, asking for my father. Mother refused to wake him, saying, "He's got to have his rest. He's going to work early tomorrow."

The next morning some of the fellows came over from a nearby workplace and told about the meeting with the boss and the proposed change.

My father asked, "And did you agree to do this?"

An old Welshman named Peters replied, "Sure, what else could we do?"

"But don't you see what you've done?"

"Why? What have we done? We haven't done anything wrong. We've held our rate at forty cents a ton."

My father began to get impatient and said, "You've given them six cents worth of coal for five cents. All the boss asked for was a five-cent cut, but you've given him six this way."

Peters was confused by this. "That's silly," he said. "We're still getting forty cents."

"No, you're not," my father snapped. "I think you're a bunch of damn fools." That was rough talk, but they were good friends and could stand it.

"Well," said Peters, "if you don't like it, why wern't you there?"

"I didn't know anything about it."

"They sent over for you."

"Yes? Who was sent?"

"I don't know, but I understand somebody sent word."

"Well, it didn't get to me. Who told you to accept this arrangement?"

They gave the man's name. "Oh, now I understand," said my father. "He wants to get a foreman's certificate and wants a good recommendation from the boss. He fooled you into taking a bigger cut than you needed to. But that's not the worst part of it. These bad times won't go on forever, and when the market picks up you're going to have trouble getting that cut removed. If I've got to have a wage cut, I'd rather have it out in the open where it's plain to be seen, instead of a concealed cut like this. When things pick up and they have to pay the prevailing rate, they can claim that they're paying the same as everybody else, and just forget that they boosted the tare. And then how are you going to get it changed back to what it was, without even a checkweighman to fight for you?"

Peters was upset and embarrassed, especially because my father put the case so strongly. He could only shrug and say, "Well, that's the way it's going to be. It's all decided." My father was boiling mad, but there was nothing he could do.

However, when the pit boss came by that morning, my father went after him. "Here," he said, "I hear you've given us a cut by a trick." He bawled him out, and I sat taking it all in. They both lost their tempers. I suppose the boss got even angrier than he might have, because he was a decent person and realized there was a lot of truth in my father's accusations. But with business so bad, he had to lend himself to such tricks in order to hold his own job.

Finally, he could stand it no longer and burst out, "Well, if you don't like it here . . ."

"Sure," my father said, "it's easy to say that. I don't like it, but . . ."

"All right. Why don't you go somewhere else?"

"I'd be damned glad to go somewhere else if I knew where to go. If there was such a place, you'd go there, too. But where is it?"

Although relations were strained for a while, I don't think Tom Bellis held any grudge against my father. But there was nothing either one could do to improve the situation, so my father eventually had to move elsewhere, looking for a better job. And he was right about the difficulty of recovering that cut. The company insisted that the rate was forty cents a ton and they were not going any higher. And it did no good to talk about changing the tare; they just refused to discuss it. In a bigger operation, my father would have been fired just for speaking his mind. Nothing but a strong union—and, of course, there was nothing of the kind, then—could have saved him.

Our first move, after Urey, was to Barnesboro in neighboring Cambria County. My father walked over there, about twenty-five miles, and got jobs for both of us in Brown's mine. It was a good, clean, thick seam, and the work was steady. We loaded our things on a rented wagon and moved, hopeful that this would be a good job.

We soon discovered that even though the mine was working steadily, it was crowded, and the turn of cars was so slow that a man did well to clear as much as a dollar or a dollar and a half a day. Other working conditions were good enough so that with a brisk turn of the cars we might have been able to make twice as much. The mine was operated by a contractor who had leased it from the owners. His interest was to get as much coal out as he could while his lease ran, so he put every man he could find into the mine, but did not invest any of his own money in equipment to keep up with production, trying instead to get the most he could out of the equipment already there. All this explains why father had no trouble in getting taken on.

After about two weeks of this, it was clear that we were in a trap. The contractor had an arrangement with a storekeeper in Barnesboro to give his men credit on the basis of their earnings. This meant, of course, that they had to buy everything at that particular store; it was as bad as a company store. The contractor got a small rake-off from the storekeeper. We learned that this had been going on for a year or more, and, worse still, that there had been no payday for six weeks. Even when men had earned more than the amount of their store bill, they could not collect the balance. There was much unrest and talk about suing the contractor.

My father soon had enough of this fly-by-night operation. He walked over to Elmora, and got jobs for both of us on the night shift in a mine there.

We had to walk four miles from our home in Barnesboro to the mine in Elmora, and another mile underground, work a ten-hour shift, and then walk all the way home in the cold dawn. We left home at three in the afternoon and got back around five in the morning. We were doing fairly well so far as getting out the coal was concerned— that is, we were making nearly two dollars apiece per shift—but it was a grueling schedule.

Along about the fifth night, I was so overwhelmed with exhaustion, in spite of my father's best efforts to spare me, that I don't recall how I got home. I must have walked the four miles down the track in my sleep, holding my father's hand. When I got home I went right to bed, not even taking time to eat. When I woke up, I found I had slept all through the following day and night, well over thirty hours.

My father decided that something had to be done. He found a farmhouse for rent, about a mile and a half back in the hills from the mine, and then went to the Elmora mine and got an advance of ten dollars to pay for moving our things from Barnesboro. This was wonderful news to me; I could not have faced that schedule again, even with the help of my long sleep.

Father still had to collect the balance due us from our work at

Brown's mine, in Barnesboro. He went to the company store and got a statement of our earnings. It amounted, as I remember, to $14.75 over what we owed the store.

He said to the storekeeper, "I wish you would cash this statement for me. Give me what's due me, and hold the rest for the store bill."

"Oh, no," said the storekeeper, "I'm not going to enter into any arrangement like that."

"Why not? What's wrong with it?"

"Just that I can't make any money out of giving you cash. Why should I do you favors?"

"All I'm asking you," my father said, "is to give me the fourteen dollars. You can keep the extra seventy-five cents. Your bill will be paid and we'll be all square. What's wrong with that?"

The storekeeper wouldn't agree. "No," he said, "I won't do it."

"If you don't," my father warned him, "I'll turn this over to someone who will collect it, even if it costs me half the balance. What's more, I'll write to your employer and tell him I offered to pay my store bill, but you refused to settle, wouldn't make any reasonable arrangement. And if he has any idea of protecting his own interests, he'll fire you for not collecting."

This flustered the storekeeper, who said, "Well, don't get sore," and counted out the $14.75. My father picked up the money. The storekeeper said, "Hey, wait a minute, you said I could have the seventy-five cents."

"I know I did," said my father, "but you didn't accept it. I had to force you to give me what was due me. I can't see why I should pay you for that, so I'm taking it all. You can be thankful that the store bill is paid. That's that."

There were two or three people in the store listening to this altercation. They followed my father outside, and one man said, "You're the first man that's gotten any money out of this outfit in six weeks. That's probably the last cash any of us will ever see." My father was very proud of having gotten his due, and liked to tell the story of his $14.75. A few months later, that contractor actually was sued, and there was a lot of trouble with him. We at least had gotten our money out in time. Part of the contractor's trouble probably was the fact that in those panic years he was having the same trouble collecting what was owed him by his customers as the miners were having collecting from him.

The Elmora mine had its drawbacks too, as we soon found out. We started work on the night shift, working in a pretty good place for about six weeks, then we were put on the day shift, working in a cross entry. Very soon, the seam "went to the dip," that is, began to slope deeper into the earth. Water accumulated in our workplace, and had to be bailed out by hand every morning before we could get any coal out. Furthermore, the dip in the seam meant that we had to push cars out to the main entry up a longer and steeper grade. The bailing and car-pushing wasted our time and energy, our earnings suffered, and so did we. The company refused to make any allowance for time lost in bailing water. Neither would it pay to have rock shot down into the roadway so that a mule could be driven in to pull our cars out. For a few days some of the other men gave us a hand with the cars, but they couldn't keep it up. They had all they could do to make their own living. We were working ourselves to death and still unable to make a decent day's pay, so we quit.

Our next job was in the Wigton mine, near Carrolltown, two or three miles away. We rented a small five-room house, about a mile from the mine, for four dollars a month. There was a good thick vein of coal in this mine. We could get out a good run of coal when we worked, but we only got one, two, or three days a week. And there were some weeks when we got no work whatever. Even though we could make two dollars a day, it did not stretch very far. The little one-room company store got in about three hundred dollars' worth of groceries and other goods every two weeks. Everybody kept a sharp lookout for the delivery. When it came, there was a grand rush to get orders in, the store was cleaned out in two days, and then there was a two-week wait for the next order to arrive. The operators were taking no chances of having anything left unsold on their hands. We got no cash, so we were completely at the mercy of that one store. Even though Carrolltown was a farming center and living conditions were therefore somewhat better than in most mining towns, we were living from hand to mouth, and often suffering real want.

While we were in Carrolltown, I made friends with a couple of boys named McDermott, whom I met again years later when I was president of District 2 of the United Mine Workers. One of them was by then the sheriff of Cambria County, and the other was active in the union. The sheriff later served several terms in the state legislature. They were both good union men, probably for the same reasons that made me a union man—memories of what it was like to grow up in mining towns without a union.

We were in Carrolltown during the presidential campaign of 1896, and I remember the miners discussing candidates and issues, though nobody seemed to be very much excited about them. Some favored Bryan because they thought the country needed a change. Others were not sure the kind of change Bryan was advocating would necessarily be a good thing. The money question meant nothing to them. My father remarked once that the Republicans were promising better times, once the gold standard was assured and their candidate elected, and he hoped they knew what they were talking about, because the country certainly needed better times. He had not gotten his citizenship at that time, so he couldn't vote. The most conservative miners were the Welshmen; they usually voted Republican out of habit. That was the stock that John L. Lewis came from, so he learned his Republicanism young. The most notable thing about the campaign was, I think, that however much excitement it created elsewhere, it was a matter of little interest in the isolated mining towns. The miners lived in a world of their own, cut off from the general population, both by geographical isolation and by the character of their life and work. It was hard for them to take much interest in matters which seemed to have no direct bearing on them and their problems.

In November, 1896, when our fortunes had declined to the point of desperation, an old friend from Urey came through Carrolltown and stopped to call. He reported that the Urey mine was expecting a good order that would provide steady work. My father immediately started out, walking the thirty miles to Urey, to see his old friend, Tom Bellis, who told him the new order was not expected until April, which was not much help to us right then. But Tom recognized our situation, and went on to say, "If you're up against it, why not come back here anyway? We can find a house for you easily enough, and your credit is good at the store until spring. It's not much help, I know, when you'll have to pile up a debt, but it's better than nothing. And I know you're good for the debt. I can get one of the local farmers to drive his team down and pick up your things."

My father did not hesitate very long. We would have enough to eat and a place to live, at least, and the assurance of work to pay off the debt. A miner could hardly hope for more than that. So we headed for Urey, right back where we had started from.

There were less than a dozen families left in the town when we got there. We shared with the others the occasional days of work until spring arrived, and with it the new contract. By the time work was steady, our debt at the company store had mounted to over a hundred dollars, a huge sum. It took several months of hard work and frugal living to get us square with the store. I remember well our jubilant celebration when we got our first cash in the pay envelope.

About a week after our return to Urey my youngest sister, Bessie, was born. There was no doctor in the town, but neighbor women came in to help out at the birth and afterward. Urey had not changed. It was still a tiny self-reliant community, living from hand to mouth, and providing all its own social and intellectual life. The people were poor, sometimes terribly poor, but they had strength and courage and self-respect to keep them from being overwhelmed and destroyed by their poverty. Things would be better some day, and it was their business to keep themselves ready to make use of opportunity when it came. Even if it never came, they would be better off for their readiness. And the friendly atmosphere of the small operation, helped by the special qualities of Tom Bellis and his wife, made the hardships of life easier to bear. Later, in larger towns, where we were confronted by an impersonal coal company, everything was run on a cold-blooded "business basis," and we remembered the personal relationships of Urey with some nostalgia.

Our security did not last long. After a few months, the company lost the good contract, and we were back to short time and the necessity of starting out again to find another job.

It was not a good time. Wages were low and work spotty. The United Mine Workers, though it had fewer than 10,000 members, was driven to call a general strike in the bituminous fields on July 4, 1897, which brought out about 100,000 men in Ohio, Illinois, Indiana, and western Pennsylvania. Very few places in central Pennsylvania were involved, so the strike didn't touch us directly. After a twelve-week strike, the union won a sixty-five-cent base rate for the Pittsburgh area, with corresponding rates in the other districts. The agreement covered the Central Competitive Field (Ohio, Indiana, Illinois, and western Pennsylvania),* providing a basis for firm organization there,

---

* The mine owners in these states had an informal organization through which they negotiated wage agreements with the UMW. This was called the Central Competitive Field (CCF), though the exact origin of the name is unclear.

but it was another year before central Pennsylvania was benefitted. The national union reported a membership of 33,000 by its 1898 convention, with the prospect of further growth. The eight-hour day was won in the Central Competitive Field in 1898.

Father heard, by the grapevine, that there was work to be had in a place called Horatio, near Punxsutawney in Jefferson County. He got the promise of a job there and walked back to Urey. The Horatio mine was working only three days a week, but Urey by then was closed down altogether and we were accumulating a new debt at the store. Father decided that the best arrangement would be for him and me to go first to Horatio, work a while to get enough money to move us and pay off the store debt, and then bring mother and the children to the new home.

We walked a few miles to a rail junction and then indulged ourselves by taking the train the rest of the way. Father probably thought it was worth the money to save me from arriving in the new town exhausted before even starting work.

It was dark when we got off the train in Horatio. Some miners were standing around the small station; father asked one where we could find a place to board. There was no boardinghouse in town, he replied, but Granny O'Brien and her son might take us in. We went to see Granny O'Brien.

She was a very large woman, and quite old. Her son was fairly well along in years, so I suppose she must have been in her seventies or eighties. At first she was not inclined to accept us, but my father was persistent and eloquent. He told her it would only be for a short time because he would soon bring his family to Horatio. And it wasn't like taking in two men—after all, I was pretty small. She asked for my name, and then my father's. Whether because of his eloquence, or because his name was Pat Brophy—obviously the right kind of name for her taste—she finally grumbled, "Oh, all right, come on in."

Granny O'Brien was a "character." She smoked a black corncob pipe, and loved to spend evenings sitting in the kitchen and talking. My father enjoyed talking as much as she did, so they had a good time, smoking their pipes and yarning about the old days in Ireland, and a multitude of other things. She claimed she was born in Ireland on the night of the "Big Wind." All the windstorms Ireland has ever had must have been collected under that name, if all the people I've known who said they were born on the night of the "Big Wind" actually were.

I sat quietly and drank it all in, enjoying it as much as they. I had to be quiet, because if I called attention to myself I would be sent to bed.

We worked four days and did pretty well, making about four dollars a day between us. The job looked promising. But on the fourth day, my father spoke to me rather sharply about something or other, and I broke down, began to cry, and would not be consoled.

I'm sure my father suspected what was wrong with me, but he didn't shame me by accusing me of being homesick. Instead, he urged me to give my own explanation.

Finally, I gulped, "It's Granny O'Brien."

"What has Granny O'Brien done?"

"Her pies are not as good as mother's."

My father didn't push the questioning any further. He said, "All right, let's finish loading this car and we'll go along out."

When we got back to the house, Granny O'Brien soon found out what was wrong, to bring us out of the mine early, and she was all sympathy. "Oh, the poor lad," she said. "I can understand it all. He wants his mommy, and he should have her." It was comforting to have her sympathy, but also a little embarrassing. After all, I was working at a man's job even if I was only fourteen, and I preferred to think that I was too big a boy to need my mother.

My father went down to the coal company office to rent a house and get an advance to pay for moving. He got the house, but no money.

The next move was to see Tom Bellis in Urey. Father said to him, "The mine here is shut down, and I'm in debt to you for twenty-five or thirty dollars. If I stay here, I'll just have to go further into debt. I've got a job over in Horatio, but I haven't been working there long enough to pay this bill and the cost of moving over there. What I want is to borrow ten dollars from you to pay for moving, and I'll send you something each payday until the ten dollars and the store bill are both paid off. I think the Horatio job will be good enough for that. What do you say?"

Tom Bellis agreed, so we were able to move in spite of being in debt. It took nearly a year for us to pay Bellis off.

We had a good year in Horatio. It was the best company town I had ever seen, though it had seen its best days before we lived there. In the eighties and early nineties, six or seven hundred men worked in its three large mines. The largest mine soon ran out, because of a fault, which cut off the vein of coal. There had been a vigorous local assembly of the Knights of Labor in the town until a bitter strike in 1894. The Berwind-White Company, which owned the mines, decided to break with the union, and brought in numbers of Pinkerton "detectives." These thugs killed a Mrs. Williams, the wife of a leading striker, and many strikers were arrested and thrown in jail.

The town never recovered from that blow. The best men among the miners, active leaders of the union, were blacklisted and left. Some of them provided leadership in other union locals, in the new fields which opened up around the turn of the century, along the line of the Buffalo, Rochester, and Pittsburgh Railroad. The men who remained in Horatio would sometimes talk about the struggles of the past, but they always dropped their voices, almost to a whisper, even when it was certain there were no company spies present, so thoroughly were they cowed. Berwind-White was the largest operator in central Pennsylvania, with mines in several counties. The company had unusual success in warding off unionism for many years, but in 1922 I was able to pull its men out on strike. I got a lot of satisfaction from that achievement.

In spite of the destruction of the union, there was much to be said for life in Horatio. The company houses were doubles, five or six rooms to a side. The gardens were fenced, and plank sidewalks were laid from the houses to the store, school, and railroad station. There were about 150 houses, kept in good repair. The company store was a large one, stocking a great variety of groceries, clothing, and even furniture.

Each miner was supplied with a "store book" in which his purchases were entered. At the end of each pay period the amount owed was deducted from his earnings. When he bought such things as furniture, too expensive to be paid for at one time, a few dollars would be deducted from each pay and entered in the back of the book until the full amount was paid. There was no interest charge for this installment buying—the interest was concealed in the high original price. Often, before one such article was completely paid for, another was needed. I remember one miner with a large family being asked once how he could afford some furniture he had bought shortly after buying a stove. He replied, "Oh, I just had it put on top of the stove!" The success of this device depended on regularity of work, and if that failed, the miner lost his new possessions.

Work was fairly steady. We never had full time, but we could almost always count on three or four days a week, occasionally even five, and since we could make about two dollars a day apiece, we not only lived fairly well, but added to our stock of furniture. We bought a new bedroom suite, a dining table, and a new stove, among other things. My father and I were fortunate in having good workplaces in the mine during almost the entire year, so we could get out a good day's work without killing ourselves.

It is a curious thing that although Horatio was much larger and more prosperous than the average of small mining towns where I worked half a century ago, it has now vanished utterly. It is still possible to find Urey and Carrolltown and some of the others on a map, if you look hard enough, but I went through Horatio a few years ago and could find no trace of houses, nor even of a mine entrance.

In addition to regular work and relative prosperity for the family, Horatio brought me a special bonanza. The other side of our house was occupied by a young couple. The man was the meat-cutter at the company store, and his wife was the daughter of a minister in a nearby town. They shared with us the use of a large back yard, so my mother became very friendly with the young woman. During a visit next door, my mother noticed that they had a large bookcase full of books. She remarked that she had a son who was fond of reading, and the young woman offered to lend me any of the books I wanted.

These young people had had more education than was the rule in such towns, and owned thirty or more books, an enormous library in my eyes. I remember a wonderful book about how Henry Stanley found Livingstone in darkest Africa. Rider Haggard's *King Solomon's Mines* and *Allan Quartermain* were marvelous adventure yarns. There were some novels by Scott—*Ivanhoe* was one—and by Charles Dickens, and a history of the United States. I read them all, good and bad alike, and then reread the better ones. I sent away I don't know how many soap wrappers for a small dictionary to help out with the hard words. It was my most prized possession, the only one of its kind in town.

We saw more newspapers than we had previously. The Philadelphia *Inquirer* came regularly, and sometimes we had a Pittsburgh paper as well. I was learning about the world I lived in, not least from the talk of the miners when they gathered for an evening of beer-drinking at one of the homes. Horatio was dry, but we brought in four- or eight-gallon kegs of beer by wagon from Punxsutawney, four miles away, for a weekend gathering. I would sit silently and listen as the older men told of the Pinkertons, how Mrs. Williams was shot and some of the men beaten up, how men were taken off to Brookville, the county seat, to stand trial on trumped-up charges of trespass or disorderly conduct, and always found guilty and sentenced to the maximum penalty for their so-called crimes.

My father was a slow but very careful reader. He never took anything on a newspaper's say-so. Because I could read faster than he, he often had me read the longer news stories or feature articles aloud, and we would discuss them. I learned from his often scornful or angry comments that even the printed word had to prove its case. Whether he intended it or not, he was providing me with excellent training.

George Pitaway and Tom Clorley, two Staffordshire men who were oldtimers in Horatio, became great cronies of my father's, spending many evenings with him, talking and singing. They were sometimes joined by a Derbyshireman named Beard and his son. Pitaway and Clorley belonged to a fraternal order called the Knights of the Golden Eagle, and persuaded my father to join the local "castle." This had been a large organization before the strike, but most of the members had been blacklisted by the company, leaving only a few to run the lodge. Many of those who had left town continued to send in dues, to retain their right to certain small financial benefits. I well recall the rapidity of my father's rise in this make-believe medieval world of castles and knights. He was shortly elected keeper of the exchequer and was overwhelmed by the responsibility of keeping the seventy or eighty dollars in cash of the order's treasury. He told Clorley, "I wouldn't care so much if it was my own, but how can I take care of all that money belonging to other people?"

"Do what I did on that job," said Tom. "I put the money in a tin can and buried it in the dirt floor of the cellar." My father laughed at this idea of safe storage, but he followed Clorley's example, nevertheless. Fortunately, my father had a good mind for figures, so he had no trouble keeping the books straight, but he really sweated over being accountable for all that money.

Another friend of his was Roger Hudson. Hudson had had his left arm amputated just above the elbow as a result of an accident. This would seem to be a fatal disability for a miner's work, but Hudson had an iron will, and was determined not to give up just for lack of an arm. He trained himself to use a shovel and even undercut the coal almost as well as men with two arms. He was a cheerful, spunky man, and welcome company on the walk of a mile and a half from our house to the mine. He would stop at our workplace when it was time to go home, and if we had a car to finish loading he would pitch in and help, making as much coal fly as either of us.

About a half-mile from Horatio was Hunkietown, a hodgepodge of shanties thrown together cheaply on company land and renting for a dollar a month. It had been put up in the day of Horatio's prosperity to house Slavs and Italians, the late-comers who gradually replaced English-speaking miners as the latter moved out to more promising jobs in the cities. Two Italian brothers from Hunkietown who worked next to us in the mine were the first real "foreigners" I had ever gotten to know very well—kind, gentle men, always eager to be friendly and helpful. Knowing and liking these men no doubt helped protect me from prejudice against people who differed from me in such non-essential ways as race, religion, and language.

There were three English-speaking Catholic families in Horatio, including five boys who, like me, worked in the mines. The nearest Catholic church was in Punxsutawney, so we got to Mass only occasionally. Father Winker, the old pastor of the Punxsutawney church, came over to Horatio regularly to give us instruction preparatory to our first Holy Communion. He rode a bicycle if the weather was fair; otherwise he walked or hitched a ride with somebody's team. We were so fond of him that we sometimes walked over to his little house in "Punxsy," just to see and talk to him. Ours was not the only hamlet he visited regularly, to care for the spiritual needs of the isolated miners. He would even go into the mines to talk to the men during the day, and he was always welcome. He was the unselfish missionary, kind, humble, and hard-working—a true miners' priest. People of all creeds respected and, indeed, loved him. His example has been one of the primary supports of my faith.

Early in 1898 the Buffalo, Rochester, and Pittsburgh Railroad started an extension of its road westward to complete a long-projected line into Pittsburgh. A mile-long tunnel had to be dug near Horatio, which would provided work for a large force of men for many months. The newspapers were full of stories about the project, and hundreds of men drifted in, under the impression that work was ready to start, many arriving destitute, weeks too soon. The railroad had not, of course, made any preparations for such a flood of early arrivals, so many of the men were forced to beg for food. My mother usually baked bread twice a week, but now she began baking every other day, and even oftener. Our house, like many others in the little town, was haunted by the hungry men until the work finally got under way.

The Spanish-American War brought a certain amount of patriotic fervor—speech-making and flag-raising—but only a few youngsters enlisted. One young man from Horatio died in the war; like most of the casualties, he was the victim of disease, not of battle. Nobody in Horatio had any clear idea what the fighting was about; it seemed very unreal.

Early in 1899 the work slowed down. My father decided to leave the mines and get work in a factory. Most miners got that idea at one time or another. Ex-miners and their sons in hundreds of thousands are scattered all over the country. My mother's brother worked in a glass factory in Jeannette, near Pittsburgh. He had written to us from time to time, contrasting factory work with the mines, and arguing that everything favored the former.

We sold off our household goods and took the train to Jeannette for what we expected to be a new and better life. But even though business was improving, there were no jobs in Jeannette. My father left us with relatives and tramped around to nearby factory towns looking for work. We finally heard from him a week later. He had found work, not in a factory, but in a mine at South Fork in Cambria County. I never found out whether he drifted back to mining because he really preferred to do his accustomed work or whether he took the job out of actual necessity. I do know that he never again tried to leave the mines.

I was just as well pleased that things had turned out as they did. I had hated my brief experience in a factory in Jeannette, when I replaced one of the regulars who had failed to show up. The shifts ran six hours on and six off—twelve hours of work out of the twenty-four. I learned why openings for spare help to work a shift or two were so frequent. I worked at a "carry-over" job in a flint-glass factory. A machine moulded and pressed a tumbler, then dropped it on a metal tray which I held ready. I walked two steps to my left and placed it on a metal table. Then I went back and did it all over again—and again, and again. The factory was noisy and hot, a bewildering world of machines. Worst of all were the broken shifts which made it impossible to get a decent night's sleep. It was an existence of weariness and boredom. I was glad to follow my father back to the mines, where we had some variety in our work, and could, within broad limits, set our own pace. And the pay was better, too—I was paid only fifty or sixty cents for twelve hours in the glass factory. After that, the mines of South Fork looked inviting.

6

IIIIIIIIIIIIIIIIIIIIIIIIIIIIIIIIIIIIIII

SOUTH FORK

I took the train to meet my father in South Fork, east of Johnstown, leaving the family to follow when we were settled. We lived for a while with an old couple in what was known as the "Klondike Blocks." This company "patch" included twenty double houses set in two rows along a bluff facing the south branch of the Conemaugh River. The name "Klondike" carried no promise of gold. It was probably invented by some wag with a grim sense of humor, because the scenery was rugged and the houses bleak and bare. But they were new and large, and the company was better than average to work for. The owner, Jacob Stineman, was a state senator; his political ambitions may have accounted for his liberal attitude toward his help. The town supported him in elections, as did the miners elsewhere in his district. We worked only a nine-hour day, but the six-day week was still the rule. Stineman let his men maintain a checkweigh association. Each miner contributed a ton of coal each payday to support the checkweighman, and since this was a large mine, there was a little left over for a beneficial fund. A miner injured at his work got five dollars a week, after the first week, from this fund. The company had a good contract with a public utility, so work was steady.

Four companies operated mines around South Fork, supporting a population of about four thousand. It was a larger community than any we had worked in, and dominated less by the operators. There was a large company store with an extraordinary variety of goods, but there was also an independent shopping center, where we could buy what we wanted. We did not have to smuggle in things bought elsewhere, as in smaller towns. Also, we did not have to rent from our employers, because there were not enough company houses for everybody. Relief from the weight of company control over our lives through monopoly of housing and stores was enough to make the move to South Fork memorable. This new freedom, added to the novelty of working regularly six days a week, made South Fork almost a miner's idea of heaven.

South Fork even had a theater, operated by a couple of Jacob Stineman's sons. Traveling variety shows and repertory companies came through, putting on their shows for a week. I soon discovered a great appetite for this world of make-believe. The companies issued coupon books for use at the company stores, with stamps in various denominations, from one cent to a dollar. Twenty-five cent coupons were accepted for admission to the theater.

We lived for a while in "Sunshine Row," a straggling line of double houses painted a hideous red. The row began near the mine tipple and fronted the railroad siding to the Pennsylvania's four-track main line. There was so little space between the tracks and the steep hillside behind the houses that there was scarcely any yard. Coal sheds and privies were less than fifteen feet from our kitchen windows. Dust from the tipple, smoke and noise from passing trains, and other smells, made this the worst place we ever lived in. Fortunately, there was enough choice to enable us to escape from Sunshine Row to a house with more comfort and a less mocking name.

While we were in Sunshine Row, I contracted typhoid fever. I had just turned seventeen. When the company doctor first told me he thought I had typhoid, I broke down and wept, saying to my mother, "Why did this have to happen now? How will the family get along without my working?" She managed, of course; somehow mother always managed. As I lay in bed during the long weeks of convalescence, I could hear the miners in the morning, gathered along the spur to see how many railroad coal cars were brought in, and waiting for the mine whistle to signal the start of work. If there were no cars at seven o'clock, the usual starting hour, the boss would tell the men to wait and see what the shifting engine brought on its first trip. The railroad's rule was that cars brought to a mine were charged against it for that day whether they were loaded or not. Sometimes the men had to wait until nine o'clock before the shifter came through on its first trip, and even then there might not be enough cars for a full day's work. There frequently were too few cars to keep up with demand, and the roads distributed those available according to their convenience. Of course, mines which owned their own cars were free of this annoyance, but few concerns had enough capital to afford them. Requiring the railroads to establish a reasonable rule governing distribution of coal cars was one issue on which the union and operators agreed, but it took years of pressure to get the roads to adopt one.

The doctor who cared for me during my illness was supported by a small monthly charge deducted from our pay by the company. Company doctors were usually young men in their first practice. The regular income gave them a degree of security while they saved to establish themselves in a more usual practice. I suppose the American Medical Association today would call this socialized medicine, but it was a boon to the miners, and had advantages for the young doctors, too. The monthly charge covered drugs a doctor might carry with him. Anything for which he had to write a prescription cost extra. The one hospital in Cambria County at that time was in Johnstown, and miners only went there to die. Nursing care was provided by the family or by neighbors. Childbirth was tended by more or less professional midwives; the doctor was called in only for very difficult cases, and then sometimes too late. This may help explain why, of my father and mother's eleven children, only five lived to adulthood. One of the others died at four or five; the rest as infants. I was the oldest, born in 1883; Mary, born in 1886, died a few years ago; Beatrice, born in 1890, is still living. But of those born in America, only two grew up—Charles, born in the terrible depression year of 1894, died in 1961; Bessie, born three years later, is still living.

Our arrival in South Fork coincided with a revival of the union in central Pennsylvania. My first five years in the mines were spent under non-union conditions. During those years, we had no choice as to where to live or to buy our supplies; we had to take whatever the company thought was good enough for its help and not talk back. As word of improvements seeped through from districts farther west, miners in our district began to stir and to think seriously of winning greater independence and a better living.

South Fork was a good place to be during the revival of the union.

The miners had maintained their checkweigh association for a number of years, and there was even a tiny local of the United Mine Workers, barely managing to keep alive. The company dealt with its help informally through a mine committee chosen by the checkweigh association. I can't say whether it was the vigor of the South Fork miners that made it possible for them to keep the protection of a checkweigh association, or whether it was the excellent quality of the coal and its command of a steady market, or the liberality of the operator and his political ambitions. Whatever the reasons, South Fork, which had done better than most of the districts during the hard years of the nineties, was now in a position to take the lead in reviving the union.

Early in 1899—I think it was in March—a conference of the few locals in our district was held at Tyrone. Fifteen delegates were present, including two from South Fork. One of the latter was Richard Gilbert, the checkweighman in the mine where I worked. The dues-paying membership represented, out of 50,000 miners working in the district, was 633. The man who held the title of president of the district, George Harris, had had enough of his empty honor. His office was in his vest pocket; there were no funds to enable him to get around to do any organizing. In fact, he had to work full time in the mines to make his living. He was tired and discouraged, and well he might be.

New men had to take over, if the drive for unionism was to get anywhere. William B. Wilson of Blossburg, in Tioga County, was elected president, with Gilbert as secretary-treasurer. Bernard Rice of Du Bois was vice-president. The convention issued a call to organize and adopted a scale of demands for wages and working conditions. If these demands were rejected, the locals were authorized to strike. It was a bold stand, and the new regime had little to depend on but the new hope that at last, with the upturn in business, something might be done.

The conference found great inconsistencies in wages and conditions. Day rates ran from as little as $1.35 to rare instances of $1.90 per ten-hour day. Rates for pick-mined coal ran from thirty-five to fifty cents a long ton. Loading behind machines paid, usually, thirty cents a ton. Reports were given of high rents and of high prices and sharp practices in company stores. There were only twenty-five checkweighmen in the several hundred mines of the district.

The standards proposed by the conference were by no means extreme. It suggested that the locals demand $1.75 for day rates, fifty cents a ton for pick-mined coal and seven-ninths of that for loading behind the machines. Even before the organizing drive got very far, some mines accepted the Tyrone scale. They could afford it in a good market, and accepting it promptly was insurance against having production interrupted by a strike. Men at the other mines could then argue that they were entitled to the same rates and would strike unless they got them. South Fork was already doing as well as the scale, so we had no trouble. Even so, the local miners had to understand that what they had could be lost unless they supported the organizing drive. If a meeting of fifteen people in Tyrone could accomplish so much so quickly, there was no telling what a strong union might be able to do.

Richard Gilbert and George Bassett led the agitation in South Fork. Bassett was the principal speaker at mass meetings in the open air along the Dunlo track, which ran through the center of town. I remember the first meeting very well, on a pleasant spring evening. The men left their work at the mines around 4:30, went home, washed up, had a bite to eat, and gathered along the track at about six. There must have been two or three hundred of them. Bassett, a fluent speaker with a talent for fervid and impassioned oratory, told about the national union's call to organize, the gains made in the West, the actions of the Tyrone convention, the gains already made in our district, including a few successful strikes that he had heard of by grapevine, and wound up with a stirring appeal to all to join up. The crowd was very enthusiastic, and when Dick Gilbert followed Bassett with a proposal that the mass meeting accept the standards set at Tyrone and submit them to the employers, there was a roar of approval. These demands, as I have described them above, became known among the miners as the "South Fork demands," perhaps because Gilbert, as district secretary-treasurer, circulated them to the locals from his "office" in his home. His union work was unpaid, so he continued to serve as checkweighman.

I developed a great admiration for George Bassett at these twilight meetings along the Dunlo track. I was impressed by his self-assurance and his ability to express himself. During this period he suffered an accident. He had just finished his day's work and on his way out of the mine stopped to talk to somebody at a curve near the mine entrance. The rope by which cars were hauled out of the mine slipped off a sheave wheel and whipped against his leg, crushing it so that it had to be amputated. He was off work for a long time and when he returned was given a job as an engine tender. He continued his union activity and was a delegate to district conventions for thirty years. During his last years, the union deteriorated and times were bad; he became a tired and sad old man. I prefer to remember him as the fiery young agitator who did so much to build the union in District 2.

Our success in building the union in South Fork was in part due to the fact that the miners were almost all of British origin; very few were native Americans or from later immigrant stocks. The bulk of them were English, from Cornwall, Lancashire, or Staffordshire, with generous sprinklings of Welsh, Scottish, and Irish. Bassett was born in England and had come over as a child. Richard Gilbert had arrived from England only a few years before the time I am describing. The British immigrants brought with them not only experience in British mines but also, like my father, the experience of British unions.

All through that summer there were mass meetings in South Fork, usually on Sunday afternoons. William B. Wilson, president of the district, came down from his home near the New York state line to speak to us. He was not so badly off as when I had heard of him last, in Philipsburg during the 1894 strike, but he still worked without adequate support from the organization. He was the district's great man, in my young eyes, confident and able, with a fine speaking voice marked by a pleasant Scotch burr. In his ideas and policies he was much like the conventional AFL leaders I met in later years. It was his energy and devotion which made him outstanding, I think, more than any special talents.

At one afternoon meeting, Wilson got into a prolonged argument with a local miner, a fine-looking young man named Quinn, who opposed the United Mine Workers and supported the revolutionary unionism of the Socialist Labor Party. The crowd was unsympathetic to the adherent of De Leonism, but I was fascinated because it was the first time I had ever heard a Socialist of any kind. It was typical of the miners that although they had no interest in Quinn's revolutionary message and found him hard to understand, they nevertheless heard him out. I remember one man grumbling: "What's he think he's driving at?" and an old Englishman retorting, "Let the beggar speak! It's all right—he'll soon work himself out."

He never joined the union, but in a year or so obtained a foreman's certificate. Many years later I met Quinn again when he had become a superintendent and I was president of District 2. I sensed that he was still privately socialistic in his ideas and not very happy about his situation. Whatever his private notions, as a mine superintendent he reacted as his employer, the coal operator, required—no worse and no better than any other man in the same position.

It was probably at about this time, also, that I first saw Mother Jones. At a mass meeting I heard her rip into the operators for their sins of commission and omission. She came into the mine one day and talked to us in our workplace in the vernacular of the mines. How she got in I don't know; probably just walked in and defied anyone to stop her. When I first knew her, she was in her late middle age, a woman of medium height, very sturdily built but not fat. She dressed conventionally, and was not at all unusual in appearance. But when she started to speak, she could carry an audience of miners with her every time. Her voice was low and pleasant, with great carrying power. She didn't become shrill when she got excited; instead her voice dropped in pitch and the intensity of it became something you could almost feel physically. She would take a drink with the boys and spoke their idiom, including some pretty rough language when she was talking about the bosses. This might have been considered a little fast in ordinary women, but the miners knew and respected her. They might think her a little queer, perhaps—it *was* an odd kind of work for a woman in those days—but they knew she was a good soul and a friend of those who most lacked friends: the down-trodden and oppressed, whoever they might be. The union used her as an organizer, and paid her when it could, but she agitated whether she was paid or not. She had a complete disregard for danger or hardship and would go in wherever she thought she was needed. And she cared no more about approval from union leaders than operators; wherever people were in trouble, she showed up to lead the fight with tireless devotion. With all this, she was no fanatic. She had a lively sense of humor—she could tell wonderful stories, usually at the expense of some boss, for she couldn't resist the temptation to agitate, even in a joke—and she exuded a warm friendliness and human sympathy. The priest who preached at her funeral in the little mining town of Verdon, Illinois, said, with all truth, that she had spent her life in God's work for the poor and oppressed. May her soul rest in peace.

I joined the South Fork local in the spring of 1899, at the age of fifteen. Those of us who belonged to the checkweigh association at the Stineman mine were entitled to join the United Mine Workers without paying an initiation fee. My father joined on the same night, along with a large crowd of men from the mine where we both worked. The union had rented a hall which belonged to some of the Stinemans for its meetings, and we gathered in the anteroom, where the doorkeeper took our names and the name of the mine where we worked and then went inside to report to the meeting. After a short wait, we were admitted and walked up to the front of the room, where Ed Fisher, president of the local, was standing. There were perhaps 150 to 200 people in the room, and about 20 of us newcomers. Fisher read us the obligation of membership, which we repeated after him, sentence by sentence. I don't remember it all, but one phrase I have never forgotten: "to defend freedom of thought whether expressed by tongue or pen." I know that whenever the union forgot this principle, whatever the excuse, it suffered for the lapse.

I was greatly impressed by the solemnity with which Ed Fisher read the obligation of membership. When we had repeated it after him, he said, "Now you are members of the United Mine Workers and entitled to all rights and privileges as a member of this body." Then we sat down among the other members. As a boy of fifteen, I was very conscious of a warm feeling of belonging, of having a common cause with the older men gathered in Stineman's Hall. I wish I could remember the date of that meeting; it would be worth commemorating for its great effect on the rest of my life.

We were given the current password, by which we were admitted to local meetings. The password was changed every three months or so. I remember that we used "United We Stand," and later its obverse, "Divided We Fall." During the bloody struggles in Colorado we used the name of that state.

The United Mine Workers was not a secret organization, as the Knights of Labor had been. In the years of the Knights' ascendancy, secrecy had had its uses, and if secrecy had been enforceable, there were still occasions when protection against spies and stool pigeons would have been welcome. But the fact was that secrecy had never been a very realistic policy, and the survival of customs like the use of a password, along with a great deal of ritual derived from the Knights of Labor, can be ascribed more to a sentimental affection for the old ways of doing things than to their utility. The men enjoyed

the ritual—it was a change from the drab commonplace of daily life—
and it probably added something to the impressiveness of the union's
work. Some of the men belonged to lodges, and I suppose they felt
that a certain amount of ceremonial was only proper in an organization
professing high ideals. There were branches of the Odd Fellows and
the Order of United American Mechanics in South Fork. A few of the
Scottish miners had brought membership in the Masons with them
from the old country, though the Masons recruited mostly from the
middle class of mining towns—storekeepers, superintendents, and
lawyers. The Knights of Columbus had not been heard from in our
area that early. There was a group called Sons and Daughters of
Patriotic Orders of America, made up of descendants of Civil War
veterans and mostly middle-class; they were very reactionary and had
little in common with the miners.

There had been a good deal of tension between the United Mine
Workers and the remnants of the Knights of Labor in the coal fields
all through the nineties. National Trade Assembly 135 of the Knights
was not a satisfactory substitute for a national union of coal miners,
and the leaders of the Knights of Labor were not flexible enough to
recognize the need for a better union. They refused to back trade
assemblies in conflicts with mixed local assemblies, and when the
UMW appeared on the scene, the Knights treated it as a dual movement. Because the UMW was more efficiently set up to deal with
grievances of the trade, it drew members from the Knights, who had
vanished from the coal fields by the beginning of the century. The
ritual used at the funeral of a miner was taken bodily from the Knights,
as was much of the obligation of membership, and the formalities involved in introducing new members. So there are traces of the long
dead and gone Noble Order of the Knights of Labor still to be found
in the United Mine Workers, and in other unions as well, I suppose.

The first leaders of the UMW received most of their experience and
training in the Knights of Labor. John Rae, the first president, came
from the Broad Top region in the southern part of District 2, where
he had been active in the Knights. I never saw him, but I remember
some of the miners talking about him and his work.

South Fork was rapidly organized, and benefits soon followed. In
1900, the eight-hour day was won for the entire district. Annual
agreements were signed between the union and employers, with uniform higher wages. Thousands joined the union. Dues were checked

off: 2 per cent of earnings from day men and 3 per cent from miners. Sub-district organizations were created, to administer funds, pay check-weighmen, and provide more help to locals than the district organization could give. Each sub-district had one or two men working full time, visiting locals and checking on the hundreds of mines. The miners paid higher dues than the day men because the latter had no need for the services of checkweighmen. With the help of extra income from the larger mines, we were able to support a checkweighman in every mine employing fifteen or more men.

I attended local union meetings only occasionally in South Fork. Perhaps because the union was successful and no burning issues arose calling for active support, I often found something else to do on meeting nights. Like most people, I took the union for granted because it was doing well.

When there were major issues, the union would call a mass meeting and everybody would attend. And elections for local offices, held every six months, brought out a good attendance. Mine committees and checkweighmen were elected by the men in each mine, usually in an outdoor meeting near the mine, after work. The mine committee was important. It took up grievances with the foreman and reported each week to the local union meeting. As a mere boy, I never served on a mine committee in South Fork. Seasoned veterans who had had long experience with miners' problems and who could be expected to deal gravely with grave problems were usually selected. When committee-men lost time from their work on union business, they were compensated by the union at the going day rate.

We got newspapers from Philadelphia and Pittsburgh. Often my father and I would read the papers together and discuss matters of interest we found in them. We followed the anthracite strike of 1902, and read the verbatim reports of arguments before the Coal Commission created by President Theodore Roosevelt. I was deeply stirred by the drama of John Mitchell's fight for the miners' rights.

The bituminous miners assessed themselves a dollar a week to support the anthracite strike. This meant two dollars out of each paycheck, which was a lot of money for us, in addition to regular dues.

My father and I worked in several mines in South Fork, and in the nearby towns of Ehrenfeld (known locally as "Scooptown") and Dunlo. We moved two or three times, but these were short moves within a small neighborhood, so life was more stable than it had been for years. We were able to buy some new furniture to replace what we had sold on leaving Horatio.

As usual, my father soon found special cronies with whom to spend his spare time. On Sunday evenings, he and I would often visit two Irishmen who lived in the two sides of a double house. Pat Ganley and Martin Coyne had come from the same village in Connaught, as young men. Both were ardent Irish patriots, whose mother tongue was Gaelic. Often they would explain things to one another in that language while I listened wonderingly, for of course I understood not a word of it.

We always went to Ganley's house. In a few minutes, Coyne would appear, saying, "I heard Paddy's voice and I knew he would be here for a chat or something special to read for the evening."

The "something special" was usually my reading from a copy of the *Irish World*. It might be a whole issue devoted to the story of Robert Emmet's effort to seize Dublin Castle in 1803, and of his capture, trial, and execution, with long quotations from his stirring speech on the scaffold. Or I might read the story of the United Irishmen of 1798, the failure of the French troops to arrive in support of the rebellion, the capture of Wolfe Tone, and his suicide. Both Tone and Emmet died at the age of twenty-five, and their stories always brought the comment from one of my audience, "Ah, the grand man he was, cut off so early in life." Other stories told about the famine years, the Fenian agitations, and the "Manchester martyrs" of 1867. On evenings when there was nothing special to read, the two Irishmen would regale us with tales from the old country. I got a vivid introduction to Irish legendry from Pat Ganley and Martin Coyne.

Father and I went to Johnstown a few times, usually on a holiday. It was the biggest place I had seen since our arrival in America. Father liked to show me where he had worked to save lives and property after the great Johnstown flood.

7

IHIHIHIHIHIHIHIHIHIHIHIHIHIHIHIHIHIHIH

GREENWICH

For some reason I do not now remember, we moved from South Fork to a company town named Greenwich, three miles from Barnesboro where our wanderings had started a decade before. We had accumulated a lot of experience since then, but were no richer. The most important change, from my point of view, was that I was now a young man and able to carry my share of work in the mine with my father.

Mining towns have much in common, but also have points of difference. Greenwich was strung out for half a mile along a narrow ravine. A railroad branch, a highway, and a few houses were lined up by the side of a small creek; the other houses, the three mine tipples, and the company store perched on the hillside. The mines employed over four hundred men when they worked full time. The town was about half the size of South Fork and very new when we went there in 1904. Like Horatio, Greenwich has now vanished from the map.

The fifteen or eighteen hundred people of the town, including a dozen nationalities, had neither a church nor a public hall of any kind. They were still struggling to establish the beginnings of community life and spirit. The most compact group of English-speaking miners came from Tioga County, in the northern part of the state. They were the first American generation, sons of British miners who had manned the early field around Blossburg in the sixties. Most of them had moved to Greenwich after a long and bitterly fought strike against the Morris Run Coal Company. They always referred to Tioga County as "back home," so they were called "back-homers" by the other miners. They had had considerable union and local political experience, which made them an asset to the town. The only community organization was the union. It was recognized by the Greenwich Coal and Coke Company, which had signed the District 2 agreement. Local meetings were held on the second floor of a house rented from the company. The hall held no more than a hundred of the four hundred employed by the mines, so we had to build a proper union hall while I was in Greenwich. Members assessed themselves a few cents from each pay, and the union sponsored "festivals" to raise money. The company owned the entire town, so the union had to hunt around and find a farmer who would sell us an acre on the edge of town. The men pitched in to cut down timber on the land and built a big one-room frame house large enough to hold the membership. From then on, that crudely built house was the one independent center of community life.

The president of the local was John Flynn, a checkweighman. He was called "Crip" because he walked with a decided limp. He was an able and experienced local union officer, above average in intelligence and possessed of a fair education, including a working knowledge of parliamentary law. Unfortunately for the harmony of the local, the back-homers disliked Flynn. He was plain-spoken with everyone, the company and his fellow miners alike. The back-homers considered him sly and distrusted him, though I think their chief objection was that he was not one of their crowd but held his position because the other miners considered him the best man available.

The Flynns lived near us, so my father and I often walked with him to work. Perhaps because he had gotten to know me well from our daily walks together, one evening Flynn appointed me acting secretary, in the absence of the regular secretary. I was overwhelmed by the responsibility, but with Flynn's help I got through the meeting all right, and when the minutes were read at the next meeting they were approved "as read." The secretary had other interests and was irregular in his attendance, so I filled in several times. Finally, he got a job in another town and resigned. The men by then were used to seeing me up front, so they elected me in his place. I was only twenty, and had a lot to learn about this new job. It gave me a new and engrossing interest. I read communications from the national and district offices, kept the minutes, and answered letters. I modeled my minutes after the old ones, and learned how to write letters by imitating those that came in. I worked hard, because I was interested in learning how things should be done and wanted to make a good showing. I was paid fifty cents for each weekly meeting, which I put aside as a fund for the purchase of books.

My reading took a new turn in Greenwich. I began to read everything I could get on history, economics, social problems, and the labor movement. The United Mine Workers' *Journal,* which was published weekly at that time, carried advertisements for pamphlets put out by the AFL. I sent away for the whole set, and studied them. Some were convention speeches, which were uneven in quality, but there were also substantial pamphlets by Samuel Gompers, George McNeil, John Swinton, George Gunton, and Henry Demarest Lloyd on labor and social questions. I found the philosophy behind these writings congenial; it resembled the pragmatic trade-unionist thinking that my father had learned in England and passed on to me. There was no such thing as a bookstore for miles in any direction, so I had to send for books by mail. I bought a couple of histories out of the Sears, Roebuck catalogue. Then I went on to read Carroll D. Wright's *Industrial Evolution of the United States,* Richard T. Ely's *The Labor Movement in America,* Lloyd's *Wealth Against Commonwealth* and *Newest England,* and Henry George's *Progress and Poverty* and *Social Problems.* By then I was emboldened to try George's *Science of Political Economy,* but there I was out of my depth. When I was working, reading had to be fitted into evenings and weekends, but I got a lot of reading done during the strike of 1906. A little later, my urge for self-improvement led me to enroll for a correspondence course in English and mathematics. I felt a need to supplement my few years of formal schooling. I read the minutes and proceedings of national and district conventions to learn about the workings of the union. The 1904 national convention and interstate joint conference were, in a way, exciting reading. The operators had pressed for a reduction in wages on the ground that the depressed conditions of 1903 required it. Thousands of workers in non-union mines had already taken cuts. A joint subcommittee recommended a 5½ per cent wage cut, which was submitted to the UMW membership for a referendum vote. The national officers recommended acceptance, and the majority of the miners followed their advice. I was not convinced of the need for this concession or of the wisdom of granting it without a struggle, so I was one of the minority who stood against it. This was the first cut we had taken since 1899. One of my reasons for opposing the retreat was the fact that District 2, like many of the outlying districts, was only beginning to catch up to the Central Competitive Field, and I was afraid that this concession would weaken us in future dealings with the employers. We had built our membership up to about thirty thousand, but they were mostly new to unionism and apt to be easily discouraged.

I was elected, I think in 1905, as one of two delegates to a sub-district convention at Ebensburg, the county seat. There I met with forty delegates from the twenty locals of our sub-district in the grand jury room of the courthouse, and got my first practical experience of convention procedure. I met David Irvine, president of the sub-district, at this meeting; he later exerted much influence over my thinking. I met Patrick Gilday, president of District 2, at the dedication cere-monies of our Greenwich union hall. He was Scotch-Irish, a careful, deliberate, conservative person. Anything but an orator, he was im-pressive to me because he created a feeling of strength, stability, and self-assurance. The friendship of these men helped me overcome my natural shyness and develop the confidence I needed for leadership.

The local secretary whose place I took had been checkweighman in the Number Two mine, where I worked. When he left, the check-weigh job was open, and I developed an ambition to succeed him in that post, too. The checkweighman, elected and paid by the miners, was responsible to them for seeing that they were not cheated by the company weighmaster as their coal came from the mine. This was a very important job, because some of the companies were not above cheating the men outrageously. Unless there was somebody on hand, alert to protect the miners, chiseling a few pennies on each car could make a tremendous difference in earnings, both for the men and for the company.

I told my father I would like to try for the job, and asked his opinion. He approved of my ambition and promised to campaign for me. The mine committee had selected another man, an active young fellow a few years older than I, as its candidate. This did not preclude com-petition, but it did give him some advantage. On a warm June after-noon, about two hundred men gathered after work at the entrance to the mine. One of the mine committeemen presided. He stated the purpose of the meeting and presented the name of my opponent as the committee's choice. There was a pause for additional nominations, and as the interminable seconds passed I began to fear that I would not even be nominated. Finally my father shouted, "I nominate our Johnnie."

The balloting gave me a good majority. The man I defeated never forgave me; he had been sure of winning, but my father was a better campaigner. He went to work half an hour early each morning, sitting in the blacksmith shop at the mouth of the mine where he could talk to all the men as they came in to get their picks. He dropped into some of the workplaces, too, and asked the men to "give the lad a vote." And in the evening he circulated around the houses, seeing anybody he might have missed in the mine. He worked at this for a week, so I'm sure he missed nobody. The fact that I was secretary of the local and thus known to everybody no doubt helped. Furthermore, I had taken the previous man's place several times when he was out, so the men knew that I could do the job. I liked that job and held it for a year, until the strike of 1906 upset everything.

Conditions in the district had been improving steadily since 1899. Membership grew from a few hundred to over thirty thousand. A district office was opened in Clearfield and Dick Gilbert moved there from South Fork to give his full time to the job of secretary. The president and vice-president also were put on salary, and each sub-district had one or two full-time workers. There were checkweighmen in most of the mines; wages were raised; the eight-hour day had been won in 1900; working conditions—ventilation, safety, compensation for accidents—were being improved. There was much still to be done, but the union was pushing in the right direction and there was hope that major problems would be dealt with, instead of depending on the operators' whim, which usually favored no reform.

In our annual (later biennial) negotiations with the employers, we were constantly confronted with the argument that low wages in the West Virginia fields to the south of us gave those mines a competitive advantage that could only be met by cutting our wages. Otherwise West Virginia would steal all the customers and we would be unemployed. There was some merit in the argument, though by no means as much as the operators liked to think.

The small wage cut agreed to in 1904 whetted the appetite of certain operators for more, but the 1906 national convention of the UMW was in the mood to recover the 1904 loss by a national agreement. This determination was embodied in the Ryan resolution authorizing a nation-wide strike call, and forbidding the national officers to make piecemeal settlements. John Mitchell, the president, and William B. Wilson, the secretary-treasurer, were not happy with this rigid position. They wanted a free hand to make whatever settlements they thought would be most advantageous to the union. So they got a man named Perry, a district officer from Iowa, to offer another resolution authorizing national and district officers to sign a two-year agreement with any district operators' association or with any individual operator who would restore the scale of 1904. Ryan, under pressure from the national office, made no fight for his position, and the Perry resolution was passed. This changed a nine-year policy of holding the miners together until the Central Competitive Field had signed and then using that agreement as a base for the rest of the country. Settlements covering most of the Middle West were reached in a fairly short time, but for District 2 the result was a long and disastrous strike. Some of the operators had made up their minds to get rid of the union at any cost, and our company in Greenwich was one of that number.

We submitted our demand for restoration of the 1904 scale to the operators' association in March. Usually, representatives of the union and of the association would meet, discuss the union proposal, vote on it (a unanimous vote was required to approve a settlement), and if it was not immediately accepted, consider alternative proposals in a series of meetings until something could be worked out which both sides would take. This time, the Coal Operators' Association flatly refused to consider a wage increase. They just would not discuss it. Instead, they demanded that two new rules go into the contract: one, that in the event of a local strike for any reason whatever, both local and district treasuries would be liable for damages; and second, a rule that would protect the right of a man to work in the mines whether he was a union member or not. Also, they began to object to the check-off of dues. These three demands were all designed to destroy the union. The operators were no more interested in the "right to work" than their successors are today. All they wanted was the chance to use weak, ignorant, or corruptible men against the majority of good union men. The demand for damages was equally dishonest. There were many valid reasons for local stoppages. Miners would sometimes re-fuse to work because of bad ventilation or lack of proper safety pre-cautions. These were temporary conditions that could not be foreseen or covered by a two-year contract, and if the boss was in a tough mood sometimes nothing but a suspension of work would bring him to his senses.

I was a delegate to the district convention, which stayed in session in Clearfield all through the negotiations. Actually, negotiations were deadlocked before we ever got to the question of wages, because the association, representing most of the operators of the district, insisted that the union commit suicide by accepting their demands before they would discuss anything else. After a couple of weeks, conferences with the employers were suspended and the convention delegates returned home, subject to call if anything developed to require convention action.

Both sides were waiting to see what happened in the anthracite field. If anthracite struck, that might open up some markets for coal from our district and the operators might be willing to settle to take advantage of this additional business. If anthracite settled, our operators had enough coal in stock to last a while, and might be able to risk a strike, without too serious losses. After a couple of weeks, the convention reconvened to discuss policy. The district officers and W. B. Wilson (who was present) wanted to apply the principle of the Perry resolution, that is, to sign up individual operators who would restore the 1904 scale. This precipitated a fight.

The opposition, of whom I was one, argued first that this would split our forces; second (really an extension of the first argument), that in towns where two or more companies operated, if one signed up and the other did not, the effect on the local union would be disastrous; third, that this would allow a company to sign up for one of its operations and not for others elsewhere in the district; and finally, that we had no idea how many operators would sign any agreement under any terms, so we would be jeopardizing the custom of negotiating a single contract covering all members of the operators' association for the doubtful advantage of persuading a few operators to break away. Wilson replied to the third point that it was his position, and John Mitchell's, that a company should be required to sign for all its operations; separate settlements could be permitted company by company, but not mine by mine. Those companies that refused to concede the 1904 scale were to be struck.

The entire district was, to all intents and purposes, on strike from the day the contract ran out. I felt that if the lines were held, we might be able to force the whole Association to sign up, which would have covered more than half the tonnage production of the district. It would not have taken too long to convince the operators that their demands were not going to be met, and with no mines operating we might have been able to put enough of a squeeze on them to get a fair settlement. As it was, only about 20 per cent of the concerns accepted the chance to sign up individually and perhaps another 5 or 10 per cent broke ranks during the strike, which dragged on for three months. The miners held firm, but the drain on the union treasury was severe. In the latter part of July a compromise settlement was offered by most of the companies, and a special district convention voted to accept. This agreement restored the wage cut of two years before, but reduced the checkoff to a ton of coal each pay, thereby cutting the union's income. There was no checkoff at all from the day men; they had to be gone after individually. The union had paid out $340,000 in relief during the three and a half months of the strike. District and local treasuries were empty. The individual miners had used up their savings and exhausted their credit. The national office had sent in over $100,000 and was unwilling to sink any more in a losing struggle. Altogether, it seemed best to take what we could get, at least hoping to salvage the union from defeat. Unhappily for me, the Greenwich mines were not covered even by this settlement.

The Greenwich Coal Company had passed into the hands of new financial interests about this time, and almost from the beginning of the strike it was evident that they intended to break the local union. When time failed to weaken the solidarity of the strikers, the company resorted to harsher methods. A number of young men were brought in from outside, deputized by the sheriff and paid by the company, supposedly to guard company property and preserve "law and order." We knew there had been no increase in lawlessness in town, but we were not left wondering very long just what the sheriff and his new deputies meant by law and order. The first job they undertook was to evict the strikers from their homes. Men, women, and children were driven out of the end of the town nearest the mine, and furniture was piled outside the houses, with a warning that it must be carted away immediately. Within ten days, nearly two-thirds of the strikers were homeless. The union rented a large field over the ridge from town from a sympathetic farmer, the same one who had sold us land for the union hall. The sub-district office shipped in tents and we set up a tent colony.

Fortunately, spring had begun, sparing us an ordeal of winter weather. But rain made the field a morass of mud, sanitary facilities were makeshift, cooking facilities were scarcely better, and altogether the tent colony was a severe hardship for the families who had to endure it. A few families were able to move to empty houses in towns four to six miles away.

We understood the meaning of this extreme action all too clearly. There had been a few evictions elsewhere, but nothing on this scale. My family was not evicted because we were not in a company house, but had a little place just over the hill from town, near the railroad. There was no passenger service direct to Greenwich but a train or two a day would drop passengers a few miles from town. A spur from this line went in to the mines, carrying only freight. One day in midsummer I saw a passenger train going along the line at an unusual hour. I suspected that this special train was bringing in scabs to the mines and cut across the hill to town as fast as I could to spread the alarm. When I got to Greenwich, I saw that the train had pulled up on the spur to the mine, where no passenger train had ever been before, and was unloading its passengers—obviously scabs. A number of strikers had gathered around, but the deputies were trying to keep them away and to herd the scabs into nearby company houses. It was a wild scene, for the scabs were milling around like lost sheep, confused by the pushing and shouting of both strikers and deputies. We tried to get among them, yelling, "There's a strike on here; don't scab! Don't take our jobs!"

The deputies tried to keep us separate, shouting, "Get out of here, you're trespassing." Legally they were right, I suppose; the company owned everything. Part of the town had been closed off by a high board fence, behind which was the mine entrance and some of the company houses. If the deputies could get the men into the enclosed houses, they could keep us out by patrolling the fence. A few of us made a detour, got through a gap at one end of the fence, and reached the newcomers. The guards threatened us and ordered us out, but as more of our men arrived and circulated among the milling scabs, the guards found it hard to tell friend from foe. We got some of the new arrivals moving away from the mine, and finally about fifty or sixty broke out of the stockade and followed us down to the center of town. The first men we talked to protested that they had no idea they were being brought into a struck mine and would be glad to get out of town if they could. To prove their good faith they worked on some of the others, so we got most of that group away from the mine. I promised to arrange for them to leave safely. I phoned the sub-district office in Barnesboro, four miles away, and talked to the sub-district president. He had heard about the train from a friendly conductor who had sent him a wire from Cresson, the junction. I told him I had most of the men right there and had to do something about them immediately, because they were just standing around and I had no way of telling what the company might do to get them back. He said, "Bring them up here to Barnesboro, and the secretary will figure out how to send them back where they came from."

So I led my raggle-taggle parade four miles to Barnesboro, feeling like the proud victor in a great battle. We gave the men lunch and train fare home and saw them off at the station. They came from non-union mines in Westmoreland County, and had been induced to come to Greenwich by tall tales of fine jobs, with no mention of the strike. If they had been professional scabs instead of just dupes, we would not have rid ourselves of them so easily. The company retaliated by evicting the few union families left in town. The company, from then on, imported scabs in small groups, very closely guarded. We never could get near them. Finally there were enough scabs to operate one of the mines in a feeble way—perhaps forty or fifty men in all. The high fence around that end of town was constantly patrolled by deputies. The new scabs were non-English-speaking, so we tried to get a few men who spoke their language inside the fence at night to talk to them. But they didn't know whom to trust and were afraid to come out of the stockade. Their production of coal was small, compared to what four hundred miners had put out before the strike, but the company was committed to a fight to the finish.

By the time fall set in, ours was the only town in the district still on strike. The tent colony began to break up. Living conditions were insufferable and getting worse. It would be impossible to heat the tents in cold weather. Men drifted out to find jobs elsewhere. Nobody could blame them. The local union was broke and there was no way of telling how long even the thin trickle of district relief could be kept coming in. I was working day and night to try to keep up morale, as were some of the other men, including my father, but there was not much to hope for. We picketed the mine, but it was hard to get anywhere near it without "trespassing." There were occasional scuffles between strikers and deputies when we pushed too near company property, but no serious outbreaks. There was not much to fight about. The company was losing money every day but showed no signs of caring. In fact, the company shortly afterward went through bankruptcy to celebrate its victory over the union. The bosses could hardly have been ignorant of what they were doing to themselves, but they were too stubborn even to look out for their own interests, it appears to me. This might explain why it is impossible to find any trace of Greenwich today. I don't know; I can only wonder, as I did over half a century ago, what makes people act like that.

During the strike, we had distributed relief to the strikers. The men were expected to live on the pay due them for the first couple of weeks; then they were eligible for orders on nearby independent stores, for which they got groceries and other goods, but no cash. We allowed two dollars a week for a man, a dollar for his wife, and fifty cents for each child. John Flynn had moved out of town before the strike, and his successor, a back-homer, presided over the relief committee. After several weeks, when men were already beginning to drift out of town, a friend told me that some of the committeemen had been seen at the hotel in Garman's Mills buying drinks and flush with money. Everybody else was broke, so this was worth investigating. One of the older men suggested I see the storekeepers and find out what they could tell me about the source of the committeemen's prosperity.

I went to a storekeeper I knew rather well, a young fellow named John Criton, and asked him, "John, there's talk going around that some people are getting cash instead of groceries for their orders. What do you know about it? What's going on?"

He looked at me strangely, and said, "You mean you don't know what's going on?"

"I know there's something going on," I answered, "but I've got to find out what it is and who is behind it. I don't want this to break the morale of the strikers. Tell me, are you giving out cash for orders?"

"Yes," he said, "I've given out some."

"Would you show me the orders you've cashed?"

"Well, I don't know about that," he said. "I will if you don't tell anybody."

"No," I said, "I can't promise that. I have some responsibility in this business. I'm the secretary of the local, and I should get to the bottom of this."

After some hesitation, he showed me some of the orders. They were signed by committeemen, but made out in other names. I asked for an explanation.

He told me the committeemen had gotten groceries for their own orders and then said the other men whose names were on the orders had asked them to get cash for them. I began to get mad, and Criton defended himself by saying that the other storekeeper was doing it too. I went to the other storekeeper, gradually bullied him into admitting that he was cashing orders, and got him to give me some to add to my evidence.

The committeemen had been keeping on the roll the names of men who left town, issuing orders in their names, and then cashing the orders. The amounts of money involved were not large, but it was about as nasty a kind of thievery as anyone could invent and had to be stopped at once.

I phoned the president of the sub-district and told him the story. He asked me to meet him in Barnesboro. We agreed that the guilty men would have to be removed from the committee, and I asked him to come to the local meeting that night to back me up. He had to go to another meeting, but he promised to send the secretary over. Before the meeting, I told the man who had first tipped me off what I had found, and he promised to back me.

So that evening I opened fire, charging the committeemen with falsifying records and stealing money from the union. I accused them of treason to the union and to the strikers who were dependent on what little we could give them to keep from starving. Some of them put on a big show of indignation and demanded proof. I displayed the orders I had collected from the storekeepers, read off the names of the men they had been made out to and showed the committeemen's signatures on the orders. With four hundred people on strike, it might have been hard to track down each individual, but as I read off the names, people began to recognize some of them as belonging to men who had left town. There was no need for any elaborate checkup to convince the membership that there had been crooked business. The committeemen blustered and threatened me, but I kept pounding away at the facts and demanding that they get off the committee and that the president be fired. The district secretary backed me up, and more and more people came over to my side. Finally, I offered a motion to remove the guilty men from their offices and to deny them transfer cards to any other local union until the district organization had gone over the records and recovered the stolen money. There was no doubt about the vote; the motion carried overwhelmingly. The disgraced officers left town.

When the discharged officers were replaced, I found myself elected president. That was a great honor for such a young man, but I cannot say that I found it an easy or privileged post. By then the strike was lost, and not even the most strenuous efforts could revive it. Men were leaving to find work elsewhere; Greenwich was a ghost town; the tent colony was uninhabitable. Even though most of the mines elsewhere in the district were working again, so that there was money coming into the district treasury, the strikers could not be expected to go on indefinitely living on what relief the union could provide and without a decent roof over their heads for the winter. The best I could do was to wind up the affairs of the local with minimum loss to the union and to the workers. If there had been the slightest sign that the company was willing to consider any settlement, things might have been different. But though the trickle of coal produced by scabs hardly paid for keeping the mines open, the company preferred to write off Greenwich altogether rather than consider any terms with the union. Greenwich was doomed.

The unsatisfactory settlement in the district as a whole provoked some expression of discontent through political action. William B. Wilson, the national secretary-treasurer, was elected to Congress from a district in the northern part of the state. And in Cambria and Clearfield counties, miners and Grangers got together to organize a labor party, called the Working Class Party. Candidates were nominated for the state legislature in both counties, including Richard Gilbert, the district secretary, running paired with a Granger in Clearfield. They got a fairly good vote, but were not elected; the farmers couldn't break their habit of voting Republican. Results were about the same for the two candidates in Cambria County, David Irvine and Ed Fisher.

The party platform incorporated labor and farmer planks, as well as a variety of reforms designed to make the government more democratic. It was headed: "Your vote and influence solicited in the interest of Labor and A Square Deal. . . . We demand representation in government for the common people, that those whose toil has made the nation rich and great, shall frame the laws and control its destiny." Initiative and referendum, direct election of United States senators, progressive income and inheritance taxes, and an "equitable Employers' Liability Law" were endorsed, along with a two-cent-a-mile passenger fare on the railroads and the right of electric trolley lines to carry freight (the latter two items for the farmers). The platform denounced the State Constabulary Law as "the climax of corporate presumption," and the use of injunctions in labor disputes as "an act of tyranny offensive to the spirit of our institutions." It was a good platform, with excellent proposals to benefit both labor and the farmers, but there were a lot of hardshell Republicans around (not to mention some Democrats, less numerous but almost as hardshelled) and the new party did not draw enough voters away from their habitual ways of voting. I cast my first vote for this labor party, being too young to have formed any iron-clad habits. Even though the party did not survive that election, it was effective in spreading progressive ideas, which were considered pretty radical then, but are now taken for granted by everybody but a few of the extreme right wing.*

I would have liked to stay in this area where I had learned and accomplished so much, but that was out of the question. Greenwich was no longer a town; the men I had known and worked with were scattered far and wide. Worst of all, my father and I were blacklisted throughout the district. After much discussion, we decided that since we had to move anyway, my father and I would go to the West, find jobs, and send for the rest of the family when we were settled.

Our family was reduced by one during the latter part of our stay in Greenwich. My oldest sister, Mary, was married to William Welsh, who had been my first childhood friend in this country, back in Philipsburg. The Welshes moved to Barnesboro and then to Nanty Glo, where I worked with Bill in the union a few years later.

Father and I left my mother with the younger children and started out for the West to see what we could find.

* The platform was printed in the Lilly *Signal,* Lilly, Pa., October 12, 1906. Union men feared, with reason, that the state police would be used to break strikes in the same way as the notorious Coal and Iron Police, who were commissioned by the state and paid and controlled by the coal companies. See *The Coal Strike in Western Pennsylvania* (Dept. of Research and Education, Federal Council of Churches of Christ in America, 1928), pp. 49–52.

8

VENTURES TO THE WEST

Father and I went to Illinois, where we had heard from a friend that some mines were being opened by one of the railroads. We took the train to St. Louis, then another train fifty miles northward to Gillespie, where our friend lived. He put us up for the night, and then took us with him to the mine. We were put on the night shift, at what was called "slate work." The seam of coal in this mine was eight feet thick, roofed by two to four feet of slate, above which was a harder rock, probably sandstone. Undercutting was done by machines, and the powder charges were shot off at night, so that the miners worked fairly steadily loading coal all day. The mine cars held three tons or more, but a limit was enforced on the number of cars a man got each day, to equalize pay and opportunities to work. Even so, the men on the coal were making more than the day men.

Where coal had been dug out, the slate roof broke and fell. A fairly large night crew was required to keep the main entries and openings to workplaces clear. We took down the weakened roof and shoveled the debris into mine cars to be dumped. My father and I worked at the unloading. Toward midnight of my first shift I dozed off to sleep while we were waiting for more loads to be brought out. The night boss came along and caught me snoozing before my father could wake me.

The boss said, "No sleeping on the job, young fellow. Anyway, I have something for you to do that will keep you awake the rest of the night. Go down to the bottom of the pit and clean out the sump."

I asked if this was punishment for being caught asleep when I had nothing to do. He answered, "No, we make a practice of using younger men in turn for a few hours at a time cleaning the sump. Older men like your father are exempt." I had to be satisfied with this explanation.

During the day, as coal was hoisted up the shaft, pieces and bits would fall off into the bottom until there might be a couple of tons accumulated there. The sump, where this coal fell, was a continuation of the shaft ten or twelve feet below the level of the seam. Water drained into it and had to be pumped out daily. We night men would slosh around in the water, shoveling out the loose coal; it was anything but a pleasant job, and a few hours of it was more than enough.

Occasionally, if one of the men working on the coal failed to show up for work, one of us would get a chance to fill in. I had several nights of fill-in work, which I was glad to have, though it was not enough to do my wages much good. We got tired of working the night shift, and as it became clear that our chances of getting work on the coal were remote at best, we began to wish that we were back home in Pennsylvania.

Our living conditions did nothing to increase our affection for Gillespie. We were in a company boardinghouse near the mine, known as "The Beanery," run by a widow and her grown daughter. Among our fellow boarders was a bunch of young mule-drivers from Kentucky, a wild and harum-scarum gang. We were told shortly after our arrival not to leave our new pit clothes in the outdoor shanty next to The Beanery where we washed up after work, or somebody else would be wearing them. Being on the night shift gave us the advantage of not seeing much of these fellows, except on weekends.

But one weekend, which happened to coincide with a payday, gave us all we could take of The Beanery. Some of the youngsters went to St. Louis to sow wild oats, and returned on Sunday evening in an ugly mood. They considered that a certain coal cutter who was on friendly terms with the landlady's daughter was getting star-boarder treatment, and they resented this favoritism. They picked a quarrel with him; insults were exchanged; others were drawn in on both sides; a stove and a table were overturned. Finally guns appeared and there was a free-for-all fight. "No place for us when shooting starts," shouted my father, and we got out of there fast. Nobody was seriously hurt in the fracas, but most of the furniture was smashed, and the boarding-house had to suspend operations. We found another place to stay in a private home, which was a great improvement. But I guess we were both a little homesick by then, and with such dim prospects of being able to move the family, we decided, after a month in Gillespie, to have another try at finding a job in Pennsylvania.

We returned home and scouted around for a while. Finally we found jobs in a mine in Nanty Glo which apparently did not know about our being blacklisted, and settled down to stay. Nanty Glo was a fair-sized town. About four hundred men worked in four mines, each owned and operated by a separate company. The number employed doubled in a few years. Each company owned some houses, but a third or more of the miners lived in houses not owned by any company. Only two concerns maintained their own stores, so several independent stores catered to the wants of the miners and their wives. Two or three churches served as community centers, as well as caring for the spiritual needs of the people.

The local union owned its own building, a large two-story frame structure. The first floor was an auditorium for meetings of all kinds: mass meetings of the miners, political rallies, plays, festivals, and gatherings of fraternal societies. Upstairs was a smaller hall for weekly meetings of the local union.

The local union seemed firmly established but I soon discovered that all was not well. Owen Roberts, whom I had met at district conventions, was treasurer and financial secretary. He was discouraged, because many of the local officers and mine committeemen were shiftless fellows interested only in the small fees they could collect from the treasury and not at all interested in doing anything to improve the condition of the members. Worse, the rank and file were indifferent and few bothered to attend meetings. Roberts was ready to quit at the end of his term, in a couple of months. He was tired of being the only one who took his responsibilities seriously. I told him I thought it would be a mistake to quit, that I thought it should be possible to rebuild confidence and interest.

"Maybe," he said, "but first we'll have to get rid of the president and some of these other parasites, especially the deadwood on the mine committees."

"If you'll agree to stay on," I replied, "we can at least make a try. I can fight from the floor, criticize them for doing nothing or for doing the wrong things, or whatever else needs criticizing. Maybe a few good floor fights will build up attendance. Everybody likes to see a fight, and if it's a good enough one, maybe some of them will get into it." He was not optimistic, but agreed to give it a try. So for three or four months I showed up at each meeting loaded with ammunition to fire at the officers. At first they just considered me a nuisance, but there was so much ground for criticism that they finally had to answer me. They tried to dismiss me as a crank, they tried to bully me, they tried to deny me the floor, but none of these tactics worked. For one thing, some of the rank and file were beginning to take interest and support me. Then the leaders adopted the pose of injured men and threatened to resign if they were to be exposed to this constant barrage of criticism. That was just what I was waiting for.

"Fine!" I said. "That's just what you ought to do. You're not serving the union; you're just wasting its time and its assets."

"Are you accusing us of taking something that doesn't belong to us?"

"I don't know whether you are or not. There's a lot of talk to that effect. But even if you do put in the time you turn in bills for, you're not accomplishing anything. You don't uphold the rules of the union. Members stay away because you don't give them any reason to come to meetings. You're not taking care of our interests, but just letting everything slide."

"Oh, maybe *you'd* like this job." This with great sarcasm, of course.

"No, I don't want your job, but it's a cinch nobody could do it any worse than you. If the local can't find a better man I'll take a chance on it."

This kind of exchange did them no good, and I never relaxed my pressure. Finally, one of the gang lost his temper and resigned at a local meeting. That broke the jam. I said, "The whole shebang of you ought to quit, too, before we fire you at the next election. Then maybe we can get something done around here." By that time the pressure had built up irresistibly, so without waiting for the regular election the whole gang quit. Roberts and I put together a good slate of officers and elected them without any trouble. At various times, I served as financial secretary, recording secretary, and president. My brother-in-law, William Welsh, got into the work of the local union too, and was president for some time. Welsh was a good miner, and a courageous, intelligent fighter for the union. He had far more confidence in my abilities than I had and I always felt better when I could count on his advice and backing. He never let me, or the union, down.

We set to work on neglected grievances and demanded more support and attention from the sub-district officers. We put good men on the mine committees, to clean up a lot of bad practices that had grown up. The mine committeemen can be the most important people in the union; if they do their work well, the members get daily proof of the union's value on the job. Within three or four months we had completely reformed the local. Attendance at meetings picked up, morale improved, and interest in legislative work and in the problems of the district as a whole increased.

I had missed the 1907 district convention, but I attended the one in March, 1908, as a delegate from Nanty Glo. There I renewed my acquaintance with David Irvine, whom I had known as sub-district president during the Greenwich strike. He was twenty years older than I, and I liked and admired him very much. He was a fair speaker, clear and deliberate in manner, better read than the average union officer, and possessed of a sharply analytical mind. Whenever we got together we found an endless store of things to talk about, problems and personalities of the union and broader subjects as well. Irvine, while not a formal Socialist, knew Socialist literature and activities and was broadly sympathetic to progressive political ideas. He thought more could be accomplished for the union by working through the major political parties than in third parties, though he had been a candidate for State Assembly on the ticket of the independent labor party for which I had cast my first vote two years before. Irvine exerted a very great influence in the development of my ideas; in fact, we worked so closely together that I became known as one of his group in the union.

The district had been shaken by a fight over a reorganization proposal introduced by district president Patrick Gilday at the 1907 convention. When District 2 was reconstructed at the end of the nineties, it was organized into a number of sub-districts built around the old checkweigh associations. Each sub-district had a complete set of officers—president, vice-president, secretary-treasurer, and an executive board of the three officers and four to six working miners, which met every few months. One or more of the officers served as a full-time paid worker for the union. The sub-district treasury collected dues from the locals for support of checkweighmen, a necessary function to equalize the burden between small and large mines. And the officers were on call to help locals when needed. This provided a useful level of organization between the men in the pits and the district office. Gilday criticized the sub-district setup as expensive, complicated, and unnecessary, advocating a single central treasury for the whole district, which, he argued, would do an even better job of equalizing the burden of maintaining checkweighmen. The sub-districts would be reduced, by his proposal, to nothing more than constituencies from which members of the district executive board would be elected. I have no doubt that in the elimination of sub-district autonomy he saw a chance to extend his own power as well as to reduce the danger of factionalism. District board members were full-time functionaries of the union, but unlike the sub-district officers they were attached to the district organization and were to some extent under its control. They would take over the service to locals provided by sub-district officers. Furthermore, Gilday's proposal gave the district president the power to appoint an assistant board member for each sub-district.

The opponents of the centralization plan were caught unprepared at the 1907 convention, with no alternative to offer. Financial disparities could have been adjusted by turning over surplus funds to the district for aid to weaker sub-districts. Even without an alternative, over a third of the delegates voted against the change. Gilday was so intent on getting what he wanted and so unwilling to run the risk of defeat that he turned down proposals for a referendum. This was a blunder, for the question continued to agitate the district for years, consuming its energies in factional squabbling. Irvine supported the sub-districts, as did most of the people in our section. He ran against Gilday for president of the district on this issue during 1907, but was defeated and returned to work in the mines.

The local issue was complicated by the struggle to succeed John Mitchell in the presidency of the national union. Mitchell intended to resign at the end of his term, in 1908. William B. Wilson, the national secretary-treasurer, announced his candidacy, in which he was supported by Mitchell. Thomas L. Lewis, the vice-president, was the candidate of the opposition. Wilson was from our district, which won him the support of the district staff. Irvine threw his support behind Lewis, both because Irvine opposed the district administration and because Lewis had stood fast against Mitchell in 1906 for a national agreement and against piecemeal settlements. I agreed with Irvine on this election. I had had a convincing lesson in the disastrous effects of Mitchell's piecemeal policy in the Greenwich strike.

It was sometimes uphill work, campaigning for Lewis in our district against a deservedly popular and respected man from District 2. Though the fact that Wilson was a local man had nothing to do with the issues, the men knew him much better than Lewis, and took pride in his rise from a Tioga County mine to international office. I could not blame them for this sentiment, but I saw no reason to let sentiment get in the way of sound policy, and Wilson was on the wrong side of two very important issues. These issues—local autonomy and the need for a solid front in negotiation of national agreements—were to play a large role in my later career.

Thomas L. Lewis won the presidency by a narrow majority of about two thousand votes. Irvine, who had campaigned actively up and down the central Pennsylvania district, became his chief representative in District 2. I had also campaigned for Lewis among the locals along Black Lick Creek, in our immediate neighborhood. I was offered a commission as a national office organizer, but declined it and suggested in my place a young Italian miner, Dominic Gillotte, from Nanty Glo. He was appointed, and for several years was an effective worker among the Italian miners.

While I was in Nanty Glo, Irvine conducted me through a short course of reading about Socialism. He sent me two books, *Modern Socialism* and *Scientific Socialism.* I forget the authors' names. I was only mildly interested, but was deeply moved by an issue of the Socialist weekly, *Appeal to Reason,* devoted entirely to the case of Moyer, Haywood, and Pettibone, who were on trial in Idaho for the murder of Governor Frank Steunenberg. Gene Debs wrote a strong editorial calling on the working people to support the victims of the mine owners. I was convinced that the three men were framed for their labor activities, and I've never heard any reason to doubt it since. I went to the local union meeting that night, and when the order of business came to "Good and Welfare," launched into the story of class war in the Far West. Our local was one of many labor organizations, including the national organization of the United Mine Workers, to support the defendants.

My extensive exposure to the literature of Socialism never won me over. I was interested in and impressed by the Socialist criticism of capitalism and its evils. Like the Socialists, I wanted social justice, and a more efficient economy free of the ups and downs of the business cycle. I wanted union labor participation in the basic decisions of industry. Above all, I was bitter against conditions in the coal industry, with its frightful waste of men and resources, killing two thousand and injuring tens of thousands of men every year. I wanted an end to reckless and brutal mismanagement of both coal and men.

Yet with all my anger at the stupidities, and even atrocities, I saw around me year by year, I remained basically a trade unionist. I had lived my life in mining towns and had seen how effective the union could be in correcting evils in both mine and community. Even when the going was bad, the union had my first loyalty as the hope for better days. I formed the habit of subjecting all ideals to the test of my practical experience as a worker and unionist, both in union affairs and with respect to political questions and parties. I have known many Socialists of the party of Gene Debs and Norman Thomas, and have usually found myself in agreement with them on their reform program. But the rigid doctrines of Marxist materialism have never had any appeal for me. My belief in Christian humanism and in political and economic freedom has made it impossible for me to become a Marxist of any stamp. If I have favored increased control by the workers over the conduct of industry, it is because of my experience with the utter failure of irresponsible power, not because of any affinity with Marxism.

Had I known of the papal social encyclicals I could have been saved much distress of mind. American churchmen were very slow about heeding the papal counsel on these important issues. I never read *Rerum Novarum* until a generation after it was issued. I heard of it only vaguely as an anti-Socialist tract, or even as an apology for capitalism. American churchmen seem not to have grasped the meaning of that great document for a long time; certainly I, like many others, was long left in ignorance of its criticism of capitalism and of its constructive counsel.

I attended my first national convention of the United Mine Workers in 1908, at Indianapolis, as a delegate from Local 1386 of Nanty Glo. This was the last convention presided over by John Mitchell.

I stayed at a little hotel, the Morton House, near the center of the city. An old miner from my district who had been there several times before started out with me from the hotel, but he got lost and wasted some time wandering around before we reached Tomlinson Hall. The convention was already under way when we entered the great auditorium on the second floor. John Mitchell had just finished an opening speech, and we walked in as the fifteen hundred delegates broke out in a thundering shout of applause. I have rarely been so stirred as I was by my first sight of that convention. It was by far the largest meeting I had ever seen. There, standing before me, was the great John Mitchell, whose career I had followed through struggle after struggle. Here was the center and citadel of the coal miner's one abiding hope, this tremendous gathering representing the power of hundreds of thousands of men united to improve the lives of all who lived in the coal camps.

I was grateful for the chance to see John Mitchell in action before his retirement. The delegates felt a great affection for him and were genuinely sorry to see him quit. He had led the union through great crises to a prospect of power beyond even the hopes of a decade earlier.

Mitchell was not the only famous man I saw in action at national conventions. At a later convention, "Big Bill" Haywood came from his acquittal in Idaho to thank the United Mine Workers for their support. He was at the height of his rugged powers, and made a dramatic fighting speech. Twenty years later I saw him again in Moscow, an exile from his country. His great frame was weakened and failing, the fires of life obviously dying out. He showed some of his old animation briefly when he discovered that one of our group was from Colorado, and talked about old scenes and acquaintances in America. I think the prisoner of inaction in a far-off land would have liked to come home. He died a few months later.

I heard Eugene V. Debs speak for the first time in Indianapolis. The Socialists ran a mass meeting in Tomlinson Hall for the special benefit of the delegates. Everybody, Socialist or not, attended, jamming the hall to the rafters. I don't remember what Debs said, though it was eloquent and powerful, but I never forgot a little incident before he spoke. The stage was crowded with people pressing to shake Debs's hand. Out of the crowd came two little girls with a bouquet of flowers to present to him. He bent down to receive them, and from the bouquet drew two flowers which he gave to the children. The action was so graceful, so obviously spontaneous and kind, that I saw why everybody who knew Debs loved him.

For ten days I was absorbed in the work of the convention, officers' reports, committee reports, and full discussion from the floor of all decisions. The other business was not overshadowed by electioneering for office, as so often happens in conventions, because the miners elected their officers by a referendum vote. I became aware of the strong Socialist group among the miners, with its center in Illinois. The Socialists took the lead in pressing for resolutions supporting a variety of reforms: political changes to make government more democratic, like referendum and recall and direct election of United States senators; civil liberties matters, like the abominations practiced against the Western Federation of Miners and the IWW in the West; even foreign issues, like support for the struggle against the Díaz dictatorship in Mexico. Though they brought up new ideas, or at least concepts not commonly heard around coal towns, they were real miners and men of standing among the workers, men who knew how to talk miners' language. These men were strengthened in their devotion to the union by their political ideas, not, like the De Leonites and the later Communists, primarily interested in using the union to advance their party.

Frank J. Hayes, secretary, and Adolph Germer, vice president, of the Belleville, Illinois, sub-district were notable among the Socialist leaders. Hayes had an emotional kind of eloquence and liked to make a rather sentimental speech about the sorrows of the poor. It was a very good speech, and we heard it frequently. As he rose in the offices of the union, he developed enough variations on that speech to last him a lifetime.

Adolph Germer I remember first as a tall stripling with a high-pitched voice. I can see him now stepping out into the aisle, raising his hand, and calling "Mr. Chairman!" in that high, thin voice that carried so well through the hall. He did this so frequently, I came to associate "Mr. Chairman!" with Adolph's efforts to get the floor, which he did often, usually to good effect.

John H. Walker was president of the Illinois District, the most powerful in the union. He did much to make Illinois the center of opposition to the national leadership in later years, not so much because of his Socialistic sympathies as because he was a vigorous man with a great talent for leadership and not easily subordinated to another leader. W. D. Ryan, secretary-treasurer of the Illinois District, was an old associate of John Mitchell, and a steady, methodical man, who was reputed to have a great store of experience and sound judgment.

William Green was president of the Ohio District. I got no very strong impression of him; Green never was a vivid personality. By contrast, Alexander Howat, president of the small Kansas District, was a powerful, flamboyant figure, whom I got to know much better in later years.

Thomas Kennedy was a rather boyish delegate from anthracite District 7. He became president of that smallest district in the union, then national secretary-treasurer, and then John L. Lewis's successor in the presidency of the United Mine Workers, though, by Kennedy's own admission, Lewis still ran the union from "retirement." I don't know whether John L. Lewis was a delegate to the 1908 convention or not. This was some years before his sudden rise to prominence.*

When I returned to report to my local I was full of the excitement of my experience. The power of the union, the many able men I had seen or talked to, what I had heard of political progressivism, both in the successes of such men as Senator La Follette and in the rapid growth of reformist Socialism, all of the hopeful energy of that decade of reform agitation, combined to make me feel that we were in a movement which, in spite of any setbacks, was going to change our country fundamentally before we were through.

I think I conveyed some of my feelings to the members, though they were most interested in the proposed wage scales. These came out of the discussion at the convention and were used in negotiating the agreement for the Central Competitive Field, which was the basis for agreements in outlying districts. In those days we were edging the rates up by about 5 per cent a year, except for the reduction we accepted in 1904.

I returned to work in the Ivory Hill mine. My younger brother Charles, now fourteen, went to work with me as my buttie. We worked together for several years, just as my father and I had done. During World War I he was overseas in the first American Tank Corps. Charles did not stay in the mines but became a salesman and continued in that line of work for the rest of his life.

The operators were cutting costs to meet competition. Like most bosses, ours tried to do it the easy way, by taking it out of the hides

---

* Lewis's name does not appear in the list of delegates in the published convention proceedings. [J. O. P. H.]

of the miners. The men were forced to push loaded cars out of the workplaces instead of having them pulled out and delivered by mules. I was one of the most vocal members of the mine committee in my protests, but without success.

When the annual agreement ended, I went with the other members of the committee to get the new agreement signed. The operator was all ready to sign, but I said, "Before you sign, write into this agreement a rule re-establishing the practice of having loaded cars pulled by mules from the workplaces." He refused, so we called a meeting of the men and voted to strike. After six weeks, the operator proposed arbitration. I refused, though the district president advised acceptance. Finally, the operator yielded the point.

A similar issue arose in another mine where I worked. The mine was being equipped with mechanical haulage on the main roads, replacing the mules. No provision was made for handling the cars in the rooms where the miners worked. The miners were expected to substitute for the mules, without pay. Again, I raised the question in the mine committee, and we entered upon a long strike. The district officers did not approve this strike, though they did nothing to oppose it, either. Without their support, the best we could get was a compromise settlement.

A few weeks after the return to work, the section of the mine where I was working was shut down while engineering changes were being made. I stayed at home for a few days, expecting to be notified of a new workplace. I spoke to the foreman, but he was evasive. I pointed out that there were places available, but he said only that they could not start me just yet. All the other men had been placed by then. It was clear that I was to be frozen out as a troublemaker, but without the formality of being fired. I decided to break the deadlock. I learned from a friendly miner where there was an empty place, walked into the mine early and started to work. When the driver came around I got a car from him, loaded it, and put my check on it. I still had a number, because I had never been fired. When the car reached the mine entrance it was discovered that I was in there at work. The boss told the driver to stop my "turn." The driver delivered the message to me, and asked what he should do. I told him to pass me by this time, but to tell the boss that I was still working and proposed to continue. I knew this defiance would enrage the boss and bring him in to order me out in person. Sure enough, he arrived on the next trip, insisting that I obey orders. He could have me arrested, he said, for violating the mining laws by working without his authorization. I told him to go ahead and try it; I would like nothing better than to expose publicly his effort to deny me work for the crime of being an active committeeman. I don't know whether he was worried by my threat or whether he had a sneaking admiration for my audacity, but he finally gave in and said, "Oh, all right, I guess you're entitled to a place." He assigned me to a fair place, and we got along very well all the rest of my time in that mine.

Until the fall of 1910 I led a very busy life in Nanty Glo, between my work in the mine and my union activities. I held several offices in the local, and always served on the mine committee. Much of our time and energy went into keeping the day men in line, for their dues were not covered by the checkoff. The depression of 1909 made the operators very active in nibbling away at the agreement, so we had a lot of small local strikes. I lost touch with my friend David Irvine, who was working as a national organizer in such remote districts as British Columbia and Nova Scotia. The district was still troubled by dissension over centralization. Thomas L. Lewis was serving his last term as national president. An alliance of several districts was forming to end his tenure.

For reasons not entirely clear to me, then or now, I decided to try another trip west to find work. For one thing, I wanted to try working in a closed-shop district, with better protection against harassment by the operators. I went directly to Iowa and called on a man named Jacob Ritter, who had been a friend of Irvine's and mine in Pennsylvania. He was superintendent of a mine in Hynes and found me a job there. For the first few weeks I did day work, then a place opened up and I got to work on the coal. This was my first experience with what was called "solid shooting." The coal was very hard, so it was not undercut, either by hand or by machine. Instead, the miners drilled and placed their shots toward the end of the day. Then special men, called shot-firers, went in at night, inspected the shots to see that they had been properly placed, and then set them off. Sometimes when we had left the mine we could feel the vibration underground as the explosions were set off. Sometimes a misplaced shot would cause a "windy," igniting the coal dust, and causing damage to the mine and occasionally injury or death to the shot-firers. We got out a good deal of coal under this system and made fair enough wages, but I did not become attached to Iowa.

Hynes was set in a depression along a small run, a hideous coal camp of straggling little one-story houses. I lived in Avery, four miles away, which was cleaner but not much more attractive. There was nothing in either town but the union. Avery's only excitement was provided by watching trains passing on the main line of the Burlington Railroad. A small branch led from Avery to the mine in Hynes. Early each morning the miners from Avery piled into two box cars pulled by a switch engine for the trip to work, returning after work in the same way. We sat on plank seats ranged around the cars, each of which had a small stove to take off the chill of winter. While we waited we talked of the union, the job, and whatever else we could think of to amuse ourselves. Several men had worked in the metal mines of the West and had belonged to the Western Federation of Miners. They tended to be Socialists and liked to talk politics. I enjoyed the talk—I've always liked to talk—but there was no other stimulation to be found in either Hynes or Avery.

When work began to slack off in March, I made up my mind to return to Pennsylvania. On the way home I thought I would stop in Bay City, Michigan, to visit Dave Boyd, brother of a man I knew back home. I thought it would be interesting to learn something about the Michigan district.

I liked Bay City immediately. It was a place of nearly fifty thousand people, with most of the advantages of a city and few of the drawbacks. Dave was a vigorous, jovial, good-hearted man, who operated a compressed-air machine undercutting the seam, at the Wolverine No. 3 mine. Dave urged me to stay, which I agreed to do if I could get a job. He took me to the mine to see the superintendent, who started me off as a track man. The superintendent, Bill Williams, was a former president of District 24, and was well liked by the men. This district was small, comprising about twenty-five hundred miners in the vicinity of Saginaw and Bay City. I stayed for about three years. I was elected to the mine committee soon after my arrival, and during my last year there was president of the local union. The mines worked very steadily during the winter and we earned good wages, but we had to sweat out the summer months without pay. The trouble was that the coal was of too poor quality for industrial uses, so its only market was as domestic fuel, which has a seasonal demand. I spent most of my two summers there in the Russell Sage Library, reading fiction, history, and economics. This was the most extensive course of reading I had ever been able to enjoy, and I took full advantage of it. During my last winter there, I joined a little debating society called "The Pros and Cons," which met in the library weekly. Most of the members were school teachers and young lawyers. I listened to the debates, learning much both from the substance and from the techniques of the debaters, but I never got into a debate myself. I never overcame a certain shyness with those people, agreeable as they were.

I took a more active part in the debates, highly informal ones, that went on during the train ride to the mines in the morning. Most of the shafts were ten to twenty miles outside the town. A special train of ancient passenger coaches left the station every morning at 6:30 and made a circuitous trip, picking up the miners and dropping them at their shafts. We took three-quarters of an hour to reach the Wolverine mines, eighteen miles out. There were wash houses at the mine heads where we could clean up and change our clothes so that we could make the return trip in cleanliness and comfort.

I enjoyed the time spent on the train. Some of the men played cards, others brought along the morning papers, and many just talked. I remember the morning we learned that the McNamara brothers had confessed to dynamiting the Los Angeles *Times* building. For days we discussed the use of violence in labor disputes and the effect of the confessions on the movement. Few of the men could see any good in the use of dynamite, even in a desperate situation.

Dave Boyd was a rare bird among my friends—a member of the Socialist Labor Party. His great good nature made his views more tolerable than might otherwise have been the case. He distributed the *Daily People* and party pamphlets assiduously. I read some of these, including *What Means this Strike*, and *Reform and Revolution,* but I was never able to figure what a good man like Boyd could see in the sterile dogmatism of De Leon. Dave was not a truly orthodox De Leonite, or he would not have been a member of the United Mine Workers, which De Leon considered several degrees worse than the House of Morgan. I learned from reading De Leon something about the uses and abuses of formal analysis and logic; grant him his premise, however absurd, and his conclusions were inescapable. Despite Dave's personality and his years of distributing literature, I never heard of another SLP-er in Bay City.

Among the men I met in Bay City was a Scotch-Irish miner named Sandy McElheney, who worked in the mines as a trapper, though he was nearly eighty years old and had a son, a mine superintendent, who was both willing and able to support him in retirement. Like many older Scotch miners, he had tales to tell of Sandy MacDonald, the great British miners' leader. He also liked to tell how bad things were in the mines of Scotland before MacDonald won decent laws regulating safety and ventilation. I remember one story he told of a man who caught a young crow and took it into the pit with him one morning. Before the day was out the crow died of the foul air in which the miners had to work. After that the miners referred to the mine as the "crow pit."

I liked Bay City so well that I wrote home to my family, urging them to join me. The family had been augmented by the addition of John and Lawrence Dagnall, the youngest children of the aunt and uncle who had first sheltered us when we arrived in Philipsburg. The parents had died, leaving several children, of whom we took in two. John, who was sixteen, drowned shortly after he came to live with us, but Lawrence, two years younger, stayed with us until he was grown. Father suggested that I find jobs for him, Charles, and Lawrence, so that the family could join me. The superintendent agreed to put my father and one of the boys to work, so they all came to Bay City. I shifted over to the No. 2 mine, working under Superintendent McElheney, and before long Charles joined me as buttie.

This district had enjoyed a pretty good contract for a number of years. As a member of the mine committee, I tried to revive one clause in the contract which had become a dead letter through neglect. It provided for additional pay for working in a wet entry. We argued the point for some time, then McElheney fired me, giving some reason or other, though it was clear he was annoyed by my persistence in pushing this issue. I appealed the discharge to the commissioners provided for by the contract—the district president and an operators' representative—and won re-instatement.

I organized a protest meeting on behalf of Preston and Smith, two IWW members who had been convicted of murder as a result of a strike in Goldfield, Nevada. At a national convention, the United Mine Workers had passed a resolution protesting the convictions. For them, as for me, this was a civil liberties issue. I arranged for the IWW to send up a speaker, who turned out to be Vincent St. John, national secretary-treasurer of one of the two organizations that claimed to be the true IWW. We met in the county court room on a Sunday afternoon. St. John was very different from Haywood, who resembled more the popular notion of an IWW leader. St. John was a calm, quiet-voiced, even somewhat mannered advocate, who made a very effective plea for the men he represented.

Once when the mines were closed down I took a job in a box factory. The work was light and clean and the factory was filled with the pleasant odor of wood. I stayed only a short time because of the ten-hour day and low wages. Another summer I worked for a while in what was known as the Industrial Works, the largest factory in town, which made power cranes and shovels. My work was heavy and dirty, wheeling a barrow and lifting heavy materials. One day Dave Boyd introduced me to a young man named Solon De Leon,* who had come to town to speak for the Socialist Labor Party, and asked me to arrange a noonday meeting for him in front of the Industrial Works. I agreed, and introduced him to the men loafing near the plant gates. It was not a union plant, so when I saw the boss eyeing me sourly, I knew my time there would be short at best. When we returned to work he started riding me, so I asked for my time and quit. He was no less pleased to get rid of me than I was to leave.

Summers in Bay City were delightful, with plenty of boating, bathing, and fishing, though I confess I was too interested in my reading to spend much time at any of these things. And the winters, though severe, were not too bad. My father never got used to the new place, however, and when the mines closed down during the second summer he moved back to Pennsylvania, taking the family with him.

I decided to remain, and got a place to board. I shared my room with a young man who worked for the local streetcar company. He had to get up at four in the morning to get to the carbarn for his first run at five. He had an enormous alarm clock, which he placed on a tin pie plate for maximum effect. He admitted that he was hard to waken, but this turned out to be an understatement. The alarm would explode like the crack of doom at four, never failing to rouse me, but usually disturbing him no more than the chirp of a cricket. Then I had to struggle to get him awake so he would not lose his job. I was losing two good hours of sleep a night by this arrangement, and I growled

---

* The son of Daniel De Leon. He later broke with his father and was active for many years in the Socialist Party.

at him for not getting a union job so he could work decent hours. Twenty-five years later I met my former roommate in Flint. He was working in an auto plant and wearing a shop-steward's button as big as that pie plate he used back in Bay City. I took great pleasure in congratulating him on the improvement in his working hours, though it was too late to do me any good.

After a while I finished off a workplace in the mine, and knowing it would be several weeks before another place would be available, I decided to return to Nanty Glo for a visit with my family. I fully intended to go back to Bay City, but circumstances worked out so that I never got around to it.

!!!

9

NANTY GLO

Nanty Glo, a grimy huddle in the narrow valley of Black Lick Creek, overshadowed by slag piles and the hills of the Alleghenies, was a contrast to the open country and lake shores of Saginaw Bay. I was certain that a stay of a couple of weeks would satisfy me; I would visit with my family, renew old acquaintances, and then be ready to return to the pleasanter surroundings of Bay City.

But my father and mother wanted me to stay. My mother's health was poor; though we could not know it, she was approaching her final illness. Both she and my father were worn out by a lifetime of hard work. Except for his army service, he spent his working life in the mines, and she was never free of the cares of maintaining a large family on very little means. My mother died in 1916, I think now of cancer. The doctor did not call it that. Cause of death might correctly have been put down as "old age," though she was only fifty-eight. My father died two years later, at fifty-nine, after an attack of pneumonia. He seemed to be recovering; some of his friends called on him that afternoon and had a very jolly time with him, then only an hour or two after they left he died. Probably the illness had been too much for his weakened heart.

When my mother felt the approach of death, in the spring of 1916, she faced it as calmly as her forebears had met the dangers of the mine. She kept up with her household duties to the last, though she was but a frail shadow of her former self. One day she said to me, "I'm about through. I'll only last a few days now." I tried to reassure her, but she insisted, "No, it's the end; send for the priest." Two days later she passed peacefully away. She left us a heritage of calm and courageous acceptance of the hazards of life. Her kindliness never failed, whether it was her family, neighbors, or the passing stranger who called on her for help. She was quiet and reserved, slow to anger, but I have seen her flare up with indignation against some injustice, especially if it struck at the center of her life—her family. She made our home a haven of love for all of us.

I was able to do one thing for my parents at this time that gave me great pleasure. I had saved up about $600 during my stay in the West. I found a house for sale at what looked to me like a bargain price, only $900. Two brothers, carpenters, had built it themselves, then their wives were dissatisfied—some trouble with neighbors, I gathered—and the men had to sell. I borrowed $300 from a bank, and with that and my savings bought the house and moved my family into it. Fortunately, work was steady, so I paid off the loan in about a year. It was the first time we had ever had a place of our own. Whatever happened, my parents would have a comfortable home to live in. After my mother's death, my father and Bessie, my youngest sister, lived there until my father was taken to the Welsh home during his last illness.

All this was still in the future when I had to make my decision, but the portents of it were visible enough to influence me. I finally told my father, "All right, I'll stay, if I can get a job. But you know no mine around here would hire me, with my record in the union." I had already done some looking around, but everywhere I was told that there was no opening, they would call me—but they never did. It would be as much as a foreman's job was worth to hire me.

My father replied, "It can be done."

He and my brother Charles were working together, loading after machines in an entry and taking up bottom for the roadway. The boss wanted that entry advanced rapidly, so there was plenty of work for three. Father asked the pit boss if he could start another one of his boys on the job. The boss was a new man in town and knew me only by reputation; also, like everybody else, he had heard that I was only on a short visit and would soon return to Michigan. So he did not bother to ask for the "boy's" name, but agreed that my father could bring him to work the next day. So far, so good, but I still had to get into the mine and establish my right to the job.

My father's advice was, "John, you just walk into the mine a little early, keep out of the boss's sight, put in a day's work and send out your coal with a private mark. Then we'll see."

Very often, men working their first day on a new job would use a private mark until they could get a regular check number, so this was not unusual. I walked boldly into the mine ahead of everybody else, and worked all day. At the end of the day, father and I walked out together and saw the boss, Charlie Davis, coming towards us. Father said, "Stay back, son. Here comes Charlie. I'll talk to him."

When they met, father said, "Hello, Charlie. I brought my other boy in today, and he got out his quota of coal."

"That's fine, Mr. Brophy."

"You'd better give me the order for his check number, hadn't you?"

"Oh, yes. All right," he said, and started writing the order on the weighmaster to give me my number. "What's your boy's name?"

Father said, "John." By that time, even though I was walking slower than I have ever done before or since, I had caught up with them. The boss stopped writing and looked up with a puzzled expression. He was beginning to get the idea that something had been put over on him. But my father kept on talking, and I practically had my hand on the slip, so the boss could hardly help giving it to me. We started out immediately to get the number from the weighmaster.

This man knew me well, had known the entire family, in fact, ever since we had been neighbors in Urey, years before. He married into the family of one of the operators and had risen in the world just a little bit since the old days. I presented my order, asked for my number, and told him I had some coal entered on his sheet under a private mark which I described. He tried everything to stall me, saying it was the end of the day and he had to make up his weigh sheets, he would take care of it first thing in the morning, and so forth. But I refused to take "no" for an answer. I had no intention of letting that order out of my sight until I had my number. I insisted that I had coal to my credit and would not leave until it was listed under my number. He finally gave in, and I went home with a number, legally establishing me in a job at that mine. So that blacklist was broken.

It was not long before I justified those bosses in their fears that they were making a mistake to let me in the mine. There was ground for dissatisfaction with the way the coal was being weighed. The cars were hauled out of the mine on a rope, five at a time. When they reached the knuckle—the top of the slope at the entrance—the rope was cut, and the cars rolled down a short incline and across the scale, coming to a halt in the tipple. The weighmaster and checkweighman had to catch the weight from the scale on the fly. If couplings buckled or bound as the cars passed over the scale, nobody could tell what the right weight of any particular car should be. Besides, the checks were handed in five at a time and a car was not always credited to the man who had loaded it. The effect of all this was constant irritation to the miners, and suspicion of short weight. The checkweighman, one of the Slavic miners, was a good enough man, but he did nothing about this trouble.

A mine committeeman approached me one day. "Brophy, why don't you run for checkweighman? The job's up for election soon."

I hesitated, so he went on, "Damn it, if you don't run, I'll have to, and I don't really want to. This fellow we've got doesn't know his job. He just stands around and palavers. It takes somebody who can make the company straighten that mess out."

I talked it over with a number of men and finally decided to run. Even the checkweighman's fellow Slavs voted for me. There was no division among the men on the question of short weight.

That put it up to me, and I lost no time getting to the point with the weighmaster. In fact, I started heckling him two or three days after I went on the job. I kept at him until he lost his temper. He decided that I was questioning his honesty, so he grabbed me, shoved me into a corner of the weigh office and threatened to knock my block off. He was big enough to have done it. But he actually knew better; when I remained calm, he cooled off and apologized.

I warned him that the miners would not think well of his trying to rough up their representative. I said, "Joe, this is the end of this argument. I'm serving notice on you. You tell the superintendent that this scale has to be moved on the next idle day. If he doesn't do it, I'll call a meeting of the men and tell them what the situation is, that they are not getting what is due them. You've taken this personally and made an attack on me. I don't like that, and I could make an issue of it. But what I do demand, right now, is that the company move the weigh scale. You tell the superintendent I said so."

The superintendent came up to see me the same day. He was Enoch

Bellis, the son of the mine foreman who had befriended us years before in Urey. We were on good terms, but he had to protect the interests of the owners, just as I had to protect the interests of the men. He said, "John, you've made trouble ever since you came. In the first place you got employment by a subterfuge. Now, I hear you're demanding that we move these weigh scales. Do you know what that will cost? Why, it will cost over a hundred dollars to move those scales."

I refused to be impressed. "I don't care if it costs five hundred," I said, "you've got to move them."

"Why?"

"In the interest of honesty and fair weight, that's why. And if you don't, I'll report it to the men and there will be a strike."

"Are you saying we are robbing the miners?"

"I'm saying the system's all wrong, and that's what's robbing some of the men of their honest weight."

"Well," he said, "all the weight records from the railroads show that we are not credited with as much as you people get credit for on these scales."

"I don't care about that," I replied. "I'm saying the individual worker is not getting what's due him and it's got to be fixed."

He began to lose his temper at this point. "You got into this mine by a trick," he shouted; "you've got no right to be here at all."

"Well," I said, "what's that got to do with it? I am here, and that's all there is to that. Are you going to move the scale?"

"O.K., we'll move the scale. But I'll never forget this."

Whether he forgot or not, the scale was moved. Several men worked a full day, and overtime, moving the scale out farther from the slope. From then on, we had no trouble about weight. The weighmaster and I got along so well that if he had to leave the weigh station to go to the office he would trust me to weigh the trips as they came out and mark them up on his sheet. I worked at that job for three years, re-elected automatically every six months.

Work in the mines was steady during these years, so we were fairly prosperous, and I was enjoying my job and the work in the local union which filled most of my spare time. I served as financial secretary, and William Welsh was president during part of this time. The other officers were good men, and the rank and file were active, progressive, and interested both in local problems and broader issues. It was not long before our local became noted, among the 160 or 170 locals in the sixteen counties of the district, as an originator of policy. When William Welsh became district executive board member, in 1915, his voice carried the influence of our local even further in district affairs. His was a full-time job, adjusting grievances for about twenty locals in Cambria County. He also helped men with compensation claims against the operators through the early stages of their litigation.

The approach of each district convention set off an active discussion of a wide range of policy questions in the locals. In our local, we chose a special committee to receive suggestions from the members and put them into the form of resolutions for discussion and action at the meetings. Those approved by vote of the membership were sent on to the district secretary-treasurer, who had them printed for distribution to the delegates in a small booklet which became the agenda of the convention.

The district convention of 1914 was typical. The question of centralization was raised again, but no change was made because the proponents of a modified scheme had not prepared their plan carefully enough. Another organizational matter which was not new was a proposal to merge District 2 with District 5 in one large district covering both central and western Pennsylvania—the entire bituminous area of the state. This would have had the advantage, for us, of incorporating us into the Central Competitive Field. However, since our employers were neither as well organized, nor as prosperous, nor as accustomed to centralized bargaining as those to the west of us, it might have weakened the union's bargaining in that basic area. There were several important non-union areas abutting on the two districts and it was thought by some that the combined resources of a new 80,000-member district would be more successful in bringing these areas into the union. However, none of the plans offered to carry out this idea was worked out carefully enough to win acceptance. The leaders of District 5 were usually favorable to the idea, but those in our district were not enthusiastic.

The question of a labor party, or, failing that, of endorsement of the Socialist Party was also raised. James Maurer, of Reading, then president of the state Federation of Labor and an outstanding Socialist leader, spoke on this subject. In the prolonged discussion of this problem, I took the position that much more education was necessary before endorsement of a minority party could be more than an empty gesture. The idea of a labor party based on the masses of the workers appealed to me, but I felt we were far from ready even for that move.

I think it was during this debate that I first approached the idea of nationalization of the mines, which later became so important in my policy. I recognized then the need for better organization of management, some centralized planning, and a democratic voice for the miners through their union, but I had not gotten beyond rather vague notions.

Every convention passed a variety of resolutions favoring various kinds of political and social reform and taking positions on major national issues. During the district convention of 1916, I offered a resolution opposing our entry into the European war and condemning war as a by-product of capitalistic rivalries, fostered by military and armament interests. Nobody opposed the resolution; most of the delegates were against war in much the way they were against sin, and felt the issue was not terribly urgent. I felt so strongly the danger of our involvement in war that I took the floor and made a very long speech on the subject. The chairman of the resolutions committee, Patrick Kelly, got tired of waiting for me to finish so he could go on with his report. We were meeting in the Opera House at Du Bois; Kelly walked into the wings while I was talking and found there, among the properties, an ancient musket. He came out to the footlights, aimed the musket at me, and said, "Stop, or I'll fire." The delegates roared, and I was squelched. No doubt I deserved it. A year later we were at war and I supported it. My views had changed; I recognized that one could not be neutral in war. Much as I abhor war, things are never equal and it does matter who wins.

We agitated in those years for a miners' certificate law. This would mean that only men certified by a state board as qualified could work on the coal. Our purpose was to protect the miners against the dangers which inexperienced men sometimes created for themselves and for others, especially in gaseous mines. Such a law existed for the anthracite region of Pennsylvania, in the bituminous districts of Illinois, and in some other states. The operators opposed the proposal on the grounds that it was not needed from the standpoint of safety, and that it would give the union a "monopoly of labor." It would undoubtedly have made it harder to bring scabs into the mines during a strike. Such a law was finally passed many years later.

The miners were interested in old-age pensions provided by the state. We always proposed an age limit of fifty for eligibility, on the ground that a miner by that age was either worn out or had trouble getting a job. This was perfectly true, but I hardly need say that we did not get very far with that radical proposition.

Another constant item on the agenda was the demand for a state law requiring coal companies to provide wash houses at the entrances to the mines. We wanted to be able to clean up for cleanliness' sake, but also for the sake of health, to get rid of dirt and sweat before starting out on the often long walk home. Furthermore, washing in the kitchen every night while the evening meal was being prepared was a nuisance. The operators fought this because it would cost them a few dollars. It is now general practice.

Union sponsorship of co-operative stores to free the miners from the oppressions of company stores was a project I supported in the 1914 convention. Later, as district president, I was able to do something about this idea.

The most important matter, on which everybody always had some opinion, was the proposed wage scale. But there were always many resolutions having to do with internal problems of the union—structure, government, and functioning—and with public issues. Our local, having a more than average interest in ideas, sent in more than the average number of proposals.

I attended the district conventions regularly. I was elected to the important district wage scale committee for the first time in 1914. This committee had the task of preparing our wage proposals to be submitted to the employers, and negotiating and approving the agreement. Two members were elected from each of the nine sub-districts by caucus of the convention delegates. With the three general district officers, this made a rather unwieldy committee of twenty-one, to meet with an almost equally large number of employer representatives. If negotiations were prolonged, they were referred to a joint sub-committee, and sometimes to a sub-sub-committee, until the agreement was brought back to the full committee, who signed it before it was submitted to a referendum of the membership. If a majority of the committee and of the membership approved the agreement, it went into effect.

At the 1916 convention, I was again elected to the wage scale committee, along with my brother-in-law, William Welsh. We met with the operators' committee in a joint conference at Philadelphia. After several days of negotiation in full committee, the breakdown to a smaller group began. This was in January and February of 1916. The First World War was raging in Europe, but the United States was not yet involved. After slack work in early 1915, the demand for coal had built up in the fall and winter as the European demand for munitions and other goods increased. With a good market, bound to continue for some time, the employers were ready to make some concessions. They offered us the same increase in tonnage rates that had already been won in the Central Competitive Field, and most of our committee were ready to accept the offer. I led the opposition, arguing that now was the time for us to catch up to the Central Competitive Field in all rates, including those for day men, and to win some other badly needed improvements.

Our rate for day men had lagged behind for years, and was now about twenty or twenty-five cents below that in the Midwest. Now, if ever, was our chance to eliminate that unreasonable differential. Even more important, to my mind, was the necessity of making a fight while conditions were favorable to get rid of uncompensated car-pushing. In our arguments within the union's committee, most of the members favored taking the gains offered us rather than risk trouble by asking for more. I insisted that we could do better, that the offer itself was evidence that the employers would not risk losing the good business available to them. But when the vote was taken, it favored acceptance by about two to one.

Customarily, all members of the committee signed the report, in spite of previous disagreements, before it was submitted to the membership for approval. But on this occasion I felt the issue was too important to be glossed over in this manner. I rose and announced, after the vote, "I'm not going to sign this agreement. I won't put my name on it, because I won't have my name appear to endorse it to the membership."

This created a problem for the officers. They could foresee dissension and criticism, which they could ill afford, for reasons I will explain shortly. William Welsh and three others joined me. Then it was proposed that the scale be submitted to the membership over the signatures of the three officers, omitting all the other members of the committee. The majority was delighted with this device to conceal the disagreement among the committee members, and voted for the unusual procedure over my opposition.

The trick did not work. Word got out that there had been dissension and the district officers became worried. They made matters worse for themselves by campaigning actively among the locals for a favorable vote. This advertised the fact that I was opposed to the settlement, even though I did not campaign outside my own local. The scale was carried by a large majority; most of the members felt they should play safe rather than risk a fight, I guess. But the controversy advertised my name and the fact that I advocated a more militant policy.

District politics were in a tangled state at this time. Patrick Gilday had finished a long term in the presidency in March, 1915. His nephew, Charles O'Neil, had been his personal secretary for a number of years and expected to succeed him. O'Neil had worked in the mines as a youth, had had some business school training, and had accumulated considerable experience working with his uncle. But the vice-president, James Purcell, insisted on his right to succeed Gilday. In order to avoid an open fight, which might let in an "outsider," the administration group arranged a compromise which made Purcell president and O'Neil vice-president. Purcell was an explosive, harsh-mannered man whom O'Neil considered—probably correctly—much his inferior in ability. Jealousy and dissension among the top officers kept the district organization in a turmoil, which was worsened by survivals of old contentions. The centralization question was settled by an overwhelmingly favorable referendum vote in 1914, but some of the leading opponents were still around and still resented the administration's role in the controversy.

At the 1916 convention, the South Fork local offered a plan to modify the centralization scheme. They proposed to reduce the number of sub-districts from nine to six, with a complete organization in each, but with the administration of funds to pay checkweighmen left in the district office. South Fork had favored abolition of the sub-districts in 1907. If the idea had been more thoroughly thought through, so that its proponents were better prepared for the objections that were raised, it might have carried. But they were unable to convince the delegates that it would be either more economical or more democratic, so it went down to defeat. Purcell and his friends won the fight, but it left them shaken and weakened.

All summer, mines worked at full capacity. The operators were benefitting greatly by increased business, but the wages of the miners were held down by the contract. Some of the men left the mines to take jobs in the booming munitions industries. The cost of living rose at a terrible rate, and everybody felt the pressure of hard times in spite of somewhat better wages. By early fall, the entire district was in a ferment; and my position at the Philadelphia sessions was confirmed by the course of events. Operators could sell any coal they could bring to the surface. The market for spot coal—sales outside regular contracts, on the spot, for whatever the market would bring—was extremely profitable, but none of that extra profit went to the miners.

In the late summer, a group of local leaders from all parts of the district met at Altoona to discuss the situation. I did not attend, but I soon heard that they had decided to put up a slate against the district officers, and had chosen me as their nominee for the presidency. They selected candidates for the three top offices and for district board members in all the sub-districts. The election was scheduled for December. The new slate would campaign primarily on the issue of the administration's failure to deal satisfactorily with wages, though there were plenty of other complaints available.

At first, I was dismayed at the idea. Though my experience was extensive, it had almost all been at the local level, and I had always thought of myself as a militant rank and filer. But it was also true that I had made myself, without consciously trying to do so, the spokesman for the opposition on a variety of issues. Most of the older oppositionists had either retired or left the district, and the fight over the wage scale had made my name widely known. So I decided to accept the role circumstances had placed me in, and announced my candidacy. I issued a circular letter to the local unions, stating my platform. I promised to push hard for a better wage scale, and criticized Purcell's failure to do anything about eliminating car-pushing. He had said he had a commitment from the operators to get this done; he may have had an oral promise or two, but nothing came of it.

The election was a close one. We knew that inertia always favored incumbents in district elections; there had been for years a kind of escalator which carried men through the levels of office to the top. I was proposing to make the leap all the way from the bottom, an unheard-of presumption. When the votes were counted, it was discovered that I had defeated Purcell by the narrow margin of six hundred votes. My running mates for the chief offices had lost to O'Neil and Richard Gilbert. We had increased our strength on the executive board by two members, but the administration group still had a slim majority there. If the democratic tradition had not been so strong in the district, Purcell might have upset this result by having enough votes thrown out on one pretext or another to ensure his election. But the membership was so aroused that, in spite of the closeness of the vote, he did not dare try it.

Thus I found myself, an habitual rank and filer, at the head of a district with 40,000 members. A majority of my board was opposed to me; I would have to depend largely on my own prestige to hold them in line. The members were expecting fast and vigorous action on critical issues. Enough local unions had endorsed a call for a special convention to make one obligatory, under the constitution. The operators' association offered a 10 per cent bonus covering all workers in the district for the duration of the contract, though with the proviso that this was not to be considered part of the contract. The proviso was designed to take the edge off the demand for a raise, without committing the employers to a new and higher basis for bargaining when the next contract came up.

‖‖‖‖‖‖‖‖‖‖‖‖‖‖‖‖‖‖‖‖‖‖‖‖‖‖‖‖‖‖‖‖‖‖‖‖‖

10

DISTRICT PRESIDENT

The district officers, reluctant to get into a fight to change the contract in the last days of their term of office, sent a letter to the locals, asking whether the 10 per cent bonus offered by the operators would suffice, making the special convention unnecessary. They also warned the members that the union must live up to its contract, which had been approved by a vote of the membership for a two-year period, and they included in their letter admonitions from the national office condemning bonuses and urging strict observance of contracts. Finally, they pointed out that the operators had made it clear that they intended to stand firm on the existing agreement. The companies might make special concessions, but would yield nothing as a matter of right. And the concessions would be based on their own needs—they were facing a shortage of help—not on the needs of the miners.

In the face of such intransigence on the part of the operators, Purcell could think of nothing better to do than to talk solemnly about the sanctity of contracts. The locals rejected all his pleas and insisted upon holding the special convention. After much haggling, the date was finally fixed for March 26. I was not scheduled to take office until April 1. Purcell had no intention of facing that convention. He asked me to take over his problem before the legal beginning of my term, but I had better sense than that, and bided my time until I should have full legal authority to act in my own name.

Purcell resigned the presidency on March 21, five days before the date set for the convention, leaving O'Neil acting president, with neither time nor power to act. O'Neil followed Purcell's example by coming down to see me at the mine where I was still working as checkweighman and begging me to take over, but I refused. If he could do nothing while legally president, I could do less from my mine tipple.

The convention could hardly have been more badly timed. With the rank and file in revolt against the contract to which we were legally tied, there was no leadership available to guide them through a dangerous conflict. I could not act legally, and the old officers were incapacitated by their lack of a policy.

Operators found it impossible to hire men for the mines when better wages were being paid in war industries. Young men left the mines; those who remained struggled to meet the rising cost of living. Operators strove to fill their contracts and to get out a surplus of coal for sale at high prices in the spot coal market. Those who succeeded made fortunes overnight; it even became profitable to make wage concessions under the table. Some locals, dealing with small operators outside the association, were "wildcatting" it, getting increases of as much as a third above the district contract rates.

By the time the special convention met we were hearing of similar troubles in other fields. Pressure was building up on the international office from all districts, and it was clear that the Central Competitive Field contract could not survive until its expiration without some changes. Even so, it was several weeks before wage talks were held for that field and modifications officially made.

President John P. White (who succeeded Thomas L. Lewis in 1911) sent William Green, International secretary-treasurer (later president of the AFL), to our convention as his representative. Green counseled moderation. He warned us of the dangers implicit in the course we were contemplating: it ran counter to the established policy of the United Mine Workers; even though the operators themselves had done much to make revision of the contract inevitable, we must under no circumstances break our solemn word. He was by no means as emphatic about this as he might have been if it had not been so obvious that the contract was dead. Having delivered his warning, he then met with the wage scale committee and helped formulate the demands of the convention: (1) immediate action on the implied agreement to abolish car-pushing; (2) a one-third increase in wages because of the rise in the cost of living; (3) a broadened checkoff, covering day men as well as the men working on the coal.

The convention asked for an immediate meeting with the operators. The Association stalled, waiting for developments in the Central Competitive Field. We finally served notice that they must meet with us by April 16 or we would order a general strike. They selected April 17, the day after our deadline, to meet with us, thus saving face, I suppose. Our committee met with them for two weeks, finally reaching a tentative agreement on April 30. Increases of 25 to 30 per cent were granted for various classes of work. The operators refused to do any more about car-pushing than they had promised before: to correct the worst abuses.

The convention turned down the offer, reaffirmed its original position, authorized a strike, and adjourned until it should be recalled. The joint scale committee went back into session.

I had taken office at the convention on April 1, with all the traditional exchange of compliments and assurance of support from the outgoing president, Charles O'Neil. He reverted to the vice-presidency, but shortly afterward went to work for the Central Pennsylvania Operators' Association as their representative in dealings with the union.

As the joint scale committee returned to its labors, an invitation came to meet with William B. Wilson, Secretary of Labor, in Washington. There, with the Secretary's help, a supplementary agreement was worked out. By then the United States had declared war, and pressure to maintain coal production was mounting. The new clauses granted five cents a ton for car-pushing throughout the district, and fifty cents a yard for dead work (taking up bottom) in one territory where this kind of work was unpaid.

Opposition to the new proposal was confined to those who were not affected by car-pushing or dead work, and those who had already wildcatted raises. Secretary Wilson, who had once been president of District 2 and still held a card in the Blossburg local, came to our convention and spoke in favor of the agreement. He made an effective speech, recalling the hard conditions of former days. He emphasized the gradualness of our gains, illustrating his point with the story from Aesop about the monkey who tried to grab too many nuts from a bottle and could not get his hand out. If we took a little at a time, Wilson said, we would gain more in the long run. We had won a good contract; it was unlikely we could get enough more to justify a strike.

Wilson's speech was not needed to guarantee passage of the agreement, but he enjoyed attending the convention and the miners enjoyed having him as their guest.

The proposal was passed overwhelmingly on May 24, 1917, by the reconvened convention. The five-cent penalty on car-pushing, while it did not eliminate the practice immediately, did encourage operators to put in better equipment, so it had the same effect in a short time. Also, acceptance of the dead-work rate meant that before long all the operators had to do likewise or lose their men in a time when manpower was very short. We had at last raised our day rate to parity with the Central Competitive Field, and gained the largest wage increases in the history of the district. Never before had we been able to get more than 5 per cent in any one year. In fact, our gain in this agreement was, on the average, better than that in the Central Competitive Field. We were helped, to be sure, by the circumstances of wartime, and our gains were less than they appeared, as rising prices eroded the value of our dollars. But it was a good conclusion, and I could congratulate myself that my term, which had started in such turmoil, was already successful and promised to be peaceful and harmonious.

I moved to Clearfield to take up my duties in the district office. Clearfield was a county seat with several small hotels, operated on the American plan, in one of which I settled down to live. The accommodations were far from luxurious—the name "hotel" was more impressive than the reality. But I was reasonably comfortable, and since I spent most of my time traveling around to the locals, I had little chance to become bored with my room. Naturally, I missed the warm, affectionate ties with my family. It was quite a change from our lively household to the life of a single man. I did not find any old friends in Clearfield. I had known Richard Gilbert in South Fork, of course, but we had not been close friends.

My starting salary in the president's job was $175 a month. I got increases as raises were won for the men, so that the monthly paycheck edged up to $225. This was more than I had been used to making as a miner, especially since it came regularly. Though my living costs were higher than at home, I was able to save some money, and to spend more on books. Being accustomed to an abstemious life, I was not tempted to spend my money on riotous living.

While I served as president of District 2, I read everything I could get my hands on that had to do with labor—particularly the miners and their industry—in Britain and America. Among the historical works I read was the *History of Labour in the United States,* by John R. Commons and associates. I read some general histories, including H. G. Wells's *Outline of History,* for a more comprehensive world view.

After 1927, I read Cardinal Newman's *Apologia, The Idea of a University, The Present Condition of Catholics in England,* and a variety of sermons on Catholic doctrine and history. Newman led me to Jacques Maritain's *Social and Political Philosophy* and *Man and the State.* Most important of all, it was during these years that I finally had a chance to study the encyclical *Rerum Novarum,* with its support for my own political and social thought, centering around the idea of democratic economic and social planning.

Though we had been elected on opposing tickets, I had no trouble with Gilbert. He was not a politician or factionalist, but a methodical, conscientious man who would have done his job well under any circumstances. Some of the people who had supported me put up a candidate against Gilbert in the 1918 election, but I kept hands off. I saw no reason to punish a man who was doing a good job just for having sided with a losing faction. Gilbert retained his job even after I had left the presidency.

Purcell, with the help of William B. Wilson, got a job with the federal Department of Labor as a conciliator and withdrew from the affairs of the district. O'Neil might have kept the opposition faction alive, but when he went to work for the operators' association, he put himself out of district politics. As for the opposition on the executive board, most of them accepted the new situation. They knew that I represented rank-and-file opinion, and whenever I chose to throw my weight they accommodated themselves to my wishes.

In short, I would have had a good working organization in the district if it had not been for the national office of the union. John L. Lewis had apparently spotted me that early as an independent who might make trouble for him. I always had opposition for the presidency, and Lewis' hand was visible in creating that opposition. For example, in 1918 I was opposed by a district board member, Frank Waite, of Du Bois. He was not distinguished in any way, and my margin of victory over him was greater than it had been against Purcell. Shortly after the election, Waite was given a job with the national organization.

I made one mistake with respect to personnel. When O'Neil resigned, early in 1918, I should have appointed my brother-in-law, William Welsh, to the vice-presidency. He had been a member of the district board for years, and was by far the best qualified person. But I was perhaps overly sensitive to the suspicion of nepotism and passed him over to appoint James Mark, who later succeeded me in the presidency. Mark was competent, but he was not as good a man as Welsh.

The district organization carried a number of people on the payroll. Besides the three general officers, there were nine board members, who worked full time for the union, and each of these had an assistant working full time. There were three bookkeepers in the district office, and auditors and tellers who worked a few day a year when needed. This provided some patronage for the president to use, if he was so minded. Maybe it was naive of me, but I never used control of jobs to advance my own interests, as some others did. When I ran against Lewis for president of the UMW in 1926, the district officers who had served under me almost all went along with Lewis, though I held strong rank-and-file support.

My work kept me on the road most of the time. There was no sitting in the office, waiting for things to come to me. I went from local to local, usually by train, though when distances were short enough I would walk, or get a ride on somebody's team. I stayed in local hotels or boarding houses, or in the homes of miners.

Negotiation of the district agreement took me to Philadelphia or Washington, and once or twice I made trips to Pittsburgh to consult with officers of that district on matters of mutual concern. Travel expenses were paid by the district, but this provided no opportunities to "live it up." It was the custom then to publish detailed expense accounts for convention delegates to examine, and there were times when a delegate would rise to protest against payment of $1.50 for a hotel room when he knew of a place where rooms could be rented for $1.00. It was expected that an official would be careful of the union's money, and while this could be, and often was, carried to ridiculous extremes, it represented a healthy attitude, in my opinion.

Most of my work with locals was helping settle grievances with which local machinery had not been able to cope. If a mine committee could not get results, the board member for the sub-district would be called in. Then the vice-president or I could be called on for further support. The ultimate resort was to refer the dispute to a joint arbitration board, headed by a neutral member, whose decision was binding. An occasional dispute over a local election might be referred to me; my job was to interpret the consitution. James Mark worked competently with me, giving the locals good service. Gilbert remained in the office, handling the correspondence and the rather complicated financial affairs of the district, receiving local per capita tax and sending out paychecks to hundreds of checkweighmen.

The conditions that had compelled us to modify the 1916 contract continued through 1917. The cost of living continued to rise. About sixty thousand men left the mines for military service, and others were attracted to other kinds of work. Operators were pushing to get out coal to fill a ravenous demand. A conference of union representatives and operators of the Central Competitive Field met in Indianapolis, September 6, 1917, to discuss the problem. Shortly after the conference opened, a message arrived from Dr. Harry A. Garfield, newly appointed Fuel Administrator, asking that action be deferred until he had time to organize his agency and make preliminary investigations on the basis of which to offer suggestions. The conference accordingly adjourned, to meet later in Washington.

By October 6, the Washington Wage Agreement, as it came to be called, was worked out. The tonnage rate was raised by 10 cents; day men were raised $1.40 a day; and rates for dead work were increased by 15 per cent. This agreement was to run from April 1, 1918, to the end of the war, but in no case for more than two years. Dr. Garfield, concerned about keeping production going, insisted on a penalty clause, assessing each worker $1.00 a day for time spent illegally on strike. No corresponding penalty was laid against operators responsible for interrupting production. The Fuel Administrator allowed operators to add 45 cents a ton to the price of coal, to cover wage increases. The penalty clause roused some opposition among delegates to the national convention in early 1918, but the agreement was finally accepted, after strong urging by the national officers.

We in District 2 were not covered by this agreement, but we moved immediately for a conference with the operators of our district. We got together with them in Washington on October 30 and after several days of argument, the terms of the Washington Wage Agreement were applied to our district. In spite of some haggling, our operators were as eager as anybody not to miss out on wartime profits.

At the district convention in February, 1918, I could review the year's work with satisfaction. Despite the timidity of some who had regarded the letter of the contract as a sacred thing, we had been able to carry the practice of joint wage agreements through a trying period without coming to a breaking point. Obviously, wartime conditions were favorable to wage increases, but they were unfavorable to orderly negotiations, with both operators and miners under pressures of heavy demand, rising prices, shifts in labor supply, and the high emotional tension of public feeling. Despite these hazards, the union emerged stronger than ever before.

We could also note some gratifying legislative gains during this year. Benefits under the Workmen's Compensation Law were raised. They were too low to start with, and their niggardliness was exposed so completely by wartime inflation that even hardshell opponents could hardly protest the increases. Also, working with the Pennsylvania State Federation of Labor, we had persuaded the legislature to authorize a commission to study proposals for old age pensions. Though it was years before anything could be done, the report of the commission was useful in educating the public to the need for this reform.

Miners had long been troubled by the shortage of hospital facilities in Cambria County. The Johnstown Hospital was a long way from the mining towns in the northern part of the county. In the fall of 1919, during my second term as president of District 2, we approached members of the Pennsylvania state legislature to get some state funds for a hospital, which were finally appropriated. Local unions assessed their membership for additional funds, and a hospital was built in Spangler. Representatives of Sub-district 1 of the union served on its board of directors. This enterprise might be considered a forerunner, in a small way, of the Miner's Welfare Fund, most particularly because the miners were proud of the Spangler hospital and considered it their own.

Our convention platform was graced in 1918 by the presence of the newly appointed vice-president of the national union, a young man named John L. Lewis. I had first met Lewis in Washington a year before, during one of the wage negotiations there. At that time he was working for Gompers as a representative of the AFL, specializing in matters affecting the coal miners.

Lewis had come into my district late in 1917 or early in 1918, to help with a wildcat strike in the Broad Top region, along the boundary between Bedford and Huntington counties. This area, composed of small operations, had struck for wages higher than the district agreement. Their local representatives in the negotiations presided over by Dr. Garfield feared the reception they would get back home, and called on me to help get the men back to work.

Lewis and I went up there from Washington for a Sunday afternoon meeting, of which I was chairman. Though the crowd was in a rebellious mood, I got them to hear a local representative, who described in some detail what had transpired in Washington and made it clear he favored going back to work. Then I called on Lewis, who backed up the local man. After he finished, a number of men took the floor to argue the matter. There was a lot of opposition to ending the strike, but as arguments grew repetitious and the day waned, I finally persuaded them to take a vote, which showed a majority for returning to work.

I can't say that I had any strong feeling about Lewis as a result of these first encounters. I accepted him at face value as a vigorous representative of the national organization. No sixth sense whispered to me of his future importance in my life and in the history of the miners. I am sure he was considering me much more seriously, estimating whether I could be useful to him in his plans.

I introduced Lewis to our district convention as a new officer of the international union, and said that we had invited him to get acquainted with him and his views. He started with the usual "review with pride" of the condition of the union, and compliments to the district and its officers. Then he came to the issue that interested me. Referring to the previous national convention, he said, "The organization also outlined its policy in regard to the possible governmental ownership or control of the mines. . . . The government has assumed control of the industry. . . . this control might not cease with the end of the war; the people might come to recognize that they have an interest in the mining of coal; the government at the end of the war might not be willing to permit the industry to again slip from its grasp." If the government did take over the mines, he continued, "the United Mine Workers must be given equal representation on all governmental boards." *
While he did not explicitly advocate government ownership, he so obviously accepted the policy adopted by the union, even looking forward to the situation that would prevail after the takeover, that none

* *Minutes of the 26th Successive Constitutional and Third Bi-ennial Convention of District No. 2, United Mine Workers of America* (1918), I: 107.

of the delegates had any doubt that he favored nationalization. It is characteristic, I think, that he did not discuss whether nationalization was desirable, or any of the intricate economic and social questions involved, but leaped ahead at once to consideration of who would hold the power once it was accomplished.

Another encounter with Lewis during 1918 showed me something of his character and, I have no doubt, raised doubts in his mind of my "reliability." The Pennsylvania State Federation of Labor held its convention in Pittsburgh in May. James H. Maurer had been president for years. He was a Pennsylvania Dutch steamfitter from Reading, and a very prominent Socialist, long a member of the state legislature and in 1932 his party's candidate for vice president. He was a very lovable man, with great ability as a legislator. His integrity and good sense won him great influence in state politics, far beyond labor and Socialist circles. His uncompromising loyalty to principle also won him many enemies. He was the best kind of public agitator and educator.

Maurer was caught in a critical situation during 1918. He had taken a strong stand in the Pennsylvania legislature against suspension of labor laws, contending this was not necessary for prosecution of the war. He successfully blocked the employers' offensive, cloaked as patriotism but designed to break down even the inadequate protections afforded to labor by laws already on the books. The press raised a barrage of propaganda against him, charging him with being "pro-German." He was vulnerable because, like the majority of the Socialist Party, he had opposed our entry into the war. After the declaration of war he ceased his opposition, but his critics were not really interested in his war position. They were out to ruin a pro-labor representative, by fair means or foul. Attorney General Palmer and others in the federal government were making fine political hay out of the red scare, and Maurer was a prime target. They wanted him repudiated by the labor movement.

I was asked, by an international representative of the UMW, to meet with "Jack" Lewis in his hotel room. Lewis had been named vice-president a few months before. He turned on his charm, which was considerable, greeted me effusively, and complimented me on my election to the district presidency and our recent good wage settlement. He pointed out that with the retirement of Charles O'Neil, the leader of my opposition, the way was wide open for me to rise in the labor movement. This attempt at buttering me up did not work, because I was amused by the idea of my rising any farther, or even holding the post I had for very long.

Lewis finally got to the point. We were now in war, he said, and it was a matter of vital concern that this important state federation be headed by a loyal American. Maurer was identified with opposition to war; his record could be used to make the unions appear disloyal. District 5 was opposed to him, and Gompers was concerned about the situation, too. Lewis asked me to help line up delegates against Maurer, especially my own miners.

I told him I could not agree, that Maurer was my friend and I believed he was perfectly loyal to his country. His anti-war activities had ended upon our entry. Furthermore, most of the delegates from my district were in favor of him, believing as I did that the attack on him was caused by the fact that he was a strong labor man. He argued at some length, but I was unmoved. At the end of our conference, he was rather testy; the warmth and friendliness had evaporated. The plot to unseat Maurer was unsuccessful, and I have always been glad that I had no part in trying to punish him for his devotion to labor. Later, Maurer told me he was convinced that if he had been rejected by the state federation, the Department of Justice would have stopped at nothing to put him in jail. In view of Attorney General Palmer's record, I have no doubt he was right.

As I look back on this incident, it seems evident that Lewis was concerned solely with his own political ambitions. He wanted to be kingmaker and to have the state president under obligations to him. Ethical and human considerations were brushed aside if they interfered with his ambitions. On many union matters I agreed with him, and would willingly have worked with him, yet again and again the ruthlessness and extreme egotism of the man drove us apart.

The large Pittsburgh district, directly west of my own district, had been torn by factional disputes ever since 1906. Without going into details of the wrangles, which were mostly of concern only to the individuals involved, I need to give some account of the situation, because of its effects on later parts of my story. Francis Feehan defeated Patrick Dolan for the district presidency in 1906 and held the job until his retirement in 1912, when Van A. Bittner, his vice president, succeeded him. In spite of repeated defeats, the Dolan faction maintained a bitter warfare against Feehan and his supporters, making it almost impossible to get anything constructive done.

Behind this relentless guerilla warfare stood a sinister figure, Al Hamilton, owner of a magazine, *The Coal Trade Bulletin,* which carried some news of the industry and plenty of advertising. Hamilton was reputed to have been an adviser of Dolan; in fact, he was said to have told him to take the stand against John Mitchell in the 1906 national wage conference which broke the united front of the miners and caused Dolan's defeat in the next district election. Hamilton had a reputation as a union "fixer" who gave the operators information secured from his contacts inside the union. In return, he could help an ambitious man to rise in the union by a variety of means, none of which would stand much public scrutiny. He could profit greatly by having the ear of the president of the important Pittsburgh district. He never forgave Feehan for unhorsing Dolan and refusing to play his, Hamilton's, game. This enmity toward Feehan carried over to Bittner. The result was constant sniping at the district officers, blurring real union issues with personal antagonisms.

The district quarrel soon became a national matter. In 1909, the Pittsburgh Coal Company attempted to install in its mines a new method of blasting which caused an increase in slack coal. The miners were paid only for lump, so their earnings dropped by about 10 per cent, and they walked out. National President Thomas L. Lewis intervened and arranged a settlement over the heads of Feehan and Bittner, which they protested as an illegal extension of his authority.

The following year Feehan made an effort to organize the non-union fields of Westmoreland County, lying between Pittsburgh and my district. In spite of poor business conditions, the miners responded. Thomas Lewis opposed the effort as ill timed. The mine owners resisted the strike with all the weapons at their disposal, including violence. The strike dragged on for more than a year, costing the national organization over a million dollars. Constant sniping at Feehan, from both national and local forces, added to the hostility between him and Lewis. Feehan joined with Illinois and some other districts to oust Lewis and elect John P. White of Iowa to the presidency. The District 5 executive board and convention held fast in support of the strike, and the national convention of January, 1911, also voted support, after a prolonged debate. But by summer, there was no hope of victory, so the national executive board ended the strike.

During the strike, many younger men had found jobs in the Pittsburgh district, and some remained there after the strike was called off. They were a small but cohesive group unconcerned with old factional loyalties. They supported Feehan and Bittner because of the effort to organize Westmoreland County. Philip Murray was one of this group. In the next district election, the Westmoreland men helped re-elect Feehan; Philip Murray ran successfully on his slate for district national board member. The opposition maintained that the Westmoreland County votes were illegal, carried the issue to the courts, and held their own district convention. The Feehan group won in the courts and in the union executive board. But the fighting went on, and at every stage Al Hamilton manipulated events to keep the union divided and weak. Finally, the worst turmoil of all broke out in 1916, when some of the rank and file objected to the agreement and to the role of Van Bittner in concluding it. The national office intervened. Bittner and his vice-president, Pat Hanaway, were persuaded to resign and accept appointments to the staff of the national union. They were succeeded by Philip Murray as president and Robert Gibbons as vice-president.

I had my one encounter with Hamilton during the 1918 wage conference in Washington, which confirmed my view of his role in union affairs. He was one of the operators' representatives. It was the only time he appeared openly in negotiations in our field; I have no idea how he happened to get in on this. Leaving aside his reputation, he was an impressive and persuasive man. His attitude toward us was friendly and ingratiating.

One item the miners wanted was a rule that disputed discharge cases had to be disposed of in five days, and if the decision favored the miner, he was to be paid for lost time. This request had been resisted in previous years but now we found an ally in Hamilton, who said the rule was a reasonable one, with proper safeguards. With his support, we won the point.

I soon learned that Hamilton was not there just to help the miners. At the close of the conference, he asked me to meet him in his room. I agreed, but took the precaution of telling my two fellow delegates about it, feeling sure that he had private reasons for the invitation. He came right to the point: he had come to Washington primarily to "establish a basis of friendly relations" with me.

He said, "I can kick people off your back. I can arrange settlements in places where you are having trouble, things important to you locally. I can intervene—not in all places, but in a lot of them—and make it possible for you to succeed where others have failed, and get the credit for it with your membership. Things like this discharge issue, that don't cost the operators much but everybody's being stubborn about it; it means a lot to you to win the point, and it's not too hard to arrange if the right person goes about it in the right way."

He said this was nothing new or unusual. I had suspected as much, even within the official family of my own district, so I was not too shocked. I quizzed him about his techniques, and he told me a series of stories of what people had done for him and what he had done in return. In most cases, he omitted names. But he did say that he was responsible for Philip Murray's appointment to the Pittsburgh school board, without specifying any favor in return. I doubt that Murray was one of Hamilton's pals, but Hamilton had pals in that district, and Murray probably knew what was going on around him. Murray was not the type to raise a row, but was more likely to steer his way carefully through a mess, trying to get the best he could for the union without upsetting applecarts. He would not welcome such operations, but would consider them something he had to live with.

I finally got Hamilton to state what was expected from me in return for his favors. He said he was a consultant for the Berwind and White Company, which operated mines in Somerset County, adjacent to my district. The president, E. J. Berwind, was determined to operate without the union, as he had done since 1894. Hamilton said that maybe after the old man died there would be a change of policy, but in the meantime it was Hamilton's job to get protection for the company. In other words, he was ready to buy exemption for one concern by betraying the interests of others. This was the counterpart, on the operators' side, of what he had been doing in the union. As long as he could keep both sides divided there would be good pickings for Hamilton, and maybe a few crumbs for those who played his game.

I told Hamilton flatly that I wanted no part of any such deal. My obligation was to all the miners, to get the best wages and conditions I could for all, and to organize the unorganized no matter where they worked. I knew the Berwind and White Company from having worked in one of its mines as a boy, and that experience gave me no reason to think it deserved any favors. I had no objection to friendly relations with operators who accepted the right of labor to organize and bargain collectively, but my relations would be the same with all, and entirely in the open.

That ended our talk. I never saw him again, but I came across his handiwork from time to time. I did organize the Berwind and White mines in 1922, but we lost the strike against them and they did not finally recognize the union until the New Deal days. Hamilton could not have helped me in that situation. I am sure he was working hard to defeat my plans.

In view of the turmoil in District 5, Philip Murray was a fortunate choice for president. He was always at his best in composing differences; this was his greatest value to John L. Lewis in later years, when Murray did most of the work of negotiating agreements for Lewis's signature. He had an easy, conciliatory manner, and never pushed things to a showdown if they could be allowed to work themselves out gradually. The first account I heard of Murray came from William Welsh. Murray was sent in as representative of President White, sometime in 1916, to straighten out a local dispute in our district. Welsh was present as district board member. He was favorably impressed with Murray's tact and Scotch-Irish blarney, and prophesied that he would be heard from in higher places. I met Murray often after we had been elected to the presidency of our respective districts, but we were not close friends, perhaps because his district was linked with those farther west, with its primary market in the Great Lakes area, while mine looked eastward. Murray took less interest than I did in the larger social and economic problems. He was very much the trade unionist, interested in day-to-day operation of the union. His pragmatic turn of mind helps explain his long and faithful, though unhappy, association with Lewis. Murray saw Lewis as a man who got things done, and was not much interested in his social views. Lewis was the one disturbing factor in my relations with Murray.

11

IIIIIIIIIIIIIIIIIIIIIIIIIIIIIIIIIIIIIIIIIII

THE POSTWAR STRIKE

The Washington Wage Agreement of October, 1917, was by no means the end of our struggle to stabilize wages. The bitterest fights were yet to come, against the Fuel Administrator and the government. During the winter of 1917–1918, the operators of my district asked Dr. Garfield to grant them a special price increase, on the ground that costs of production in the thin seams of central Pennsylvania were higher than elsewhere. Garfield gave them sixty cents a ton, starting February 16, 1918, on all coal mined in the area, high-cost as well as low-cost. The fact that central Pennsylvania coal would be the highest-priced in the country made no difference; coal could be sold at almost any price. No provision was made to pass on any of the bonus to the miners. Our convention, in session at the time, demanded a share.

I went to Washington, with Gilbert and Mark, to plead our case to Garfield. We had scarcely begun when he produced a chart showing that half the tonnage in our district was produced at a profit of 60 cents to $1.25 a ton, a fourth at 38 to 60 cents, and the rest for less than 38 cents. This, to his mind, was all the justification needed for the bonus to the operators; he rejected our request for a comparable raise.

It seemed to me that his case was less than perfect. While obviously some operators would make less than others, this was nothing new.

A government-fixed price which guaranteed a profit to everyone would also guarantee exorbitant profits to some. Federal Trade Commission reports showed that average profits for the whole industry had increased from 15 per cent in 1916 to 24 per cent in 1917. Since then, prices had been boosted by 45 cents, and now our operators were getting 60 cents more. None of them were suffering, and some had multiplied profits by as much as 350 per cent. If prices and profits were to be raised by government action, at the expense of the people, I saw no reason why the miners producing high-priced coal at wages pegged to lower prices should not get equal consideration.

Dr. Garfield was a very stiff, formal, dogmatic person. He had arrived at a conclusion which satisfied him, and questions and arguments simply annoyed him. It was soon clear that nothing was going to break his conviction of his own rightness, though I admit I kept on trying, because it was unthinkable to me that anyone could fail to see the justice of our cause.

When we reported back, the reconvened convention voted reluctantly to swallow this injustice rather than call a strike in wartime, but the resentment of the delegates was freely expressed. We sent an appeal to the Administrator for investigation of the question, with representatives of the union participating. He turned this request down; he considered the matter closed and saw no need for further investigation.

We were not the only ones dissatisfied with the Fuel Administrator's decisions. Unrest spread among the miners in other districts, leading the international to make its own move for a wage adjustment. A conference of the miner's National Policy Committee with Garfield was called for August 22, 1918. We demonstrated to him how drastically the cost of living had increased since the last wage increase, and how the profits of the operators had multiplied. It was impossible, we argued, for the miner to watch the value of his wages shrink while others were making vast fortunes out of his labor. Dr. Garfield was unmoved. He contended that we were legally bound to work at the prevailing rates and he could see no need for change.

On November 1, we appealed from this decision directly to President Wilson. We pointed out that an increase had been granted, very justly, to the anthracite miners, and asked for the same consideration. We pointed to a rise in the cost of living in excess of 20 per cent during the last year, and to the astonishing production record of the nation's bituminous miners. The President's reply, on the fifteenth, was couched in friendly terms and acknowledged that the miners had made a splendid record of production, but it upheld Dr. Garfield's decision. The war had just ended, and there did not seem to be any next step to take.

The end of the war made things worse. Industrial cutbacks were swift and merciless. Many mines shut down altogether. Short time became general, and the miners' income declined. But the cost of living did not come down. There was widespread distress in the mine fields.

The executive board of the UMW called a meeting of representatives from all the districts, to gather in Indianapolis May 18, 1919. After extended discussion, the conference proposed the following demands: (1) a six-hour day and five-day week; (2) substantial increases in all rates for tonnage, day work, yardage and dead work; (3) nationalization and democratic management of all coal mines in the United States.

The conference called for a special convention in Cleveland to plan action to secure these demands. The date was left for the officers to set. The demands agreed upon at the May conference were not all regarded with equal enthusiasm by the officers of the union. Everybody agreed on the thirty-hour week as a device to spread work and reduce unemployment. Though thousands of miners have made the shift to other industries in the last half-century, it has not been an easy move to make. It is no small matter for a man to give up the experience, skill, and habits of a lifetime and become an apprentice in a new kind of work. It takes time to find a job. It takes even more time to recover the status lost by giving up the advantages of experience and seniority.

The demand for higher wages was an obvious effort to keep up with rising costs of living, and there was no disagreement about that. But there were mixed feelings among the officers on nationalization. I will discuss this subject at greater length in the next chapter. Personally, I felt that this was the key to the entire problem of the miners.

At the Cleveland convention, which met in September, 1919, John L. Lewis, as acting president, took a strong stand on wages. He recommended that the contract be terminated on November 1 if no agreement was obtained by that time. His wage proposals called for a 60 per cent increase in tonnage, day work, yardage, and dead-work rates, the thirty-hour week, time and a half for overtime, double time for Sundays and holidays, and elimination of the penalty clause.

An interstate joint conference had already been arranged with the operators, which met in Buffalo on September 25, and continued until October 2, without agreement. Another three-day meeting in Philadelphia also made no progress. The operators took the stand that the contract was still in force and they would consent to no changes. In accordance with the Cleveland decision, the union ordered a national strike to begin on November 1. Secretary of Labor Wilson made a final effort to get agreement in a four-day conference with both sides, but this meeting also broke up without accomplishing anything. On October 25, President Woodrow Wilson stepped into the dispute, with a statement demanding revocation of the strike call, and denouncing the strike as "not only unjustifiable but unlawful." He made no equivalent demands upon the employers. The Lever Act, which, among other things, had given the Fuel Administrator control over wages and prices during "wartime," was still legally in effect, although the fighting had ended with the Armistice a year before.

On the basis of this legal quibble, that the war had not been officially ended, Judge Anderson of the Federal district court in Indianapolis, at the request of Attorney General A. Mitchell Palmer, issued a temporary order to the union officials to withdraw the strike call. After a hearing on November 8, Anderson issued an injunction forbidding the union officials and everybody else to do anything whatever to support the strike, and giving us until 6 P.M. on the eleventh to get the men back to work. The executive committee of the AFL called Anderson's order "so autocratic as to stagger the human mind."

However autocratic, the injunction was, in fact, irrelevant. On November 1 the miners stayed home. The strike was almost 100 per cent effective. I believe I was in my office in Clearfield on the day the strike began. I had sent letters to all the locals informing them of the union's decision, and I knew that was all I needed to do. The miners were so infuriated by the way they had been treated that they needed no urging to strike. And the legal fraud of the Anderson injunction just made them madder. The strike had been well timed, and I was sure the men would stick it out. The time had come when finally something had to be done.

At the meeting of the national policy committee in Indianapolis, it was soon clear that there was no sentiment for obeying the order. We met on November 10 in the Lincoln Hotel—in a low-ceilinged room on the mezzanine floor, which got pretty hot before we were through. The scale committee of the Central Competitive Field and three delegates from each of the other districts were there, about 125 people altogether. Lewis reviewed the situation and then, without committing himself, called on us to give our views. As delegate after delegate spoke, some quiet and brief, others more excited and long winded, it became clear that sentiment was for standing fast against government interference. Alex Howat, president of the Kansas District, was characteristically the most vehement. He damned the judge and shouted, "To hell with him and anybody else who attacks the miners' rights. We're not going to be robbed by any legal fiction about the war still going on when even the biggest damn fool in the world can see it is over!" When I got my chance to speak, I expressed the same sentiments, but in milder language. Most of the other men felt as I did, that with the miners as firm and united as they obviously were, we should stand fast, not denouncing anybody but insisting on our rights. The government could put a few of us in jail, but as long as we stood firm, the men in the pits would stand with us, making the injunction a useless piece of paper. Putting men in jail would not mine coal.

After several hours, Lewis called on the union's counselor, "Judge" Henry Warrum, to give us his opinion. He could see no legal alternative to compliance.

Finally, Lewis had to make his position known. It came as a shock. He said, "We've got to face this situation. The obligation is upon the national officers. The injunction is directed against us specifically, to comply by a certain time. That time is tomorrow, so we have to act at this session." He had made his decision, he said, "with as much resentment and bitterness as was in the heart of anybody present, to do his duty, which was to comply with the injunction and cancel the strike order."

He went out and told the reporters his decision, with a rhetorical flourish to the effect that he could not fight his government, the greatest government on earth, because the miners were good Americans. I did not hear him make this famous remark, but I never forgot it, or forgave it. He was not so hesitant about fighting the government later on, when it suited his purpose. It apparently did not occur to him, or to those who applauded his "patriotism," to demand that the operators also sacrifice something to prove their Americanism.

I was disappointed by the decision to call off the strike, but I was disgusted by the cheap hypocrisy of the talk about patriotism and law and order which came from all sides to cover up the naked brutal rejection of the miners' demand for a decent agreement.

As it turned out, the miners were better men than their "leader," which did not surprise me, knowing the miners as I did. The papers made a great hurrah about getting back to work, but the miners just stayed home. I returned to Clearfield and caught up with my office work. I made no effort to get the men back to work, because I knew they would pay me no attention and I knew they were right. The order had been issued, in obedience to the court; I couldn't stop that; neither was I obligated to make a fight for an order I considered indefensible. My men stayed out 100 per cent, and so did those in most of the districts. A few people in some of the Southern fields drifted back, but the country was still not getting any coal.

The powers of government were used ruthlessly to break the strike. Wyoming was placed under martial law, and troops were used in Alabama, West Virginia, Tennessee, and Kentucky to drive men into the mines at the point of a bayonet. The press let itself go in a vicious campaign of villification against the miners and their officers. The public, kept in ignorance of what was going on and unable to hear the miners' side of the story, blamed us for the shortage of coal, which soon became serious. Numerous officers of the union were arrested and threats were made to throw more of us in jail. Worst of all, no strike relief could be paid, because all funds of the union were tied up by the injunction.

On December 4, Judge Anderson cited eighty-four of us for contempt. I let the union lawyer appear for me, as did most of the others, except for a few who lived in Indiana. We could not have sent the men back to work if we had wanted to, and the judge still had not given us any good reason to want to, so this changed nothing. On the sixth, Joseph P. Tumulty and A. Mitchell Palmer announced that the President was determined to end the strike, and produced the first reasonable proposal which had come from the union's opponents. The miners were to return to work immediately, with a 14 per cent increase, and a Presidential Commission would consider further claims, their decision to be the basis for new wage agreements. The policy committee accepted this, and the national convention supported their decision by an overwhelming vote in January. So ended a strike which neither Lewis's shilly-shallying, the operators, the courts, nor the President could break.

The AFL had stood solidly behind the miners. At the November 10 meeting, Robert Harlin, then president of the Washington State District, reported that he had talked to Gompers, who had promised him that the AFL would issue a statement urging defiance of the injunction. Lewis, instead of being pleased by this promise of support, seemed resentful. Perhaps he thought Gompers should ask his permission first. Anyway, Gompers issued the statement, showing more guts than Lewis.

Before the strike, Secretary of Labor Wilson had proposed a raise of 31.6 per cent. Dr. Garfield, who had been resurrected for the occasion, perhaps to maintain the fiction that "wartime" law still applied, though the Fuel Administration had been disbanded, produced charts to show that the weighted average increase in the cost of living since the last contract had been only 14 per cent. The operators rejected both figures.

The new commission finally came out with a rather complicated award, granting additional raises. These came to about 34 per cent for tonnage men and 20 per cent for day men. There were wildcat strikes of day men here and there, which finally won them an additional $1.50 a day. The new contract ran until April 1, 1922. Altogether, it was not a bad result, but nobody could claim any credit for it but the miners themselves.

Through all the demands of my first two years in the district presidency, I had been preparing to make the most important and, I am sure, the happiest change in my life. The story began back in 1908, when I had spent a weekend visiting a young friend named Carl McGrath, in the little town of Gallitzin. We went to Mass together on Sunday. As we came out of the church, we met two young girls, cousins of Carl's. One of them was Anita Anstead, just sixteen, with dark brown hair and eyes and fresh red cheeks. I was so taken with her that I hardly noticed what her cousin looked like. The four of us chatted for a few minutes, then decided to call on Mrs. McGrath. There we had a late breakfast, and sat for a couple of hours, talking and sipping coffee.

That afternoon, Carl and I visited the Ansteads. Others dropped in, and, with three of Anita's sisters, we had a fair-sized party. Anita played the piano, an accomplishment I found very impressive, and we all sang.

The next morning, on the way to the train for home, I realized I was "smitten" when I met one of the young men who had been at the party and found that I was jealous of him! He could stay in Gallitzin, while I had to return to my home and my job twenty miles away. I wrote Anita several postcards, then a letter asking if I could come to call again. Her parents decided that she was too young to have a strange man (I was all of 24) coming to see her from out of town, and as an obedient daughter, she accepted their decision. She moved to Pittsburgh shortly after that and we continued to exchange postcards. Sometime in 1910, I renewed my request for permission to call, and this time it was granted. I made several trips to Pittsburgh, taking her to dinner and the theater. Then I departed on my travels in Iowa and Michigan. We exchanged letters, but after a while she sensed that my interest in her was more serious than hers in me and cut off the correspondence.

I heard no more from her until 1917. Anita finished high school and passed the state teacher's examination. Despairing of finding a teaching job, for there were too many teachers available in spite of poor pay, she went with her older sister, Mary, to Pittsburgh to take a business school course. The two girls bought a small stenographic and multigraphing business and after a year of struggle, managed to make a living out of it. One of their customers was the district office of the United Mine Workers, which at one point sent in a list of names of people to whom some circulars were to be addressed, among them one John Brophy. On the chance that it might be the same man she had known, she put one of her business cards in my letter, with the note, "It's a small world after all, isn't it?" I had never forgotten her, though it had seemed there were too many obstacles in the way of keeping up a courtship.

That card was all I needed to overcome my fears. I went to Pittsburgh as often as I could manage it; soon we were engaged and several months later were married. During our courtship we tried going to dances. Anita liked to dance and was very good at it, but I had no talent—she declared I had two left feet and gave up on me. We would have dinner together and occasionally go to the theater or to visit friends. But mostly we walked and talked, enjoying each other's company without any entertainment. We shared an interest in reading and, above all, our common faith.

Our wedding was a small one, at St. Peter's Church in Pittsburgh, on August 13, 1918. William Welsh came from Nanty Glo to be my best man; a girlhood friend of Anita's from Gallitzin, May Burke, was bridesmaid. The rest of the guests were members of our families and some of Anita's friends. After a wedding breakfast at Anita's home, we went on a trip to New York, Philadelphia, and Washington. Significantly, I had to interrupt the honeymoon briefly to attend a wage conference in Washington. Then we returned to Clearfield.

Houses were hard to find because of the war, so we lived for a while in a small hotel. We had scarcely unpacked our bags when I had to leave on one of my trips to visit the locals, neglected while I was busy getting married. Living in a hotel room, poor Anita had nothing to do. Clearfield had no library and only one movie. There was a piano in the hotel on which she could practice, but there were limits to the amount of time she could put in on that. Finally, she took a temporary job as secretary to the committee running the local Liberty Loan campaign. We found a furnished house offered for rent because the widow who owned it was going to live near her soldier son's training camp. But we were no more than settled when the war ended and she returned, with her son, to claim her home again. We rented three unfurnished rooms for a while, and at last a house in which we could begin to live a normal life.

Although there were mines around Gallitzin, and her father had worked in one when she was very small as a "stable boss," caring for the mine mules, Anita knew little about mines or miners, and even less about the union. Her father had become a contractor, so it was in this work that she remembered him. She has said that she never heard of the Mine Workers' Union until she sent out the mailing for District 5. But now she had every chance to learn fast.

In December of that year I was up for re-election and facing formidable opposition; they were working hard, and though I knew I had good rank-and-file support, it was necessary to see that that support was translated into votes. Anita was invaluable in helping me get out my campaign material. She helped with my more complicated correspondence and newspaper articles. We would often chuckle together over some exchanges with John L. Lewis.

We lived in Clearfield for nearly nine years. Anita's sister Stella worked as my secretary and lived with us for several years. With her help as babysitter, Anita was able from time to time to accompany me to conventions and other union gatherings and advance her education in unionism.

Anita and I had two children. Philip Noel Brophy was born on July 30, 1919, and Jacqueline on March 11, 1923. We were able to give them a better education than either of us had had. Philip graduated from Georgetown University in 1941 and immediately enlisted in the Naval Air Force. At first, he was a flying instructor in Pensacola. Then he was assigned to a squadron based at Klamath Falls, Oregon. There I had an opportunity to visit him and his new bride, Beryl, a great-grand-daughter of Samuel Gompers. Later he served as a fighter pilot with the Pacific Fleet in a number of actions. By then, he had become a lieutenant. He happened to be on leave and visiting us when the war ended. Because of his length of service, decorations, and foreign duty, he was able to go on inactive duty at once and entered the George-town University Law School. After he obtained his law degree and was admitted to the bar, he served on the legal staff of the District of Columbia for several years, and then was an attorney in the Office of Price Stabilization. Since the end of the Korean conflict he has been in private practice in Falls Church, Virginia, where he and his wife live, with their eight daughters and one son, John A. Brophy II.

Jacqueline attended the University of Maryland, where she became interested in newspaper work, and rose to the editorship of the college newspaper. After college, she worked a while for the United Press, then for a year as my secretary, and then held a State Department job in Lisbon, Portugal. During one of my trips to Europe, she got a short leave to join me in Paris. She resigned the State Department job to study at Columbia University for a year, then worked for several years on trade papers and the IUE *News*. She won a two-year Fulbright scholarship to England to study British labor journalism and workers education. When Anita and I were on our way back from the dedica-tion of the Philip Murray memorial in Israel, we spent several weeks with Jacqueline touring England and Scotland in a hired car. She earned her master's degree at Michigan State University, where she is now on the faculty of the School of Labor and Industrial Relations.

Anita apparently was never concerned about the hazards of life with a man already marked as a "troublemaker." When we had to face hard decisions, she never once faltered. She backed my decision to run against John L. Lewis, risking my safe job, because she shared my feeling that this was something that ought to be done. And when I was unemployed, she became the breadwinner until I could find work. Most important, she gave me strength to face all decisions and hardships; when I had fought for my principles to the point of exhaustion and, apparently, of defeat, it was she who restored my strength and enabled me to continue. That bright, cold winter day in front of the little church in Gallitzin was the most important and most fortunate of my entire life.

12

THE MINERS' PROGRAM

John L. Lewis played such an important part in my life from this time on that I should pause to give a brief account of his rise to the presidency of the Mine Workers.

Lewis started in the mines of Iowa, then moved to Illinois. His highest post in Illinois was membership on the legislative committee of District 12. He was an officer of a local union and a mine committeeman, but never held any higher elective post. Then, as some of the Illinois boys put it, he "decided there were ways of getting ahead in the labor movement besides elections," and used his legislative work to court John H. Walker, president of District 12. He got Walker to recommend him for a job on Gompers' staff. Gompers had several men who did odd jobs for him: legislative work, visiting conventions, reporting on strikes, etc. With the entry of the United States into the war, Lewis specialized in liaison between Gompers and the United Mine Workers. John P. White, president of the UMW, was putting in almost full time as labor representative with the Fuel Administration. White was tired of his union job and wanted to become a full-time consultant in the Fuel Administration without losing contact with the union. He discussed the problem with his new friend, Lewis, who had some helpful ideas as to how he could move over and still hold his influence in the union. Frank Hayes, the vice-president, was one of the Illinois group, an ineffectual person who had won his eminence by a gift of florid oratory. After a few years in office, he was notable principally for his efforts to keep up with the boys in drinking. He had previously been very abstemious, and did not have the head for heavy drinking, but once started was apparently unable to quit.

The plan Lewis and White worked out was that Lewis was to be appointed statistician in the national office of the United Mine Workers and business manager of the UMW *Journal*. Both jobs were sinecures, if the holder chose to treat them that way. The staff could do the work, and Lewis could give almost full time to building himself up with the membership. In July of 1917, Lewis received his appointment and White started negotiating for his government job.

White was appointed in October and resigned the presidency of the union. Hayes moved up to president, with the power, under the constitution, to appoint a new vice-president. In accordance with the terms of the understanding with White, Hayes appointed Lewis vice-president. The only hurdle to be topped was getting approval of the appointment by the executive board. There was considerable resentment against the choice of this unknown man. Walker and Farrington of Illinois, who knew Lewis better than anybody else on the board, were strongest of all against him. They may have had ambitions of their own for the post; I don't know about that. Whatever their reasons, they never forgave Lewis. Illinois, under their leadership and after they were gone, remained solidly anti-Lewis for a generation.

Philip Murray, president of District 5 and a former board member, made a special trip to Indianapolis on the eve of the board meeting to win over a number of his friends. From what he told me later, I gather that he felt the union needed somebody with Lewis's vigor and drive to make up for the weakness of White and Hayes. Murray was not privy to the deal that had been worked out by Lewis; I think he really thought this was a good appointment. His work was successful; he won over a majority, the opposition collapsed, and the stage was set for the next move.

In the absence of Frank Hayes, who was reported to be "ill," Lewis presided over the 1919 convention of the United Mine Workers. From what I have heard, Hayes's illness would nowadays be called alcoholism, and it was not necessary for Lewis to get him drunk, as some have charged. If White had had any ideas of being the power behind the throne, he was soon disabused. Lewis ran his own show, as acting president and as president, which he soon became. Hayes was out of circulation from September, 1918, until he resigned his position, in February, 1920. Lewis then succeeded to the presidency and appointed Philip Murray vice-president.

Like most miners, I had no very strong feelings about Lewis as a prospect for the presidency. His way of getting the job, without ever submitting his name to the members in an election, was unprecedented in the history of the union, and was understandably resented, not only in Illinois. But the important fact was that he had no record, so there was no way of telling whether he was qualified. We could only wait and see. The one thing that was not obvious to us was that he had already done what was most important to him, namely, getting the job, from which only death or old age would ever remove him. He had managed his intrigues, and was hard at work completing his control of the organization. He paid little attention to the duty of providing the membership with a program. Instead, he passively accepted what had already been decided.

Looking back, it now seems to me that his attitude toward policy could have been discerned from his conduct at the 1919 convention. He took a strong stand in favor of a raise in wages and shorter hours, but he was indifferent to the proposals for nationalization of the mines. The miners were committed to nationalization by earlier actions. Lewis presented the report of the president, which had been written for Hayes by Robert Harlin, Lewis's predecessor as statistician. Lewis read it off and presided while the report was discussed. He made no comment for or against nationalization. There was strong sentiment for the idea, so he let it go through, but did nothing to help or to hinder.

The proposal to nationalize the mines came out of a trip Hayes and Robert Harlin had made to Europe shortly after the war ended. Their purpose was to get certain European countries, who were suffering from a shortage of coal, to buy some of the surplus piled up in this country. Hayes and Harlin, after conferring with Woodrow Wilson in Paris and receiving a promise of his help, went on to visit Germany, Belgium, and England. While in England, they attended sessions of a royal commission investigating the state of Britain's coal industry. The British miners' union was pressing for nationalization, and Hayes and Harlin were deeply impressed by the union's case. Hayes was a sentimental socialist of sorts, who would respond favorably to such an idea anyway. Harlin, the brains of the combination, had worked in the mines in the north of England before coming to America as a young

man. Both returned from Europe convinced that arguments for centralized planning and control of the industry applied with equal valid-
ity to America. Harlin drew up the proposals, and they were given an
equal place with the wage and hour demands in the discussions of the
May, 1919, conference in Indianapolis. At the conference, which I attended along with a large number of leading officials of the union,
sentiment was strong for a vigorous move forward.

It was soon common knowledge that Lewis was unsympathetic, but
not because he stood out in opposition. His position in the union was
still too uncertain for him to risk fighting the trend. He just sat and
glowered, sullenly biding his time. He played no particular part even
in formulating the wage demands. This sitting on the sidelines was not
his usual style. Some of the more conservative men sniped at the program. One jibe I remember went, "Here we hit the operators with the
biggest wage demand in history, and follow it up with a threat to take
the mines away from them altogether. What are we coming to?" And
some argued that the nationalization idea was the best way to solidify
operator resistance to our wage demand; by asking for too much we
were likely to end up with nothing. It was true that this was the strongest stand the miners had ever taken, but the circumstances of the time
justified it. The idea of nationalization had been in circulation among
the miners for years, especially where the Socialists were strong,
though this was the first time that a proposal to achieve it had been
presented.

During these same years, the railroad unions were supporting the
Plumb Plan for nationalization of the railroads. Both the miners and the
railroad workers, after their experience of government controls during
the war, were reluctant to return to the wasteful anarchy of private
operation without adequate guarantees against losing their gains of the
past couple of years. Glenn Plumb spoke to the 1919 convention of the
United Mine Workers on the plan for nationalization of the railroads
and urged an alliance between the coal and rail unions for mutual
support. His speech won a rousing ovation.

Harlin, who had been elected president of District 10, in the state of
Washington, was secretary of the resolutions committee at the 1919
convention. He reported that eleven resolutions favoring nationalization had been received from the locals, not a great number, but indica-
tive of some interest. He drafted a substitute, which was adopted by
the convention. After stating the basic importance of coal in the na-

tional economy and indicting private exploitation of our coal resources, the resolution proposed: (1) that the government purchase all coal properties, paying actual market value for them; (2) that the mines be thenceforward operated by the government through a commission which would include full representation for the miners, with guarantees of collective bargaining; (3) that the international officers and the executive board do all possible to win popular support for our proposals, including an alliance with the railroad unions committed to the Plumb Plan for mutual support.

During the discussion, questions were raised about the right to strike. Lewis gravely assured the delegates that "we will never agree to any measure that will set aside or transgress the inherent right of every free born citizen of the United States to strike if he so desires." One delegate, after praising the Harlin report, asked if it would be published. He was told that it would be printed in the proceedings. This could hardly be avoided; what the delegate wanted was a pamphlet which could be distributed, but Lewis never provided any such thing.

It was pointed out in the discussion that adoption of a resolution was not enough, that the miners would have to make their power felt in elections. As one delegate put it, we should "send a few coal miners and men from the ranks of labor to sit in the halls of Congress." An amendment was passed to include Canada in the resolution, and the amended resolution was passed by a unanimous rising vote. Opinion was not quite as strongly in favor of the idea as this might appear to indicate, but there was a large body of support, strengthened by the example of the Plumb Plan agitation. Opponents did not make a clear fight against the proposal; they preferred to drag their feet and quietly sabotage all efforts to do anything. This was Lewis's policy.

In spite of the failure of the national office to obey the convention's mandate, the nationalization issue would not down. It came up at the AFL Denver convention in 1921 and in later conventions of the United Mine Workers. I did my full share to keep the idea alive, and others agreed with me that this was the one current proposal which offered hope of a better regime for the coal miners.

Nationalization was pushed into the background by the struggle over wages which I have described in the previous chapter. At the special convention in Columbus, Ohio, in January, 1920, Lewis had a hard fight to get approval of his actions during this struggle. Both he and William Green reported that the sentiment of the November 10, 1919,

conference in Indianapolis had been overwhelmingly in favor of com-
plying with the Anderson injunction, which was untrue. Green said he
and Lewis "paced the corridors of the hotel for more than an hour
debating in our minds as to whether or not we would yield to what
seemed to be the overwhelming sentiment of that conference."

Although many delegates recognized and resented Lewis's attempt
to create an alibi for himself, they were confronted with a *fait accompli*
and could only vote to accept the compromise offered by the government, though a few carried their bitterness so far as to vote against the
whole proposal.

In such an atmosphere, serious thought and study of the nationalization program could hardly be expected. Lewis's contribution was confined to booming speeches rehashing what everybody knew—too many
mines, too many miners, too much coal, disorderly production and distribution, wretched conditions for the miners—coupled with exhorta-
tions to stand firm while time and the processes of the market cleared
up the situation. His economic ideas never got beyond the primitive
level of laissez faire—old fashioned even by comparison with those of
his Republican heroes.

After the nationalization idea had been silently sabotaged in the national office for two years, I decided to use my position as president of
District 2 as a platform from which to revive it. The occasion I chose
for this effort was a special convention held at Du Bois, February
22–24, 1921. The convention had been called by some of the locals to
consider raising the pay of checkweighmen and district officers, bringing them into line with the miners' increases and with the rates paid in
other districts. Naturally, the hottest debates raged around this question, which required an increase in the checkoff of dues. The convention
finally referred the matter to a referendum of the membership, which
approved the increases.

Even though the opposition to the raises, largely by remnants of the
old Purcell machine, focused on me as the visible symbol of officialdom,
I was able to get substantial discussion of what I presented as "The
Miners' Program." I had consulted with James Mark and Richard Gilbert beforehand about the program, and they supported it at the convention.

My program was presented in five parts. The first part argued that
our efforts to deal with grievances as they arose had won us some gains
but had not won us a good life by American standards. In fact, such

grievances as car-pushing were still with us, in spite of years of effort to negotiate them out of existence.

The second part pointed out the strategic position of District 2. We had 43,000 organized miners, who produced 50,000,000 tons of coal a year, supplying the greatest industrial area in the world. Although the larger program of the miners could not be realized by one district alone, if we pushed the program resolutely, other districts would have to follow our lead.

Third, I said that we could win only when we made it clear to the public that their grievance and ours were one and the same. Almost always, when we demanded raises or other improvements, the operators, with the help of the reactionary press and politicians, had been able to persuade the public that the miners were responsible for shortages of coal and for high prices because of our "unreasonable" demands. The actual cause of the trouble was the greed and incompetence of the owners. The true interest of the public would be served by our proposals to end the waste, unreasonable profits, exorbitant prices, unemployment, outrageously high accident rate, and planlessness and indifference to public needs characteristic of the industry.

The fourth section I devoted to a statement of the program itself: nationalization of the mines under government and worker control, and the thirty-hour week. A unified industry under intelligent management would reduce the cost of coal and at the same time provide a decent American living for the miner. With collective bargaining, and with the miners having a voice in decisions on industry policy, we could give the public an assured supply of its essential fuel at reasonable prices, without interruptions of work by conflicts between the men and management.

Finally, I said that the first step toward achievement of these goals must be education of the miners themselves in the importance of the program. We must issue a series of pamphlets on the subject, to be distributed through checkweighmen to the rank and file. Workers' education classes in the locals should be organized to provide information on economics, politics, and the problems of the industry. The State Federation of Labor was already organizing such classes throughout the state, and the coal miners' locals should all participate. We should back the proposal of the State Federation to set up a state-wide daily labor paper. And we should undertake a program of research to find and organize the facts needed to support our proposals.

A few delegates, who would have opposed me if I had said no more than that the sun shines by day and the moon by night, tried to ridicule the proposals. And some were worried that the program might cost money. But a number of delegates pointed out that money spent on research and education was a sound investment, bound to pay off in the long run, and the convention accepted that common-sense conclusion. The sections were adopted in order, and when we came to adoption of the whole, the vote was unanimous. The three hours of discussion obliterated the opposition, which had no program at all to offer and could only resort to niggling complaints about details, which carried no conviction, even with those who made them. I don't claim that the "down-with-anything-Brophy-wants" group were convinced, but they were silenced.

After the convention, the report was printed in a pamphlet under the title, *The Miners' Program,* with an explanatory addendum covering some of the objections that had been raised. It was distributed to the locals as a basis for further discussion.

!!

13

CAMPAIGNING FOR
NATIONALIZATION

An unexpected assist to my campaign for nationalization came out of the 1921 AFL convention at Denver. John L. Lewis was an avowed candidate for the presidency of the AFL, which Gompers had held, except for one year, since 1881. In support of his candidacy, Lewis was patching together an alliance of elements who had nothing in common but dissatisfaction with Gompers. The United Mine Workers, largest union in the Federation, was the core of his support. The "Indianapolis group" of unions with headquarters in that city (the Miners and Carpenters were the largest—an odd alliance in view of event of the 1930's) was ready to vote against Gompers. These unions represented no policy; their officers had developed personal ties during Sunday evening poker games at the English Hotel, and thought it would be useful to have one of their gang in the presidency.

The other important faction whose votes Lewis had to win was the group of Socialist-led unions who had been critical of Gompers for years. To satisfy them, Lewis had to announce a progressive platform. He declared on June 23, "I stand for government ownership of the railroads, nationalization of the mines, and other progressive legislation that would give the workers and toilers of America the freedom and justice in industry they deserve. I stand for health insurance, old

157

age pensions for the working masses. The enactment of laws covering these subjects would give the workers adequate protection and reward them for the service they have rendered industry."

When I read this statement in the newspapers, I sent Lewis a telegram, congratulating him on his stand. The same afternoon, I got a wire from Thomas Kennedy, saying that Robert Harlin, Alex Howat, and Frank Farrington, of the miners' delegation, were reported to be ready to vote for Gompers, and urging me to wire them, "demanding that they vote the sentiment of the miners by standing for Lewis." Lewis also sent a telegram, saying, "Greatly appreciate your splendid telegram and am fighting in this convention for progressive principles to which our organization is committed. Regret that I am being opposed here by some delegates of our own organization but that fact will not deter me from carrying on. Best Wishes."

Rarely, if ever, in democratic politics, does one find the perfect combination of candidate and platform. Lewis might not be the candidate of my dreams, but the stand he had taken was so clearly superior to the stand-pattism of Gompers that the choice seemed to me clear. It was time to rise above personal feelings and old disagreements to advance a sound policy. Therefore, I sent wires to Harlin, Howat, and Farrington, saying, "Lewis public statement favoring nationalization of mines and railroads and other progressive measures and Gompers silence on these questions I believe warrants solid support of miners delegates for Lewis." I also sent Kennedy a wire quoting what I had said to the three recalcitrant delegates. They persisted in voting against Lewis, who was defeated by a vote of about 25,000 to 13,000. Undoubtedly, their defection was a major factor in his defeat, because a number of delegations which might have supported him were reluctant to follow a man who could not command the united support of his own union.

Lewis wrote to me on the twenty-seventh:

I have your telegram of June 25th, quoting telegram which you had forwarded to Messrs. Howat, Harlin, and Farrington, in relation to my candidacy against Samuel Gompers.

I express my sincere appreciation of your splendid action in this matter, and greatly regret that the above three gentlemen saw fit to permit their personal feelings toward me to sway their judgment upon a matter of utmost importance to the United Mine Workers and the entire labor movement. Without question the fact that these three men publicly worked in favor of Gompers had much to do with influencing the vote of a number of delegations. It is indeed a sad commentary upon the intelligence of our representatives to the American Federation of Labor convention when we cannot reconcile our own differences to a degree where we would be able to extend a complimentary vote to the President of the organization in his candidacy against the present incumbent of the presidency of the American Federation of Labor. I suppose the coming international convention will deal with the whole subject matter, and it will therefore be unnecessary for me to make further comment thereon.

I again extend my appreciation of your action in the premises and with personal well wishes, I am

Yours very truly,
JOHN L. LEWIS, *President*

This letter reveals much about the man. I had made it as clear as I could that my support was for the program; without that, Lewis's ambition to step into Gompers' job was a matter of the most complete indifference to me. Yet his argument was that differences should be reconciled in order to give a "complimentary vote" to the president of our union! Evidently he appreciated my action, but I wonder if he ever understood it.

Tom Kennedy was another of the anti-Lewis people who supported him at Denver. When John H. Walker of Illinois ran against Lewis for the presidency of the UMW in 1920, Kennedy was on his slate, running against Philip Murray for vice-president. Though Kennedy lost to Murray, he won election as a delegate to the AFL convention, with the help of a large block of votes from Illinois. Like me, Kennedy had been influenced by James Maurer, and was genuinely concerned with committing the president of the Miners to a progressive platform. He had no more hesitation than I in choosing between the Lewis and Gompers platforms, even though it meant for him a break with the Illinois group, to whom he had political obligations. I had no such obligations, so I was in an easier position. Unlike me, Kennedy maintained his alliance with Lewis and broke permanently with the progressives when Lewis found it expedient to abandon the forward-looking program.

The next convention of the UMW, in October, 1921, followed so soon after the Denver meeting that Lewis had to reaffirm his support of nationalization. Besides, he could use the progressive program to deprive his opponents of their best arguments for voting against him at Denver. The resolutions committee report reaffirmed the statement of the 1919 convention favoring nationalization, and then went on to recommend preparation and publication of "a treatise . . . setting forth arguments as to economic conservation made possible by government ownership . . . together with all pertinent authentic data . . . and that copies of this treatise be distributed to all members of Congress, prominent welfare organizations, state legislatures, and members of organized labor, our own membership especially, and further that all district organizations are hereby instructed to give their unqualified support in the matter of education and furtherance of this subject."

The Committee on Officers' Reports endorsed a proposal in Lewis's report for a committee of three to "give study to the problems and perform such other services in this connection as may be of value in the propagation of this much needed reform." The proposals of both committees were approved without a dissenting vote.

Toward the end of the convention, I had a talk with Lewis about the convention action on nationalization. I told him I was deeply interested in the subject, was pleased with what had taken place. He said he thought I would be. I then asked what his plans were for setting up a committee. He said he thought of me as a member of the Research Committee in view of my interest, and asked if I would serve. I agreed to do so. He then asked for suggestions as to the others, and I replied that they ought to be people who were committed to nationalization and suggested Thomas Kennedy from anthracite and William Mitch of Terre Haute, Indiana, in the Central Competitive Field. These two, with me, from an outlying bituminous field, would make a fully representative committee. He approved of these names. I raised the question of the Committee's duties. Lewis asked what I thought about it. I then read him a memorandum I had written of what I conceived to be their duties. He asked if he could have it, and I turned it over to him.

When Lewis went to see Kennedy, he said he was unable to serve because of wage and organizational problems that required his full attention. He proposed Christopher J. Golden, president of District 9, anthracite, as his substitute. The formal letter of appointment, dated October 7, 1921, read as follows:

GENTLEMEN:
    The recent international convention adopted the Report of the Committee on Officers' Reports, which concurred in the recommendations of the president dealing with the question of nationalization of mines. The convention further adopted supplemental resolutions transmitted by the Committee on Resolutions. In conformity with this action by the convention, which constitutes instructions to the officers, I am appointing each of you gentlemen as a member of the committee to be designated as the Nationalization Research Committee of the United Mine Workers of America. The duties of your committee will be to carry out the instructions of the international convention

Patrick Brophy

Mary Dagnall Brophy

Anita and John Brophy
on their wedding day,
August 13, 1918

John Brophy, about 1920

Powers Hapgood, John Brophy, and Adolph Germer
in Akron during the 1936 struggle
to organize the Rubber Workers

John L. Lewis and John Brophy
at the CIO convention in Atlantic City,
October, 1937

Photo by Central Studios, Atlantic City, N.J.

John Brophy, Secretary of the CIO
Free World Labor Fund, and Walter P. Reuther,
President of CIO, place a wreath at
the Independence Monument in Mexico City,
December, 1954

Anita and John Brophy
at the AFL–CIO merger convention, New York City,
December, 1955

Photo from Ransdell Inc.

John Brophy making a speech

Luncheon held in Washington, D.C., August 12, 1961,
marking John Brophy's retirement after sixty-two years of membership
in the labor movement. From left: George L. P. Weaver,
Assistant Secretary of Labor; Brophy; James B. Carey, Secretary
of the Industrial Union Department, AFL–CIO; Arthur Goldberg,
Secretary of Labor; Mrs. Brophy; Msgr. George Higgins, of the
National Catholic Welfare Conference.

with reference to this subject matter and to familiarize yourselves with various phases of the problem as they may be encountered with a view of formulating a detailed practical policy to bring about the nationalization of the coal mines and to aid in the dissemination of information among our members and the public and the crystallization of sentiment for the attainment of such end. In this work the international union will assume the financial expenses incurred by your committee in the nature of salary and expenses during the time you are employed in holding meetings, conferring with authorities and other necessary work. The international officers will be glad to cooperate with each of you gentlemen in the fullest possible way to aid and facilitate any definite accomplishment and will be pleased to confer with you upon the work at any time.

I express my hopes for the success of your efforts.

Very truly yours,

JOHN L. LEWIS, *President*

This letter seemed to me to give us all the authority we needed. I had laid the foundation for our study with *The Miners' Program,* so the directions the study should take were already clear in my mind. I had sent *The Miners' Program* to Ellis Searles, editor of the United Mine Workers' *Journal,* shortly after its adoption, asking that he publish it in the *Journal* to encourage discussion among the miners. Nothing happened. I wrote a second time. Searles's reply was evasive, saying he felt it was unwise to publish the program because it appeared to be "to some extent a denunciation of the policies of the union." This referred to my argument that collective bargaining, as we had been practicing it for so many years, was inadequate to deal with the basic problems of the industry. I sought to allay his fears, but without success; he thought the program was "too controversial," even though I pointed out that it followed the principles laid down in the resolution of the 1919 convention. I knew that he would not take this stand without consulting the national officers, so I concluded that they (meaning Lewis) were opposed to the idea and concentrated on educational work within my district.

With Lewis's commitment at Denver, the ban on "controversial" matter in the *Journal* was lifted, and Searles backed Lewis's stand enthusiastically. Though I knew that Lewis had made his commitment for personal political reasons and was, in fact, unenthusiastic about nationalization, the exigencies of his situation were creating breaks favorable to my purpose, and I wanted to take full advantage of those breaks. I knew I would have to walk warily to avoid trouble, but I wanted to get as far as possible with the job while things were going my way. Lewis may have thought of the committee as a device to pigeonhole the matter, but in that case he shouldn't have appointed me. I had made no effort to conceal my desire to do a thorough and effective job. I am not sure who made the mistake at this time: whether Lewis underestimated my enthusiasm, expecting me to act as a well-trained bureaucrat should, or I overestimated his need for a program. Whatever the facts as to that, I decided to take Lewis's letter at face value and get on with the work.

I called the first meeting of the Nationalization Research Committee in New York, on October 25 and 26, a time when we would all be there anyway on other union work. I submitted an outline of work for the Committee, which was accepted as follows:

1. The jobs before the Nationalization Research Committee:
   a. The "treatise" on nationalization—how to get it written.
   b. Material for bills for Congress—a nationalization bill or prelim-liminary legislation.
   c. Preliminary reports—how to publish them and in what shape, for the miners and for the public. The treatise will probably grow up by assembling the Committee's preliminary periodical reports. The bills for Congress would come last of all.
2. What methods can the Committee use to collect material for the pre-liminary reports and to get them written, then printed—in the UMW *Journal,* in pamphlets, etc.
3. First report at Chicago—my speech, and discussion by each member of committee.

The outline continued with further detail on the kinds of data we would need: on wages, costs, profits, value and basis of valuation of properties; the problems of transportation, capitalization, freight charges, executive salaries, spot coal operations, speculation, stocks on hand, reserves, etc.; also legal problems—how to prepare a bill for Congress, the question as to the need for a Constitutional amendment, the creation of a federal fact-finding agency and its relationship to existing bodies such as the Bureau of Labor Statistics and the Federal Trade Commission. I proposed that we consider some tactical problems: collaboration with the railroad unions supporting the Plumb Plan; some kind of affiliation with the Public Ownership League; the mechanics of Committee supervision of research and what kind of help we should get in research; a survey to determine what Congress, the public, and the miners would want to know about the problem; and finally, how we should go about getting information from district offices of the union and feeding them reports in reciprocation for that aid.

Mitch, Golden, and I all had a heavy load of work in connection with our district responsibilities. The end of a wage contract was impending, and negotiations with the employers were going badly. We expected a great strike in the spring. Unemployment was growing; employers were pushing for wage cuts, and had already imposed some in the non-union fields. Holding the line on wages would absorb our attention for months to come. I proposed that we use the Bureau of Industrial Research to do the research and writing for which we, as individuals, had neither training nor time. Mitch and Golden agreed to all my suggestions.

The Bureau of Industrial Research was an independent non-profit research service supported by Mrs. Willard Straight, the principal backer of the *New Republic*. I had made use of it in the preparation of *The Miners' Program*, on which Arthur Gleason, of the Bureau, had been my chief technical consultant. Gleason was a very able economist and journalist, who had served as correspondent in Great Britain for the *Survey* and *Survey Graphic*, and had written extensively for *Collier's* and other muckraking magazines. He had studied the British labor movement very closely, and had developed a great interest in the campaign for nationalization of the British coal mines. His thorough knowledge of economics and public affairs, both in America and abroad, made him an ideal advisor. Furthermore, he was a modest man, more interested in doing a good job than in advancing his own fortunes. Unlike some others I had to deal with during this period, he understood that the duty of a consultant was to consult, not to try to mastermind the union. We had a very good understanding, Gleason and I; he respected the labor movement and the men like me who bore the responsibility of leadership. He never tried to impose his notions upon me, but recognized that ideas and policy had to come from the union. My job was to interpret the needs of the workers; his to supply the facts and to help present them in convincing form. Gleason understood this delicate relationship thoroughly.

My first contact with the Bureau of Industrial Research was in the spring of 1921, when Heber Blankenhorn visited me at my office in Clearfield. Blankenhorn had a talent for promotion. Though not a man of great depth of knowledge or understanding, he was useful to the Bureau in ferreting out opportunities for it to do its kind of work.

Unfortunately, his promotional instinct could run away with him, as it did later in District 2. He told me how the Bureau had helped the Interchurch World Movement prepare its great report on the 1919 steel strike. He had heard of my work in District 2 and of the interest I had shown in ideas of reform, largely through my appearances at annual meetings of the League for Industrial Democracy to talk on the labor movement and the need for better planning in industry. He asked what specific views I had about a large program for the labor movement, and how the Bureau could co-operate. We talked for several hours about the need for better planning in the coal industry, the Plumb Plan, and prospects for a labor party. He had been told, he said, that I was the only person in an official position in the miners' union who was both interested in social problems and to be depended upon to stick to his guns on a matter of principle. I had to confess, with all modesty, that I had very little competition for that distinction.

A little later, Robert Bruere came up and spent two or three days, talking about all kinds of things relating to the labor movement in general and the United Mine Workers in particular. Bruere was an able man with a great enthusiasm for his work. He got all fired up about the idea of working with me and making District 2 a sounding board for the nationalization campaign.

As a result of these encounters, Arthur Gleason came to Clearfield and did the substantial work of liaison between the Bureau and District 2. Bruere and Blankenhorn were in and out; I was never sure just how much of the actual work they did. Besides these three, an economist named Savel Zimand did some of the research.

The opening gun of our campaign to publicize the union's demand for nationalization was my speech before the annual meeting of the Public Ownership League at Chicago in November of 1921. John L. Lewis authorized my appearance there as an official representative of the United Mine Workers, and Mitch and Golden also attended. My speech emphasized the lack of accurate knowledge about the coal industry. I argued that a permanent fact-finding agency should be created by the federal government, with power to compel the industry to collect and turn over essential information about costs, wages, profits, stocks of coal on hand, working conditions in the mines and many similar matters. The operation of coal mines was so clearly a matter of public concern that the public was entitled to know the facts, on which effective legislation could be based. Only a public agency with ample powers could collect the needed information and make it public, thus providing light on the problem. I said I was confident that the facts would support our contention that only nationalization and democratic management could clean up the mess in the industry and serve the public interest.

The speech was well received and got considerable attention in the newspapers. I sent Lewis a copy of it with the first report of the Committee. His reply approved of our work, and he ordered the speech printed in the UMW *Journal.* The Committee had the speech published in a pamphlet as our first report to the membership; Lewis approved payment of the printing bills for the pamphlet.

Early in 1922, the Committee put out a report in pamphlet form, under the title, *Compulsory Information in Coal—A Fact-Finding Agency.* As the threat of a national coal strike developed, this pamphlet attracted public notice. The District 2 convention in March, on the eve of the strike, adopted a call to the public to join with the miners in forcing out the facts on coal through federal action. The threat of the coal strike, and, when it was called, its success in pulling out almost all the miners in the country made our policy statements news.

The strike began on the first of April. Against the background of the walkout (that story I will tell in the next chapter), the Labor Committee of the House of Representatives held a series of hearings on a bill to set up a commission of inquiry into labor conditions in the coal industry. In spite of incessant demands on my time and energy by the strike, I managed to get to Washington to testify before the committee; such a golden opportunity to advertise the miners' grievances and program could not be neglected. John L. Lewis appeared before the Committee on April 3, and I gave my testimony on April 7.[*]

I opened my testimony by presenting a tabulation of wages earned by the tonnage miners of District 2, based on fortnightly reports from checkweighmen at 364 mines, all but a tiny fraction of the district production. This did not, of course, include the earnings of day men.

This report covered: tonnage produced (pick and machine production listed separately), number of days each mine operated, wages received, number of miners employed, total earnings per year per miner, with average income per week (for 52 weeks, not just those

---

[*] *Hearings before the Committee on Labor, on H.R. 11022* (House of Representatives, 67th Congress, 2nd session). Lewis's testimony starts on page 192, mine on page 309.

worked, since this was designed to show what the miners had to live on), and the number of days worked during the year 1921. The district produced about 25,600,000 tons of coal, nearly 7 per cent of the national total; more than 60 per cent was machine mined. The 31,979 tonnage miners averaged $760 a year, or about $14.60 a week. They worked an average of 122 days a year, about 2⅓ days a week year-round.

The enormous variation in what an individual miner could expect was partly revealed by breaking down the figures to show totals for each of the nine territories of the district. Average yearly wages varied from $532 in Territory 8 to $1052 in Territory 3. Likewise, the number of days worked varied, from 91 in Territory 4 to 188 in Territory 9. The figures did not include a small additional income from yardage; that would be balanced by charges for supplies—powder, picks, blacksmithing, etc. Thus I was able to demonstrate that the tonnage miner had an income of about $2.08 a day, for 365 days, on which to support his family and himself. Day men averaged about $17.50 a week, so they could dispose of the luxurious sum of $2.50 each day of the year. And these were the wages the employers wanted to cut by over 30 per cent, on the excuse that labor costs were "inflated." Thomas S. Watkins, of the Central Pennsylvania Operators' Association, had presented his argument, the day before I appeared, for reducing the tonnage rate from $1.28 to 86 cents, to match post-war "adjustments in every line of industry except in coal wages in the union fields." *

Watkins bore down heavily, in his testimony, upon generalities about "inflation" and "readjustment to more normal circumstances," now that the war was over. My figures forced the committee members to look behind these plausible theories to the reality of life in a coal town.

From this demonstration of the usefulness of facts, I went on to say:

The miners demand the facts of the coal industry. Coal facts have never been made public. Mining is carried on in the darkness of underground. The business of coal-financing and coal-selling is carried on in the darkness of secret speculation, secret profits and secret resales. The result is a sick industry. Coal has the dropsy. It is bloated with water and over-development. There are too many mines, too many miners. Waste is the rule of the industry, . . . an industry which is able to pay only $760 a year to its workers and which gives them only 122 days of work in the year, . . . needs a reorganization. To make that reorganization requires the facts. To get the facts we suggest two proposals—one for an emergency commission and one for a permanent federal fact-finding agency.

* *Hearings . . . on H.R. 11022,* pp. 276, 283.

I described the proposed commission in detail. It should be made up of an equal number of men representing management and the union, one each from the five major areas of the industry: anthracite, the Central Competitive Field, tidewater, the other union districts, and the non-union fields. With joint chairmen, this would make a "jury of twelve Americans sitting on the case of coal." The commission should not attempt to arbitrate differences, but only to investigate and make recommendations for legislation. The commission should have the same powers to require that facts be made available as the FTC had. I suggested some particularly pressing problems on which the commission should prepare recommendations:

1. Restrictions on "such bad mining practices as the irresponsible opening up of new mines by shoestring speculators." Mines already operating could produce several hundred million tons a year more than the public would consume. Every new mine accentuated the twin problems of over-production of coal and under-employment of miners.
2. Methods of storing coal near centers of production. Though this was feasible, speculators preferred periodic shortages to drive prices up.
3. The pyramiding of prices by resales, to squeeze the public.
4. Most important, the commission should recommend a plan for a permanent fact-finding agency. No emergency action could cure the the ills of an "industry sick with a spring fever every year."

I was equally specific about the fact-finding agency, asserting that it must have the power:

1. To lay down and supervise the conduct of uniform systems of accounting;
2. To require continuous reporting of facts;
3. To require by subpoena the attendance and testimony of witnesses and production of documentary evidence;
4. To go into the books of the coal companies;
5. To invoke the aid of any court of the United States.

I then gave the members of the committee copies of our pamphlet, *Compulsory Information in Coal—A Fact-Finding Agency,* for the record. I pointed out that this pamphlet demonstrated the need for no less than twenty-seven categories of facts not available to the public at that time, and that the operators were fighting, even by appeals to the courts, to keep information essential to public policy secret.

The hearings often wandered from the point of setting up an investigating commission to the situation created by the strike. However, even though the strike was the news of the day, I was able to get considerable public attention for the Nationalization Research Committee's proposals. We felt that the opportunity given us by the hearings had been well utilized.

I had had some uneasiness over the amount of public attention the Nationalization Research Committee was getting, and its effect upon Lewis. The hearings gave me further grounds for concern. Lewis testified at length on the mismanagement of coal, but when the committee members questioned him on the subject of nationalization, his answers were equivocal. He said at one point:

I think that Government ownership is an impossibility under present circumstances. The people of the country are not in a position to acquire title to the mining deposits of the country or the developed mining properties. It would be a tremendous financial burden upon the country, and it would be extremely difficult to secure any appraisal of the valuation of the mining deposits and the developed properties. . . . It would possibly take many years to determine that particular point. On the other hand, the question of the government taking over and operating the mines after the manner in which the railroads were operated during the war period is repugnant to many; as a feasible proposition it seems that the creation of some board of control, if a proper legal premise can be found, would be the most practical method of stabilizing the industry and bringing it into some degree of proper regulation.

The congressmen tried, on two occasions, to get more particulars as to what the proposed board should control. The one thing that emerged from the jungle of Lewis's rhetoric was that the board should "prohibit the unwarranted development of the industry." * Whatever that might mean, it was straying far from the fact-finding commission, and equally far from nationalization. Lewis's argument that it would take years to determine the value of the mines and the coal deposits was absurd. Much of that information was already available, and completion of the data was entirely feasible in a reasonable time. But in spite of the facts, this argument of Lewis's turned up again later on. The significant thing about his testimony was that his words could so easily be used by the opponents of nationalization to discredit the whole campaign for the union's program. This was coming perilously

* *Hearings . . . on H.R. 11022*, pp. 233, 251.

close to open sabotage, and was a clear indication of the line he would take to destroy the nationalization campaign when he decided it had gone far enough.

I had to live with this uneasy situation, hoping to be able to build enough support for nationalization to make Lewis feel he had something to gain by giving it lip service. The worst thing about this was that Lewis, because he had not identified himself with the issue, as I had, was bound to feel that sentiment for nationalization threatened his position as president. In other words, the issue would become, in his mind, a personal one, rather than one of principle. I was perfectly happy to work with Lewis or anybody else in the presidency of the union so long as the larger program could be advanced. But Lewis could not conceive of anybody refraining from using a programmatic victory to enhance his own position. The limitations of his mind forced him to translate all issues into personal terms.

Despite the extraneous issues brought into the hearings, the United States Coal Commission was created and began its investigation in August, 1922, which was an achievement in itself, although labor was not represented as we had suggested.

Even during the frantically busy days of the 1922 strike, I managed to find some time to work on a plan which I called "How to Run Coal," designed for discussion by our Committee. I intended that we should submit a final corrected draft of this plan for consideration at the 1924 convention. I sent a first draft of the plan to the other Committee members. Both approved of it, though Mitch suggested a few minor changes, which were made before it was printed. Golden and Mitch also approved of having the first four chapters published in the *Survey Graphic*. Mitch, who was to be a delegate to the International Mining Congress in Frankfurt, Germany, that summer, wanted "How to Run Coal" printed as a pamphlet in time for distribution at the Congress, which was done. In August, I sent copies of *How to Run Coal* to Lewis, Green, and Murray, as the second report of the Nationalization Research Committee. All three men wrote to thank me for sending it, and Lewis and Green honored the printing bills for it. Thus I made sure that the international officers were fully informed of each stage of our work.

The stresses of the 1922 strike and the settlement, which left the Somerset County strikers in my district out on a limb, caused strained relations between Lewis and me. I realized that this would add to the difficulty of maintaining a co-operative relationship between Lewis and the Committee. On January 11, 1923, I wrote to Mitch and Golden, reporting on a meeting with Lewis in Chicago, during which we had discussed whether the Nationalization Research Committee should appear before the U.S. Coal Commission. Lewis asked that we discuss this question with the national officers during the conference on the contract in New York. It seemed to me that there would be some publicity value in going before the Commission, but that it might be bad tactics, because *How to Run Coal* was tentative, adopted only by the Committee, not by the union. I thought we should wait until we had the backing of the rank and file, and a convention endorsement. This precaution was too late; Lewis already had the weapon in his hand which he would use to destroy us, though he did not reveal his intention to use it until two weeks later. I knew Lewis was cooling toward our work, though I had no idea how far he was already prepared to go.

Chris Golden, who had worked closely with Lewis in many matters, had no qualms. He believed, correctly, that our instructions were clear and definite. He also believed that Lewis meant what he said in those instructions, but Golden was soon to learn otherwise. In fact, it was Golden, who was closer to Lewis than either Mitch or I, who gave Lewis the excuse to break with the Nationalization Research Committee.

Golden was invited to be the principal speaker at the annual dinner of the League for Industrial Democracy in New York on December 29, 1922. His talk dealt with nationalization, and he described our tentative plan for operating the coal industry. The press covered his speech liberally, there was much public discussion of our plan, and response to it was generally encouraging. For a month Lewis was silent.

When the official union reaction to this speech appeared, it came in an unexpected fashion. Ellis Searles, editor of the United Mine Workers' *Journal*, issued a statement to the papers on January 29, 1923, denouncing the Nationalization Research Committee for "prematurely" giving out its plan at "a meeting of Greenwich Village radicals in New York." The UMW as an organization, he said, had never approved, endorsed, or adopted any plan for nationalization. The Committee should have made its first report to the next national convention of the union, and no one knew what the convention might do about it. He went on, "Our information is that the plan announced by the committee at the recent meeting of radicals in New York was prepared largely by a bunch of Greenwich Village reds who do not belong to the UMWA and who have not the slightest right or authority to represent or speak for the miners' union. This crowd has long made it a practice to butt in on the affairs of the miners' union. These Greenwich Village parlor coal diggers, who might better be designated as gold diggers, represent nothing."

Obviously, Searles was speaking for Lewis: he would not dare move without Lewis's permission. A few months later, on May 23, Searles made public Lewis's alternative to our plans, in an interview with a reporter from the New York *World:* "Shut down 4,000 coal mines, force 200,000 miners into other industries, and the coal problem will settle itself. The public will then be assured of an adequate supply of low-priced fuel." When the reporter asked about union resolutions favoring nationalization, Searles said the 1919 convention had voted for a resolution "that meant nothing. They decided to place themselves on record as favoring the principle of nationalization. What they would do if a concrete proposal were placed before them is questionable." Searles repeated Lewis's argument before the House Labor Committee that "coal is underground," so that nobody knew the value of the coal deposits, although we had demonstrated that the figures could be obtained from the U.S. Geological Survey, free of charge.

Norman Thomas, director of the LID, wrote to me expressing regret that his organization was the innocent cause of this storm, and saying he had tried to get Searles to withdraw his statement, but had succeeded only in getting him to make some unimportant modifications. Thomas also issued an open letter to John L. Lewis, pointing out that the UMW had been committed to nationalization for four years, that Lewis's instructions to the Committee gave it authority to publicize its work, and that the tentative plan had been circulated for criticism and discussion only as the work of the Committee, and despite what certain newspapers said, was not presented at the New York dinner as official UMW policy. He offered Lewis or his spokesman the same platform Golden had been given "to set the public right on an issue which cannot wait for the Miners' convention in 1924. You may prefer less 'radical' auspices, but whatever platform you choose, can you be content to let Mr. Searles' statement stand as your last word?" Needless to say, Lewis did not deign to answer Thomas's letter.

Heber Blankenhorn rose to the defense of the Bureau of Industrial

Research. He pointed out that the Bureau had provided data for the Committee's use without charge. The Committee had also made use of data from other research organizations and from government agencies. Altogether, he said, the Committee "went at their task in a manner which any open-minded man should applaud. . . . Members of the Bureau, who believed the workers in the non-union fields were justified in striking, cooperated as requested with friends and acquaintances in raising $55,000 in cash donations or loans sent to officers of the United Mine Workers for the strikers in Somerset. Perhaps this is what Mr. Searles means when referring to us as gold diggers."

Though it was easy to demolish Searles's arguments, Lewis refused to budge, and so long as he opposed us, the Committee could no longer function. We met with Lewis in New York to try to straighten out the mess. Lewis made it clear that our work was objectionable to him and that Searles had attacked us with his full approval. Lewis opposed our doing any educational work either with the miners or with the public. He said we had no right to commit the union to anything whatever, not even policies the union had already officially approved, but that we could only prepare a report on facts for submission to the next convention. Since, in view of Searles's attack, we could not even use outside sources for the "facts" he was talking about, there was nothing left for the Committee to do but to wait for the convention to dismiss us with a resolution of thanks—for doing nothing.

Chris Golden was the first to resign from the Committee in protest against Lewis's torpedoing of its work. After reviewing the instructions given us, he said he was surprised to hear from Lewis fifteen months later, that our findings were not supposed to receive any publicity, even in the UMW *Journal.* "Had I understood your letter to mean that membership in the Nationalization Research Committee precluded all discussion or public statements concerning the subject of its research until such time as it could report to a convention, I could not possibly have accepted your appointment." Golden was much angrier than his letter sounded, partly because he had been the direct object of Searles's attack. In a letter to Blankenhorn written on the same day, which Blankenhorn later turned over to me, Golden said, "if it was left to the rank and file of the UMW, Mr. Searles would not be one of the leeches on and a gold digger of the UMW. He is not a member, and knows nothing about the mining industry. The Greenwich Village Reds are the same people who did so much for the striking miners and the most progressive friends the United Mine Workers have. By the next convention the UMW will have swept out all the weaklings who vote for nationalization with no intention of carrying it out." Unhappily, Chris was again too optimistic.

Though I tried my best to figure out some way to make the Committee effective under the new restrictions, I was finally forced to conclude, reluctantly, that I would accomplish more by a vigorous protest which would leave me free to act on my own responsibility. My letter of resignation, dated February 5, 1923, said in part:

I submit my resignation as chairman of the Nationalization Research Committee of the United Mine Workers of America. We have done our job. We have drawn up a concrete plan for nationalizing coal. . . .

We could not better your instructions, because they were all inclusive. But we fulfilled them with results that surpassed our hopes. We consulted experts—miners, economists, statisticians, government officials, lawyers, administrators, technicians, engineers. . . . The only other way of making the Plan would have been to let it drop into our minds as a perfect abstraction from a timeless world, or else turn over the job to some group of professional liberals and let them project a theory. We did neither. We preferred the method of hard work and expert advice. We have presented the American Plan for nationalizing coal in a pamphlet "How to Run Coal," in which every detail is hammered home, and the full union strength and bargaining power of the UMWA are maintained and safeguarded for all time. Your Committee challenges critics of the plan to point out a weak place. The only possible opponents of the plan are those who are opposed to the principle of nationalization. All such opposition we desire to locate and to face in the open. We offer the American Plan for Nationalization as the only adequate solution for the present chaos of coal. We submit that in it we have met your conception of our duties.

As to the dissemination of information "among our members and the public," we have obeyed your orders. The Miners' American Plan for Nationalization has been published in newspapers throughout the country. Editorial comment is almost universal. Every prominent union official is being flooded with inquiries.

Will you throw open the Mine Workers' *Journal* to our plan? The newspapers of the country are willing to devote columns to our findings, but our own official organ refuses to carry a paragraph. The editor, Ellis Searles, attempts to discredit our efforts by using a "red" herring. Our plan was not "in part prepared for the committee by some well known New York radicals. . . ." To permit outside organizations to butt into labor policy is the destruction of trade unionism. The methods of the Nationalization Research Committee, in preparing a case, have been the same as your own methods— no recognition of outside organizations in union affairs, consultation with individual experts on details, a trade union decision on policy.

I challenged Lewis to mail out copies of the plan to the nation's 600,000 miners, saying, "If they don't like it, they will kill it." And I urged that the national union continue the work of education and publicity, not because I expected Lewis to do any such thing, but because I was determined to use my letter of resignation to appeal over Lewis's head to the rank and file of the miners.

William Mitch was badly confused about the situation. He wrote to Lewis, after the New York conference, saying he felt there was some misunderstanding, that Lewis's letter of instructions to the Committee was not in harmony with the interpretation put on it by Lewis in the conference. He even proposed to me that we confer again with the national officers at Indianapolis, to clear things up. He had the impression, after the New York session, that Lewis had no objections to publicity in the UMW *Journal.* Mitch wrote to me that he was sorry Chris Golden had resigned "before we talked the matter over again as it might be construed that he quit when the fight was on," though he thought the Searles statement was so bad that Golden could not be blamed "for making his reply."

Lewis's reply to Mitch's protest said that the original instructions "might have been stated . . . rather imperfectly at that time, being somewhat in haste, but the intent was to convey to the committee that after they had formulated a specific plan or bill for nationalization which could receive the endorsement of the UMW they would then aid in dissemination of information among our members and the public and the crystallization of sentiment for the attainment of such end." Mitch evidently was impressed by this explanation, for he sent a copy to me, and when he heard of my resignation, wrote that he thought I should have given the matter more consideration. He held to the position that the Committee had done no more than it was instructed to do, and saw nothing he could do but to resign, though he did not "propose to function independently of the organization unless our district board agrees to follow that program." Neither Mitch nor Golden made any further efforts to push nationalization, though both affirmed that they still favored it.

I was the only one who tried to continue the campaign. The principal medium available to me was the *Illinois Miner.* Oscar Ameringer, the editor, printed my contributions and supported them in his own vigorous editorials.

When the next convention met in 1924, Lewis's biennial report was silent on nationalization. Chris Golden was ill and did not attend. William Mitch was secretary of the resolutions committee, which reported out a resolution reaffirming the "principle" of nationalization of the coal mines under democratic management, designed to put the best face on the collapse of the Nationalization Research Committee. It read, in part, "progress has been made in the past two years in the matter of education and research on this subject, and while honest differences of opinion have developed, we believe that all concerned are actuated by the desire to give the best that is in them to further the matter, and we recommend that such education and research be continued." The resolution was adopted, but the national organization made no effort whatever to translate its pious generalities into activity. It was not intended, by the administration, to be a plan for further education and research, but rather as an epitaph over the grave of the nationalization idea. I kept hoping that we could reform our lines and resume the campaign, but that hope was never realized.

II

THE SOMERSET
COUNTY STRIKE

The long and frustrating fight for nationalization would seem to have been enough to occupy me throughout 1922, but along with that I faced an even more exacting struggle, the great strike which not only closed down the union mines but for the first time paralyzed non-union areas adjoining us on the west and southwest. Almost all of Somerset County, part of Cambria County around Johnstown, and most of the Black Lick Creek field north and west of Nanty Glo were non-union. So long as the bosses held these anti-union bastions, the miners of District 2 could never be safe. In fact, the neighboring fields were more of a menace than the unorganized fields in West Virginia and farther south, if only because of their proximity. Besides the Somerset, Johnstown, and Black Lick fields in the territory of District 2, District 5 included unorganized fields in Westmoreland County and the coke region of Fayette County, centering around Connellsville. Altogether, there were nearly 90,000 non-union miners in these areas, as many as the combined union membership of the central and western Pennsylvania districts.

As early as the 1919 strike I had pointed out the overriding need to organize the unorganized. We signed up a few thousand members and established about twenty-five new locals in the 1919 drive, but were unable to overcome the employers, who had small armies of guards and spies on their pay rolls and controlled absolutely the local and county officials. Organizers and strikers had no rights; officers charged with keeping "law and order" drove union men out of town, beat them up, arrested them on trumped-up charges, and maintained a reign of terror against anyone who dared call his soul his own. Courts eagerly provided the most extreme injunctions against any person or activity the operators objected to. Men who went on strike were brutally evicted from their homes; no mercy was granted to young or old. Even pregnant women were turned out to bear their children in tent colonies or in chicken coops and other temporary shelters.*

Indignation was not enough; there was never any shortage of people ready to denounce the outrages perpetrated against the workers and their families in the non-union fields. But it would take more than speech-making or editorial-writing to change things. Only by combining the full resources of District 2 and District 5 with the maximum support of the international union in a well-planned and vigorously prosecuted campaign could we hope to clean up this situation.

John L. Lewis declared, at the September, 1919, convention in Cleveland, that organizing the non-union fields of Pennsylvania must be one of the great future tasks of the organization. I hoped that this indicated a willingness to do something substantial. At our district convention that year, in Johnstown, we pledged our fullest co-operation. By October the steel workers were on strike in Johnstown and other steel centers, and enthusiasm for unionization was running very high. An alliance with the steel workers was strategically sound, because many of the non-union mines were "captive mines," owned by the steel companies. In addition to U.S. Steel and Bethlehem Steel, ownership of the non-union mines was linked to Morgan, Rockefeller, and Mellon interests. The power of capital aligned against the exploited miners was overwhelming.

As I have related in an earlier chapter, the outcome of the 1919 strike was not such as to enable us to maintain a strong campaign to organize the unorganized. Lewis's pusillanimous surrender to the Anderson in-

---

* Heber Blankenhorn wrote a book about the Somerset strike, consistently critical of me and the district organization, called *The Strike for Union* (New York: H. W. Wilson, 1924). Though much of his editorializing is rather sophomoric, he did do a good journalistic job of describing what the strikers were up against. The great fault of the book is that Blankenhorn never understood the difference in position of the union officer, responsible to and for the organization and its members, and the outsider with nothing to lose.

junction destroyed the effect of rank-and-file courage and solidarity. Coupled with the defeat of the steel strike, this was enough to destroy what gains we had made—mostly in the Johnstown area—in 1919.

All through 1920 and 1921, the operators campaigned tirelessly for wage cuts. As demand for coal diminished, mines were shut down and there was slack work at most of those that remained open. Increasing numbers of miners drifted out of the coal camps to nearby cities looking for work. Nobody knows how many ex–coal-miners have gone to steel, auto, rubber and other industries all through the Northeast and Midwest, but they must number hundreds of thousands. I know I was constantly meeting ex–coal-miners who had taken the lead in organizing the new industries during the CIO drives of the thirties. But in the early twenties, there was nothing as hopeful as the CIO in the non-union towns, only desperation in the face of grinding poverty, and burning rage against the iron rule of the operators.

One of the most energetic campaigners for wage cuts was Thomas H. Watkins, president of the Pennsylvania Coal and Coke Corporation in the central Pennsylvania district, whose attitude I described in the previous chapter. We had had fair relations with his concern until he launched his wage-cutting campaign after the war. Watkins had one of his speeches on the subject published as a pamphlet and distributed to the press and to anybody else who could be induced to accept a copy. He said that the union operators could not compete with the lower labor costs in non-union mines, especially those in West Virginia; that unless wages were cut, buyers would go elsewhere, and the union men would be cutting their own throats because they would get less work; and finally, that the men could make more money at lower prices because they would have more work. This argument had a certain plausibility about it which could appeal to miners on short time in the impoverished coal towns. Work, even at lower rates, was preferable to no work at all, and Watkins insisted there was no other alternative.

To counteract this propaganda, I had a leaflet printed, under the title, *No Broken Contract—No Wage Reduction!* and saw that it was even more widely distributed than his pamphlet.

I pointed out that we were bound, as were the operators, by a contract which did not run out until March 31, 1922, and that we were determined to maintain that agreement. The prevalence of slack work was not caused by wage levels but by lack of a market. Work was just as scarce in Somerset County and West Virginia as in the union fields.

The only significant changes that could come out of a wage cut would be even more bitter poverty for the miners and greater profits for the operators.

The membership of District 2 stood firm, as I expected them to do, and we did not permit any violation of the contract.

Late in 1921, I sent an appeal to President Harding, asking him to take steps to relieve the suffering of unemployed and underemployed miners in union and non-union fields alike. Copies of my letter were sent to the Vice President, the Speaker of the House, and members of the Pennsylvania Congressional delegation. I pointed out that the miners had been living on one to three days' work a week for over a year. They lacked even the money for coal to keep them warm during the rigors of a particularly hard winter. Local and district union organizations were drawing on their limited funds to provide some unemployment relief—a job the industry and government, with vastly greater resources, should have undertaken long before. I said:

Through no fault of their own, miners in this district who, during the war, strained every muscle at the government's call to "produce, produce," now find themselves with nothing to live on through the winter. . . . The present managers of the coal industry have shown themselves helpless even to plan relief. Nursing their unconscionable war profits and watching only for rising prices with vague expectations of a harvest reaped from a coal scarcity, they answer all our efforts for betterment with calls for reduced wages. . . . The operators' only cry is that we are to blame, and that our wages must come down to the level of the non-union fields, even though they know that, should such a thing happen, the non-union wages would promptly sink to new levels, and we should be called to drop again into a bottomless morass.

Finally, I pointed out that four months after the President's unemployment conference we were worse off than ever before. None of the "local measures of relief" called for by that conference had been taken in our district, except for the little that the union could do. It appeared that the only way the miners could get the government to notice them was to strike, and then the notice consisted of efforts to suppress the strike. If the government was unable to put forth any plans of its own, the least it could do was to hear the plans the miners had to offer.

My letter got only the barest acknowledgment and none of those to whom I sent it made the slightest effort to do anything for the miners.

Bituminous coal production in 1921 was 407,000,000 tons, compared to 556,000,000 the year before. Production continued to drop in 1922, as market demand grew even weaker. Distress increased in the mining towns. Union funds could not begin to cope with the need.

The 2,200 delegates to the February, 1922, international convention at Indianapolis stood firm against wage cuts and demanded a six-hour day and five-day week to reduce unemployment. They decided that the outlying districts should not undertake negotiations until agreement was reached in the Central Competitive Field. And if that agreement was not reached by April 1, a general suspension of work should be ordered.

Certain of the operators' associations in the Central Competitive Field refused to take part in the traditional four-state wage conference, as required by the previous contract, on the excuse that they would be subject to anti-trust prosecution, even though the Justice Department had taken no action and soon made it clear that no action was ever contemplated. The defection of the recalcitrant operators was caused by their desire to smash the union and the well-established pattern of collective bargaining. Some of them announced their intention of imposing large wage cuts and of ending all relations with the union; others bided their time, though their intentions were no different.

Against this background of hard times, unemployment, open-shop propaganda, and the inevitability of a hard-fought strike, I made my report to our district convention in March, 1922. The delegates voted solidly to stand by the national program.

The union's national policy committee met in Cleveland on March 24 to review the situation and make plans for defense of the union. It was not an encouraging prospect. We were entering a strike under the most adverse circumstances. Some critics of the union's stand pointed out that between the large stocks of coal on hand and what could be produced by the non-union fields, the market could be supplied for many months. To counter this, district and national officials were authorized to spread the strike to the non-union fields. But no plan or direction for such action was adopted. The motion was an afterthought, adopted to save face rather than to provide a program of action.

Riding alone on the train back home, I had plenty of time to think. How could we inspire miners trapped in a deep depression to fight through to victory? I became convinced that the spread of the strike to the non-union fields on a big scale was our only salvation, and that publicity had to be used to the utmost to that end. As soon as I got home I sent out telegrams to all field representatives in the district to meet me in Altoona March 29, prepared to spend several days away from home on special field work. I made no explanation, not wanting the mine operators to learn what I was up to.

I set up an office in Cresson, to be nearer the non-union fields than in Clearfield. We had a little weekly paper which was distributed from Cresson, called the *Penn Central News*. I met with the men who put it out and arranged for a special strike number of 20,000 copies to be ready for the first of the month. I prepared a strike call, which was released to the papers on March 31. It stated, very briefly, the union's arguments against driving the miners' standards any lower. I appealed to the union miners to stand against wage cuts and for maintenance of the union. I called on the non-union miners to come out on strike, because a defeat for the union would mean that their already bad conditions would become worse. And I appealed to the public to support us because our fight was right, seeking only to defend an already too low standard of living. If we were driven any lower, everybody in the coal areas would suffer, and harmful effects would radiate out throughout the nation. The two Johnstown dailies printed the statement in full, thus covering the non-union areas. Many other papers in central and western Pennsylvania carried it, including some of the foreign-language press. As evidence of a serious intention to invade the non-union areas, the appeal was news and could not be ignored.

We prepared 20,000 throwaway cards with a strike call, which read:

STRIKE CALL
TO NON-UNION MEN

Miners of Non-Union Fields of Pennsylvania:—
Fellow Workers:—
RISE!
STRIKE!
This is your fight.
You have had wage cuts in the last year.
Do you want another?
You'll get it if the Union gets it.
QUIT WORK APRIL 1ST!
Join our fight.
Make it your fight.
You will get
     A checkweighman.
     Correct weight.
     Decent wages.
     Your independence as free men and miners.

DROP YOUR TOOLS!
LEAVE THE MINE!
The Union welcomes you.
600,000 miners are out to maintain wages for all miners.
Miners united win.
Miners divided lose.
Don't scab on Men Who Are Fighting Your Fights.
Your only reward for scabbing will be
    Short weight.
    More Wage Cuts.
REFUSE TO BE ROBBED!
COME OUT APRIL 1ST!
STRIKE!

With this material—the strike cards and the special edition of the *Penn Central News*—I was ready to meet our field men on the eve of April 1. There were about a dozen of them, all experienced miners with no illusions about the difficulty of the job to be done. I showed them the stuff we had prepared, and told them bluntly that if we failed to pull out the non-union fields there was little chance of winning a decent settlement. They were to go quietly, in ones and twos, into the non-union areas, particularly Somerset County, from widely separated starting points. Some would be stopped by police and mine guards, they might even end up in jail, but if they put in an appearance and got some of the papers distributed, the strike sentiment in the air and the feeling of grievance among the miners would assure that their message would be spread. And if any of our organizers got arrested, we would be ready on a moment's notice to provide bail and legal support for him.

It was anything but a cheerful group. One man asked, "Do you think we can break through the private guards of the coal companies and actually reach the miners?"

"Perhaps not all of you," I had to say, "but some of you will. And remember, strike is in the air. It will be front-page news for the papers, their biggest story."

With only this consolation—that whatever might happen to them, their appearance in the coal towns, however brief, would almost certainly ignite the fires of discontent—the organizers set out. One or two went on foot, but mostly they used Model T Fords, the most luxurious transportation available to us. Sometimes the best they could do was to turn over a batch of papers to a friendly miner or two before the police locked them up. One man was seized before he could speak to

STRIKE CALL
To Non-Union Men

Issued by District Two, United Mine Workers of America.

JOHN BROPHY,
President.

JAMES MARK,
Vice President.

RICHARD GILBERT,
Secretary Treasurer.

Clearfield, Penna.

Rise!

Strike!

Drop Your Tools!

Leave the Mine!

Don't Scab on Men Who Are Fighting Your Fights!

NEW GUIDE PRINT ALTOONA, PA.

anybody, but he managed to drop his bundle so that it broke and the wind took care of distribution faster than the cops could pick up the papers. Then he added to the confusion by yelling loud protests all the way down the main street to the jail. He was, of course, taking a chance on getting his skull cracked to shut him up, but that town got the message and the miners spread it for him.

The work of our union missionaries in the non-union fields produced results beyond our wildest hopes. The miners were uneasy, resentful of the treatment they had suffered, and eager to respond to any hopeful lead. Some of those who walked out first took to the roads and pulled out neighboring mines. There was no stopping the spread of the strike. The miners poured out of the mines, held impromptu meetings in the fields, and sent appeals for organizers to come and take them into the union. From the very first day of the strike, the officers and organizers worked around the clock, missing meals and sleep in the effort to answer all the demands upon them. Within a week, all the coal mines of Pennsylvania were shut down tight, anthracite and bituminous union and non-union fields alike, for the first time in the history of the state.

Among the men who worked with me during this strike was a youngster named Powers Hapgood, who deserves some special notice, for his own qualities and because of our long friendship. He was not one of the original group who invaded Somerset County, because he was working at the time in the anthracite region. I sent word to him, on April 11, that there was union work to do in our area, if he would like to help. He came immediately, and served throughout the strike as a volunteer organizer, getting expenses but no salary.

I had first met Powers the previous spring through Arthur Gleason. Gleason was a friend of Powers' uncle, Norman Hapgood, the editor of *Collier's*. He asked me one day whether I could make use of a young fellow who was anxious to do some work for the labor movement.

I asked, "How far would he go?"

"I think he would go pretty far."

"Well, for instance," I said, "would he be willing to try to get work in a non-union mine and write up conditions as he found them there? To go into the mines and work?"

"He's worked in union mines, in Montana and Colorado," Arthur replied. "He's never worked under non-union conditions, but I'm sure he will do it, because he is very idealistic. He told me he's very anxious to get a foot in the door of trade unionism."

I said, "If he'll come up here to Clearfield, I'll take a look at him, talk it over with him, and offer suggestions as to where he might go in the non-union fields. He'll probably not be able to stay anywhere very long before he'll be fired, but if he can describe the conditions he meets it will be a refresher even for our own people."

Powers came up to Clearfield. He was a very nice, unaffected boy who had graduated from Harvard a short time before. He came of a wealthy and distinguished family. His father ran the family business, the Columbia Conserve Company, in Indianapolis, which had been given to the employees and converted into a co-operative. One uncle, Hutchins Hapgood, was a novelist who had also written on social problems; the other, Norman, besides being a noted editor, had been an ambassador. All of them had lively social consciences, so Powers came by his interest in labor legitimately. It would have been hard not to like Powers. He was sincere, friendly, and courageous to the point of foolhardiness. By that I mean that he would sometimes drive ahead in a situation without considering sufficiently what he was up against. As a result, he got some pretty hard knocks at times. He became a Socialist, not so much because he was persuaded by Socialist economics as because he naturally gravitated toward a party that stood for the underdog, and he was too decent to be able to swallow the Communists. One of his handicaps in the miners' union was that everyone knew he could always pull out and return to the environment to which he was born. The Lewis crowd resented him especially because they considered him an outsider; perhaps that is why some of them beat him up so brutally at one of the national conventions.

Powers went into some of the Berwind and White mines and some belonging to the Vinton Colliery Company, during August and September of 1921, and described the conditions he found, in a pamphlet published by the Bureau of Industrial Research, called *In Non-Union Mines—the Diary of a Coal Digger*, by "Powers Hapgood, of the United Mine Workers of America." I thought his report was very good in its simplicity. The Socialists and groups like the League for Industrial Democracy circulated the pamphlet. I don't suppose it got out to a very great number of people, but it was a good job, well worth doing.

If we were surprised by the magnitude of our success in pulling out the non-union men, the employers were thunderstruck. They were by no means prepared for this universal rebellion against their rule.

However, they were in a better position to make the adjustment to the situation than the union was. They had vast funds at their disposal and could hire all the men they needed for any kind of work, no matter how sinister. The one thing they could not hire was experienced coal miners. The small number of strikers who gave up and returned to work was astonishing, considering the overwhelming pressures put upon them by the companies, and by the public officials and courts who eagerly did the companies' bidding.

Unlike the operators, the union had limited funds and limited personnel. We could expect no help from District 5, which had its hands full in the coke region and Westmoreland County. The national office sent us just over $100,000. In Somerset County alone, leaving aside the old union fields, District 2 spent five times that much on relief alone. Through friends of Hapgood and Mrs. Willard Straight, about $25,000 was raised in New York; they were also responsible for our getting a gift of $2,000 and a loan of $25,000 from the American Fund for Public Service (more commonly known as the Garland Fund), through its secretary, Roger Baldwin. The district also borrowed $50,000 from a bank in the latter days of the strike. Both loans were repaid after the strike was over. We spent every cent in the district treasury, raised more by a special assessment, and went deeply in debt, but our resources were never adequate to meet even the minimum needs of the strikers. Our staff, from the inexperienced but enthusiastic young Hapgood to grizzled veterans of many struggles, worked tirelessly and devotedly. And hundreds of strikers gave uncountable hours of heroic work to the cause. I can safely say that no better set of men ever conducted a strike. But there were limits to what naked human idealism could accomplish against the money, the courts, the newspapers, the clubs and guns at the disposal of the operators.

Strikers were evicted from company houses by the thousands. The union spent over $5,000 for tents and over $11,000 for lumber and tarpaper with which to build barracks, as winter approached. The sick and the well, the newborn and the dying alike, had no other protection from the weather than these emergency shelters during the long months of the strike. The strikers themselves had been on short time for a year before the strike began, at wages that would allow no margin for saving even on full time. They had no resources but their courage and their willingness to suffer for the cause of unionism.

We set up new union locals, often giving the obligation of membership to hundreds of men at a time, in vast outdoor mass meetings. We toured from meeting to meeting, making speeches explaining to the men, over and over again, the principles and policies of the union, until our voices failed us. Sometimes, we could not raise our voices above a whisper after a day of this kind of work. News of how the strike was going, of the hearings of the House Labor Committee in Washington, of the efforts to negotiate settlements, was brought to the strikers by these mass meetings and by the union newspaper, the *Penn Central News.*

Local strike committees handled distribution of food and other supplies sent from the district headquarters. They also often had to arrange for medical care. Some doctors were generous with their time; others were less humane.

Through the local committees, constant appeals for legal help poured into our office. The companies got injunctions from complaisant judges, under the interpretation of the Sherman Act in the Hitchman Coal Company Case, which made any effort to unionize workers without their employers' consent illegal. We were forbidden to hold meetings, to pass out leaflets, to picket, to use union funds to house and feed strikers, or to do almost anything else the bosses might object to. The injunctions were defiantly violated by the strikers, because the only alternative was to give up the strike, and that the men would not do, no matter what penalties judges inflicted upon them.

Hundreds were arrested for "trespassing" on company property and on other trumped-up charges. They were thrown into jail, always found guilty, and usually given the maximum penalty. The judges contributed their bit to bankrupting the union by the size of the fines levied.

Company guards were free to ignore the law and the rights of Americans in any way they chose. Strikers were beaten up, their homes invaded, their wives and children terrorized, without any recourse. We were driven from meeting places, even outside company-owned land, on the excuse that our meetings "might lead to violence," or with no excuse at all. Outsiders traveling the roads of Somerset County were stopped by police or mine guards, questioned as to their business, and warned to get out of town. On one occasion, more or less by accident, I found the right way to deal with that. Late one night I was driving through one of the little mining towns when I was stopped by three or four State Policemen and some company guards. They wanted to know who I was and what my business was. I told them I was looking over the countryside; I was John Brophy, president of District 2, UMW, and I was interested in what the miners were doing. They began to swell up, and one of them said, "You've no business here."

I said, "That's what you say, but I'm here." They wrangled about that, getting tougher all the time, until one man asked, "Who are those other people?"

"If you really want to know," I said, "they're newspapermen, and they'll probably write up this story for their papers."

A guard said, "Is that the way you travel?"

"That's the way I'm traveling now," I said. "Now, have you any business with me? If not, clear out of the way, because we're going along." They let us proceed.

We made every possible use of publicity. Our own little paper could not reach beyond our own area, but the strike was news and reporters from outside came into the district. For a long time, relatively little of what the reporters sent in was actually published, but gradually more and more of the facts got out to the public, and the local authorities began to get the word, I suppose from offices in Pittsburgh and New York, that newspapermen were dynamite. Reporters were constantly spied on, their telephone calls listened to, and their contacts with local people thoroughly checked. They were stopped and questioned on public roads, and driven away from company property to keep them from taking photographs.

The Johnstown *Democrat* was the one newspaper that gave us consistently fair coverage. Its editor, Warren Worth Bailey, was a single-taxer who had been elected to Congress in spite of the vehement opposition of the local operators. He was always ready to publish news of interest to the miners. The other Johnstown paper was not as friendly, but had to publish miners' news to avoid losing all its circulation to the *Democrat*. Thoreau Cronyn, of the New York *Herald*, wrote a series of articles on the strike in the latter part of April, which was the first real account to reach the outside world. And the Federated Press, an association of labor papers, kept its correspondent, Art Shields, on the scene for several months. In spite of these leaks, it is hard to believe how thoroughly the operators were able to shut off their private barony from the rest of the United States. One would find it hard to prove that Somerset County was under the jurisdiction of the United States Constitution during 1922. The Commonwealth of Pennsylvania was no more interested than the federal government in the rights and welfare of the coal diggers. State Policemen and militia were as eager as county and private police to do the bidding of the operators. Republican Governor Sproul, in spite of protests from labor and liberal groups, sent the state militia into the non-union fields (but not into the old organized areas) and issued a proclamation prohibiting public meetings, on the excuse that they might lead to "disorder."

It is impossible to give the story of a great strike like this in a summary. The true essence of the history is in hundreds of incidents in the lives of obscure people. Blankenhorn's book records a sampling of these incidents, but most of them are lost to history. Yet it is the courage and devotion of such humble men and women that has built the labor movement.

My trips to the Somerset strike scene could not be very frequent. Somebody had to "keep the store" at headquarters, to see that the constant flood of appeals was answered, to send men where they were needed, to maintain contact with our lawyers, to handle relations with the locals, the national office, and the public.

At the end of the first month, we were doing rather well. Over 40,000 in the old union fields were solidly united, and more than 20,000 new members were just as firm, giving every indication that they would stay until the end. At the beginning of the strike there were about 45,000,000 tons of coal stockpiled. This was being nibbled away at the rate of about 4,000,000 tons a week. We looked forward hopefully to a settlement when the public began to feel the pinch, if our old and new members could be held together. We knew that if we did not get a real settlement covering everybody who had gone on strike, the newly won fields would soon revert to non-unionism, and that they, with the non-union fields of West Virginia, Kentucky, Tennessee, and Alabama, would then be the operators' weapon to destroy whatever the union fields might gain.

The strike of the railroad shopmen, in July, hampered the shipment of scab coal to the market, thus adding to pressure on the government and the public to push for a settlement before things got too bad. The operators were confident when the strike began, but by August they had reason to worry. President Harding called a conference of operators and union leaders at the White House in July. The operators got some comfort out of this. The first effect of the President's call was to raise the hopes of the strikers that this was the point at which public pressure would force the operators to settle. But the latter managed things adroitly, with Harding's help, to confuse the situation. After some preliminaries, the operators, with a great show of making a concession, offered to submit the issues to arbitration—by districts, intending to use the weaker districts to break down standards in the strong union districts. Harding seized upon the magic word "arbitration," and used it in all his proposals and suggestions. The union wanted to know whether the arbitration proposals would cover the newly organized fields as well as the older ones; the operators rejected this, and Harding simply clung to the empty generality about arbitration, showing no consciousness that the desirability of the procedure would depend on how it was used. Many of the strike-bound operators were not even represented at the conference, and a minority even of those who were there refused to commit themselves to arbitration or anything else.

There was nothing in this situation for the union to accept but surrender. The conference broke up with Harding expressing the hope that now operations could be resumed. I suppose he had to pretend that something had been accomplished, though it was plainly not true. Some operators chose to interpret Harding's statement as a mandate to reopen their mines in defiance of the union. And some governors rushed to support their efforts with state militia. Sproul, of Pennsylvania, was not the slowest to move.

By the first of August, steel furnaces were being shut down, and coal was being rationed to public utilities. The need for greater coal production was becoming acute. The miners were still solid; the back-to-work movement was a fiasco; the public was confused and resentful, not sure where to put the blame. The operators were divided and squabbling among themselves. If the union leadership had been as firm as the rank and file, victory might still have been achieved.

The fatal break in the situation occurred at the meeting of the union's General Policy Committee early in August. Here Lewis proposed to call all operators willing to sign up with the union to a meeting in Cleveland on the fifteenth. The operators' associations of the Pittsburgh and southern Ohio districts, under pressure from the steel companies, had refused to take part in a new agreement for the Central Competitive Field. Lewis represented his move as a way to force them into line by signing up with their competitors.

I put up a fight for the principle that no agreement be signed with an operator unless it covered all of his mines that were on strike, both in the newly organized and in the old, established fields. This merely reaffirmed a precedent set by John Mitchell as far back as 1906, when the Central Competitive Field was split by the operators and the union authorized national and district officers to make separate agreements with operators willing to accept the union's demands. Mitchell asserted at that time that there would be no signing up with any operator unless the agreement covered all his operations. I was unable to get Lewis to be as firm as John Mitchell had been.

Instead, Lewis accepted any and all who came to his Cleveland conference. Most of the operators would sign up only for mines covered by agreements before the strike, but not for those newly organized. In his anxiety to collect as much tonnage as possible, Lewis signed the partial agreements, leaving thousands of the new union men stranded, not only in Somerset but in all the new fields.

Why this indecent haste to sign agreements which threw away all the achievements of the organizing drive? Lewis represented his agreement as a victory, because it "held the line" against wage cuts. Actually, the reason for his action can be found in his personal rivalry with Frank Farrington, president of District 12, in Illinois. Farrington was ambitious to succeed Lewis as president of the national union, and was angling for a district agreement, which would have been the basing point for other settlements. Lewis was afraid to let Farrington have the credit and prestige that might go with making the first settlement. Even if Lewis held firm and got an agreement covering a wider area, as he almost certainly could have done in another week or two, Farrington might still have bragged that Lewis had not been able to do anything until Farrington showed the way. It was not much of a brag, but Lewis could not stand even the appearance of playing second fiddle.

There was not much choice between the two men. Farrington did not back my fight in the General Policy Committee. He knew that if my principle was adopted, a couple of union mines operated in Illinois by a subsidiary of the U.S. Steel Corporation would have to remain idle until the coke region got a settlement, and he had no more stomach than Lewis for a fight.

Lewis not only pretended that this contract with about one-tenth of the national tonnage was a victory, because it continued the wages and working conditions of the 1920 contract until March 31, 1923, but he also argued that when the union districts went back to work they could give the remaining strikers greater financial support. He ignored the fact that now the public would be able to get as much coal as it needed, thus eliminating that essential pressure on the operators. And some of the operators would fill their orders from their union mines, letting their striking operations go until the men were forced back to work; then they could use the non-union mines to undercut the union mines. There could never be any safety for union men as long as non-union fields were producing hundreds of millions of tons a year. The whole tremendous effort of 1922 was a failure, because of Lewis's shortsightedness. Why a man so forceful and astute as Lewis was in many ways should have made this colossal blunder can only be explained by some fatal defect in his character. He had done the same sort of thing in 1919 and was saved from disaster only by the solidarity of the miners who refused to be driven back to work by an injunction. And he was to collapse again in other situations.

Upon my return from Cleveland, the Operators' Association of the district approached us, and we signed an agreement with them, renewing the old contract. Thus their wage-cutting campaign was defeated, but I was still left with the problem of salvaging something for the strikers of Somerset County. If I had rejected the District 2 contract, I would have put the whole union area of my district in the same predicament as the non-union fields.

I called a convention of the Somerset County locals, to review the situation and determine their future course of action. I also sent telegrams to all the operators of the county, inviting them to meet with us and their employees to negotiate an agreement covering wages and working conditions, on August 29 or any later date that would suit them. A few small operators having mines in other parts of the district signed in order that their Cambria County mines might work, but the other non-union operators ignored the invitation.

When the delegates arrived for the Somerset County convention they had already discussed their problem in their local meetings. Almost as one man they were for continuing the strike. I pointed out to them the hardships they would encounter, but assured them that if they wanted to carry on the struggle I would support them as long as our means lasted. And I promised to recommend to the district executive board the levying of an assessment on all working miners in the district. After a very full discussion, they voted unanimously to continue the strike.

The executive board endorsed the assessment, and we sent a circular to all the locals describing the condition of the Somerset men, reporting our expenditures up to that time for relief and other strike expenditures, and estimating what it would cost to keep the strike going. The members voted overwhelmingly to assess themselves $2.00 out of each fortnightly pay (which was 10 to 20 per cent of their pay, in most cases), and paid the assessment with a minimum of complaint. The assessment raised over half a million dollars, every cent of which went into relief for the Somerset County strikers. The district convention in April, 1923, voted unanimously to continue the strike and district support as long as the Somerset men thought they had a reasonable prospect of victory.

In October, James Mark and some of the Somerset men went to New York, where, in their mining clothes, they picketed the head offices of Berwind and White on lower Broadway. They also made strenuous efforts to get representatives of Berwind and White and of the Rockefeller-backed Consolidation Coal Company to meet with committees of the strikers. They got an elaborate runaround, and even that they got only because the newspapers (especially the Socialist New York *Call,* a short-lived daily) treated the picketing as news, for a change.

For a while, the strike became a public scandal in New York, and politically important, because Berwind and White was the principal supplier of coal for the Interborough Rapid Transit Company, of which E. J. Berwind was a director. He was doing business with himself for 750,000 tons of coal a year, at an enormous profit. Mayor Hylan yielded to public indignation by appointing a special commission to investigate the strike and report on whether the city should do anything about the matter. The Commission came to Pennsylvania to hold hearings. The only hall they could hire was a union hall. The operators complained bitterly about their meeting there, though efforts to get one of the operators to admit them to his hall were in vain. Operators' representatives, when quizzed by the Commission, could not remember even the address of the companies they worked for. The members of the Commission reported that they were followed around town, that their telephone calls were listened to, and their mail opened before they got it. Newspaper photographers and reporters complained of being constantly under surveillance. Operators denied that they employed guards, or that they had evicted their miners, and then made strenuous efforts to keep anyone from checking on the truth of their statements. The efforts to blanket the investigation were unsuccessful;

the Commission turned in a report which documented the abuse of the miners and charged Berwind with keeping its workers "in bondage worse than the serfs in Russia or the slaves before the Civil War." Berwind's annual profits on coal sold to Interborough were estimated at over $1,600,000. In spite of this strong report, nothing was done by Mayor Hylan which benefitted the Somerset strikers. He got his political capital out of the report, and that was all he was after.

Lewis's divisive policy was responsible for an incident in District 2 which caused a great deal of dissension. The J. H. Weaver interests operated a mine in Nanty Glo (the Heisley mine) and another in West Virginia. But they also had connections with two non-union mines near Revloc and Colver, which we pulled out during the strike. I met Mr. Ball, the head of the Weaver Company, at the Cleveland conference, and told him I would sign no agreement which did not cover all three of the Pennsylvania mines; I also told Lewis of my position on this matter. Lewis went ahead and signed a contract with the Weaver concern, covering its old union mines, but leaving out the Revloc and Colver operations. Ordinarily, the district officers were a party to agreements covering members of the district organization, but I refused to sign and the district executive board backed me. Lewis went over my head to conclude the agreement and then demanded that I force the Nanty Glo strikers back to work. The workers in all the mines involved stood firm for three weeks to get an inclusive settlement, but Mr. Ball threatened legal action against the union unless the Nanty Glo mine resumed work.

Even though Lewis had no moral right to do so, his signature had created a legal contract which the courts would have upheld, so for the sake of the union I had to submit. With a heavy heart, I sent a telegram to the Nanty Glo union:

During the recent Cleveland conference in order to secure a sufficient tonnage to insure an interstate conference, International President Lewis agreed with the Weaver interests that all their operations would be immediately returned to work if those interests would enter the conference and sign the contract agreed upon. After the settlement was reached the Weaver representative was willing to sign for all of their mines but Revloc, whereupon I refused to sign the agreement. I met President Lewis at Wilkes-Barre, September 9, at his request, and it was then I learned of the obligation made to the Weaver interests in order to secure their participation in the interstate conference. Mr. Weaver insists that he does not have control of the Revloc mines and Mr. Lewis states emphatically that the union is obligated to return the Heisley mines to work. We may not think that President Lewis was right in incurring such an obligation but under the circumstances there seems to be only one course to pursue and that is for the Heisley miners to return to work and I so advise.

Of course, my critics seized upon this incident as evidence that I was playing the game of divisiveness, just like Lewis. Lewis was furious with me for my "non-co-operation"; my critics in the district attacked me for the opposite reason; I was in the middle. The worst thing about the incident was that it was used by the Somerset operators, with the help of certain self-righteous "rank and filers" among the district staff, to undermine the confidence of the strikers in the district organization.

The international union finally announced a general assessment of $4.00 a month in support of the strikers, beginning in December. This money would be used not only in Pennsylvania but also in the other non-union fields. We obviously could not collect that amount from our members in addition to the district assessment. If we gave up the district assessment, giving priority to the national, there would be delays and complications at a time when promptness in paying out relief was essential to save the strikers from starvation. I appealed to Lewis to exempt District 2 from the national assessment in order that we might continue the job we were already doing.

The national board member from District 2 brought up before the board our request for exoneration from the national assessment so long as our district assessment continued. In view of the fact that our members had been paying a $4.00 per month assessment for two months before the national organization got around to acting, there was no possibility of suggesting that District 2 wanted preferential treatment. Although there was ample precedent for such an exoneration, the request was denied. During the two months that the national assessment was collected, District 2 sent $147,000 to the national office, considerably more than the total amount of money sent into the district during the entire strike from the national office, although we had one of the largest and toughest non-union areas in the country on our hands.

In January, 1923, the international executive board voted to call off the strike in the coke region of Fayette County. There was much dispute about this decision, as might be expected. Some people claimed that it was a surrender, but the international officers argued that there was no hope of winning contracts, that the wage scales would be preserved, and they were simply protecting the union and the strikers against further unnecessary losses. Whatever the right of that might have been, the effect on the Somerset County strikers was extremely bad. Not only were they disheartened by the appearance of being left to fight on alone, but also they were subjected to barrages of propaganda from the operators to the effect that the union was not going to back them, and to even more damaging controversy in their own ranks over the responsibility of the national and district organizations for what seemed to the strikers a defeat.

We held a special convention of District 2 at Du Bois, April 17–21, 1923, in response to a request from a number of locals, to take up a dispute over payment of back pay to the district staff for the period of the strike. The officers, board members, organizers, and other employees had received two months' pay, but the board had voted to suspend payments for a period of two and one-half months, in order to conserve the resources of the district. Now it was proposed to reimburse the staff for the lost pay. A lot of people argued that the staff should sacrifice that pay, just as the strikers had given up their pay for the duration of the strike. Some even went so far as to say that the staff should return the two months' pay they had received. It had long been customary for staff people, in many districts, to postpone their pay during a strike, but they received it after the strike was over. Gilbert and I opposed raising the issue, but Mark and some of the district board were adamant in their demands. It was a small matter, but it was blown up to a grand battle royal by the bitterness created by internal troubles which I will describe in the next chapter. We never got the back pay, incidentally, though a couple of men who took the matter to the courts got their pay, plus 6 per cent interest. Most of us were not willing to take the union into court, so we were not paid.

Far more important was the question of continuing the Somerset strike. Delegates were present from most of the Somerset locals. From the incomplete reports they were able to provide, it appeared that there were some five to six thousand men still on strike, almost all of them entirely dependent on relief funds from the district. The Somerset delegates seemed to think there was still a chance of winning, even though the operators were bringing in scabs, a great many strikers had left the area to get jobs in union mines and elsewhere, and a few—very few, let it be said—had returned to work. The debate was complicated by a great many charges and counter-charges, mostly having to do with the activity of the international organizers in Somerset, with re-lations between the district and the international, and questions as to who was responsible for the lack of co-operation between the two.

After prolonged debate, the delegates voted unanimously to con-tinue the strike and the assessment on our members for its support. A referendum vote of the membership went overwhelmingly in favor of continuing the assessment.

Unfortunately, the good will of our members—in the union mines as well as in Somerset—was not a strong enough force to overcome the powers lined up against us. The union mines were only working part time throughout this period. The assessment, which continued to be paid with astonishing fidelity for nearly a year, became a great burden on the working members, even after we reduced it to $2.00 a month. More and more men drifted out of the strike area to other jobs. The number of scabs increased, though they did not produce much coal in proportion to their numbers. Persecution of the strikers by police, com-pany guards, and the courts was intensified.

Economic conditions were consistently against the union. When market conditions were fair, at the beginning, there was a shortage of railroad coal cars. When the supply of cars began to return to normal, demand fell off. The operators, not having orders for full time work anyway, were not disturbed unduly by the fact that their production, with the crews at their disposal, was less than a third of normal. They would not have produced much more if the strikers had returned to work.

In August, 1923, after seventeen months of vain and heartbreaking struggle, the district executive board voted to end the Somerset strike and permit those who still stood fast to return to work. Some, who had been marked as agitators, could not get work in the Somerset field, but we made every effort to find places for them elsewhere.

Delegates from the Somerset field met at Johnstown, August 14, 1923, to discuss the situation, and accepted the decision to call off the strike. They passed a resolution which seems to me worth quoting; the last paragraph represents, very exactly, the spirit of the brave men and women who made that magnificent fight for unionism in Somerset County:

Whereas: The long strike of almost seventeen months in the coal fields of Somerset County has been terminated, and

Whereas, we recognize the circumstances making necessary the temporary abandonment of our fight against the coal operators for Union recognition, and realize that the failure of the strike to secure our full demands was not due to any defects in the principles of unionism, but rather to the brutal tactics and tremendous financial strength of the coal companies, as well as to the weak mindedness, selfishness and un-Americanism of strikebreakers who took our jobs, and reaped the benefit of the wage increases which not they, but we and the Union were the means of securing from the coal operators of Somerset County, and

Whereas, we appreciate the help that all the members of District No. 2, United Mine Workers of America, have given us, the miners who, in spite of slack work, paid the assessment to support us and thus sacrificed along with us, and the officers of District 2, who left nothing undone that was in their power to do for our benefit, therefore, be it

Resolved, That we, the delegates from the Somerset County Local Unions, in convention assembled in the city of Johnstown, Pennsylvania, this fourteenth day of August, 1923, reaffirm our belief in the principles of unionism and declare our intention of keeping alive our Union, even though we are working on an open shop basis, and await the first opportunity of winning a contract and Union recognition.

Few indeed were the men who were able to hold jobs in Somerset County and maintain union membership, though the principles of the union survived in the minds of many. It was a long decade later that these fields were finally organized, in the days of the New Deal.

The district organization had poured $903,119.54 into relief for the strikers, over half of which was derived from the assessment, according to Secretary Gilbert's report to the 1923 district special convention. Donations of food, money and clothing from other sources swelled the total to $1,000,000. Almost unbelievable sacrifices had been made by the strikers and their wives and families, and the miners of the district had stood behind them far beyond the usual limits.

The Somerset operators were united and well organized. The only "break" that occurred in their solid front against unionism came after the picketing on Broadway, when John D. Rockefeller, Jr., sent a letter to a representative of the Federal Council of Churches, saying that the grievances of the strikers were "well founded," and that he believed workers should have the right of "representation in the determination of those matters which affect their own interests." Rockefeller was the largest stockholder in Consolidation Coal Company, one of the major Somerset operators, but his pious generalities did not lead to negotiations with the union. If anything had come of this, it would more likely have been something like the notorious company union scheme in the Rockefeller mines in Colorado. None of the major operators made any response to our repeated efforts to get them to confer on a settlement. Because of Lewis's Cleveland settlement, Consolidation, Hillman, Bethlehem, and other major operators could operate under union contracts in other areas and refuse to meet with the union under any circumstances to discuss conditions in Somerset County, Fayette County, and West Virginia. The most powerful weapon available to win the non-union fields was thrown away in Cleveland. The very steadfastness of the Somerset strikers was a reproach to the national office; it is hardly remarkable that the Lewis supporters were indifferent, if not hostile, to the Somerset strike, and did everything possible to discredit everybody connected with it.

The Somerset strike was an inspiring demonstration of the heights of self-sacrifice and devotion that ordinary people can attain for a noble cause. The failure of the strike was a correspondingly crushing disappointment. An opportunity had been missed, the like of which could not be expected again for years. Though we maintained what contacts we had in the area, a real organizing drive had to await a major change in circumstances, such as appeared in 1933.

I had to recognize that the organization of the unorganized, one of the major items in the larger program to which I had dedicated myself, was for the time a lost cause—lost, like the nationalization campaign, by the indifference and lack of constructive policy among the national leadership. And there was worse to come, both for me personally and for my hopes for the union.

!!

15

CHALLENGING

JOHN L. LEWIS

It is an unwritten law of the labor movement that lost strikes produce an aftermath of recrimination. It may be no more than a minor rumble, or it may be a public explosion of major proportions. Even under the best circumstances, the handling of some phases of so big and bitter a strike as that in Somerset County would have been criticized. There were innumerable opportunities to make mistakes, and any human being would fall into some of the traps awaiting him.

I expected criticism and I got it hot and heavy.

Not only were there the usual growls, but I was under concerted attack from two sources. One was a group of malcontents in the district, headed by Thomas D. Stiles. The other was the international office.

Stiles had been employed by the district to conduct educational work in support of co-operative stores. At the district convention of 1918, Secretary Gilbert proposed the encouragement of co-operatives, which was approved along with an authorization to allow the district officers to provide advice and educational help to such a movement. Capital was raised among the miners; union funds could not be used for that purpose. When we came to select a man for the educational work, Gilbert, who had talked to Stiles, suggested that he be made chairman of a committee of three. The others were men who spoke Italian and Slovak, chosen for work with non-English speaking miners. Neither was very active, so Stiles was soon running the show. Although he had little experience in the mines, he spoke the miners' language and knew their problems. About twenty little co-operative stores were started.

Co-operation on the Rochdale plan, although a sound idea, was hard to practice in coal towns. Miners had little money to invest, and when they moved, had to take out their small investment. When times were bad, they expected the stores to give credit, like the company stores, but their needs often exceeded the capacity of the co-operatives. If a mine shut down, the store shut down too. It is remarkable that, in spite of years of hard times in the mines, there are still several stores operating in central Pennsylvania towns. The problem was not incompetent or dishonest management, though some managers were better than others, but the depressed state of the coal industry and consequent irregularity of work.

To help the education program, a little paper called *Pick and Plow* (changed later to *Penn Central News*) was started, with Stiles as editor. The paper was controlled by the co-operatives and local unions, which bought stock, usually ten dollars' worth. It was a four-page sheet with news of the union and the stores, some personal news, and editorials. It had no advertising income to speak of, and was circulated mostly by bundle orders from the local unions or stores. During the 1922 strike, Art Shields, of the Federated Press, was in the area and contributed some excellent articles. John P. Geyer, who worked for the co-operatives and had some newspaper experience, wrote the co-operative news.

When the 1922 strike began, the *News* enjoyed its greatest circulation and prosperity. The district bought 20,000 copies of a special edition, to blanket the strike area. Because of the near blackout of news about the strike in much of the regular press, the *News* could have been invaluable. Unfortunately, Stiles got notions of himself as a labor statesman. Instead of supporting the district's efforts to win the strike, he operated as a free-lance critic of one and all, basing his ideas on a Never-Never Land conception of mass movements, which was also characteristic of Blankenhorn's book. In such a view, the responsible officers of the union, who had to make all the tough decisions, became the villains of the piece. And chief among the villains was the president.

Stiles produced a series of denunciatory editorials, mostly directed against me. He accused me of selling out the Revloc strikers. When the international office settled the Fayette strike, he called that a sellout, too, and somehow I shared in the blame. Then he turned around and accused me of prolonging the Somerset strike for my own political ends, to discredit Lewis. This last charge was picked up by the operators and used to help break the strike. He finally surpassed himself with an extravagant editorial on the issue of back pay for the district officers.*

Such editorials were not only an indefensible attempt by an employee of the union to control its policy, but they had a disastrous effect on morale. I had to take steps against Stiles, both to clear my own name and to protect the union. But Stiles did not lack friends. One was Heber Blankenhorn, who had his own ambitions. He wanted a center for research and education in District 2, financed by outside money and free of union controls. He and Stiles applied to the Garland Fund for a loan of $45,000, to support the paper and the research and education work. The application gave a detailed budget of expenditures, but no hint as to how the loan was to be repaid. The money was to be handled by an "advisory committee" representing the League for Industrial Democracy, Cooperative League of America, Bureau of Industrial Research, Rand School of Social Science, Penn Central Cooperative Association, *Penn Central News,* and Pennsylvania Federation of Labor, but without anyone from the United Mine Workers, national or district. I first heard of this from President Maurer of the State Federation, who asked me what he should do about it and was astonished that it was news to me. Later Norman Thomas, chairman of the Fund, wrote asking that I send Roger Baldwin, the secretary, my opinion.

I replied that the co-operatives had been created by District 2; that we had been paying salaries to Stiles and a stenographer and other expenses amounting to about $30,000; that we had lent the organization $10,000 a year before, which had not been repaid; that the *News* was set up by the district with the understanding that a meeting of stockholders would be called to create a permanent organization, but Stiles

---

* Quoted in Blankenhorn's book, p. 210. I do not think any file of the *News* has survived.

had never called such a meeting; and that the district knew nothing of this scheme to squeeze the union out.

Arthur Gleason had been aware of Blankenhorn's disaffection since late in 1922, and urged me then to go to Herbert Croly, editor of the *New Republic,* and ask that he and Mrs. Straight get Blankenhorn out of the district. I tried to talk to Blankenhorn and thought at one time that I had worked out an understanding with him, but soon learned that I was mistaken. Gleason was as shocked as I by the application to the Garland Fund and told me to see Croly immediately. I did so, and explained my position, which was that I was responsible, as elected head of the district, for union policy, and that I could not tolerate an invasion of meddlesome outsiders. Whatever their motives, I could not let them impose their notions upon the union, which had its own democratic machinery to represent the miners.

Croly understood the problem and advised Mrs. Straight to withdraw support from the Bureau. She gave it a year, on reduced funds, to wind up activity, after which the subsidy was cut off. Furthermore, Thomas and the directors of the Garland Fund rejected the loan application. But Stiles was resourceful and found another way to finance himself.

He went to Philip Murray and told his story. According to his own account, he told Murray that I intended to call a stockholders' meeting of the Penn Central Association to throw Stiles out. (A meeting was called, by demand of a number of stockholders; Stiles tried to cancel it, but we met anyway to find out what was being done with the organization and its assets. Stiles offered his resignation, after a long wrangle, and left the district payroll at the end of May, 1923.) Stiles said that we were ready to let the co-operatives die, so he wanted help in saving them. Murray took Stiles to Lewis, who said there was a by-law forbidding lending union money to co-operatives, but he thought the work should be taken care of and would give Stiles an organizer's commission, at ten dollars a day and expenses. Stiles accepted, and returned to the district in a new guise.

Lewis's decision to put him on the payroll was characteristic. Although Stiles had attacked Lewis in the past, Lewis expected to keep him under control and to use him to foment dissension in my district. Lewis never doubted his ability to use anybody and then discard him when his usefulness was over; his over-confidence in this respect accounts for some of the Communist troubles in the CIO. The showdown between Stiles and me came in the district convention of March 11, 1924, which went on for over a week. At the end, the delegates approved my report by resounding majorities, and the Stiles opposition was finished. Lewis promptly dropped Stiles from the payroll, since his influence in district affairs was clearly ended.*

My troubles with the international union were harder to clear up than the Stiles-Blankenhorn cabal. Lack of co-operation between the international and the district was a major cause of the Somerset defeat. I have mentioned the impasse over assessments, and the fact that we paid the international over $40,000 more in assessments during the strike than we received in contributions. This does not include per capita tax paid in as usual.

International organizers sent in during the Somerset strike were more trouble than help. I tried repeatedly to get an agreement with the international whereby these men could be used more effectively, but without success. At first I proposed that, since I was on the scene, I be permitted to send the men where they were needed, supplementing district organizers instead of duplicating efforts. This was rejected, on the ground that the international could not surrender jurisdiction over its own men. I then proposed that the international take responsibility for part of southern Somerset County, bordering the Maryland district, where the international was in charge. Since we did not have enough men to organize that distant area, help would have been welcome. This was also rejected. The international organizers spent most of their time visiting locals in union fields, making speeches in praise of the international in general and John L. Lewis in particular. Delegates from certain locals charged later than these speeches included advice to vote against the assessment for Somerset, on the ground that the strike was hopeless anyway and was just my grandstand play, to lay a basis for running against Lewis. I did not hear any such speeches, but I would not be surprised if the charges were true. One of the organizers got a little overheated in his defense of Lewis at the 1923 special district convention and declared that he and his fellows were sent into the district to counteract the "dirty, rotten lies" about Lewis that were being circulated in the district. A year later, in the 1924

* For the full discussion, from both sides, of the Stiles-Blankenhorn affair, see *Minutes of the Proceedings of the 29th Consecutive and Sixth Biennial Convention of the United Mine Workers of America, District No. 2. 1924. 2 Vols.*

convention, another organizer identified the source of the lies as "the political agent of John Brophy"—none other than T. D. Stiles! These men worked hard at defending Lewis, but their contribution to the cause of the strikers was negligible.

Ellis Searles, editor of the United Mine Workers' *Journal*, made his contribution to the Somerset situation in a letter addressed to J. C. Brydon, president of the Somerset County Operators' Association, which was published ostentatiously in the UMW *Journal* of April 2, 1922. The letter said, among other things, "Communists and reds are in Somerset County . . . working under the direction of a headquarters in New York. . . . Unfortunately a few of these reds have worked their way into the membership in the United Mine Workers. . . . If your report of dynamitings and other crimes is true, then these crimes can be traced to these red agitators." It would be hard to imagine a more treacherous or damaging thing to do. Coming from the international union itself, at a time when the country was still obsessed with the red scare and the bosses were using it on every hand against labor, this letter had a devastating effect on public opinion and on the morale of the strikers, laying a basis for the charge that anybody who supported the Somerset strike and its implied criticism of the Cleveland settlement was a Red.

This is not to say that the Communists were not trying to get into the United Mine Workers. They were behind a convention called in Pittsburgh in the spring of 1923, under the name of the "Progressive Miners' Movement." Powers Hapgood and two or three others from District 2 attended the convention as observers. I did not go, both because I was too busy and because, not knowing then who was behind it, I was suspicious of it. The international executive board promptly denounced the "Progressive" movement as dual and ordered the expulsion of all UMW members who had attended.

Ellis Searles used the *Journal* of April 1, 1923, for another attack on me. J. J. Kintner, the attorney for District 2, had let himself be led into a concession, at some hearings of the Interstate Commerce Commission, that the miners would be able to make a living wage at rates 20 per cent below the union scale, if the supply of coal cars was sufficient to permit the men to work steadily. Kintner had no right to make such a statement. He was ignorant of the subject and was fooled by the way a hypothetical question was framed. I repudiated his statement, in a letter to the Commission, and dismissed Kintner. A few weeks after my action, a circular letter was sent to all locals, and printed in the *Journal*, stating in bold print that "President Brophy's representative" had advocated a 20 per cent wage cut. Kintner's name was only mentioned once, but mine was in every paragraph, to suggest that this was my program for the miners' union. A long editorial never mentioned Kintner's name at all, but used mine six times. The *Journal* ignored my repudiation of Kintner, refused to publish my letters, and went on repeating the lie long after Searles and the national officers knew it was a lie.

We persuaded representatives of the international office to meet with the district board in Altoona, in the fall of 1923, to try to straighten things out. No issues were settled, of course, but we did get an agreement for a cease-fire, which unfortunately was not honored.

Lewis kept on attacking me, because I stuck to the platform I had been advocating all along and lost no opportunities to press for the policy I felt was necessary to put the union back on its feet. The real issue between Lewis and me was my insistence on a constructive and aggressive policy for the union, while he preferred to drift along, waiting for the "law of supply and demand," in which he had great faith, to settle the problems of the industry.

Under this policy of drifting the situation did change, but only for the worse. Dues-paying membership declined from the 500,000 of the war years to scarcely 100,000. A great many unemployed or fictitious members, none of whom paid dues, were carried on the books. The non-union fields, organized briefly in 1922, returned to their former condition. Maryland, West Virginia, Tennessee, Alabama, and other fields became solidly non-union again. Most of these losses were traceable to Lewis's weakness in the 1922 settlement. It would be absurd to expect the non-union fields to respond to an organizing drive so soon after the sad experience of that year, unless some dramatic new factor could be introduced to kindle new hope. And that factor was not easy to find.

Lewis boasted to the 1924 international convention of the great victory the union had won in 1922, by defeating the operators' campaign for wage cuts. The volume of business was increasing, he said, and we could face the future with confidence. He went through the ritualized recitation of the ills of the industry: too many mines, too many miners, too many operators, excessive capital investment (real and watered), excessive management costs, too much speculation, too violent ups and downs in output and prices, and all the rest. What the industry needed, he said, was a prolonged breathing spell, free from "labor unrest," during which it could readjust to present-day conditions. The union should help the industry straighten itself out by accepting a long-term agreement, perhaps for four years. He ignored the non-union fields, which meant that half or more of the coal production of the country was left out of his plan.

The scale committee accepted Lewis's recommendation that an agreement be offered in the Central Competitive Field to maintain existing wages for four years. If this offer proved unacceptable, nobody knew what could be done. We could not repeat our 1922 struggle; nobody even suggested such a thing. For a time, at least, the stronger districts might save what they could; the rest would have to take what they got. Lewis gave a cold reception to demands from a few Illinois delegates for an effort to get the thirty-hour week and thus spread the work, and quietly ignored all proposals for a program of social planning for the industry. The delegates realized that there was no vigor left in the organization, that the most the leadership hoped for was to hang on in the union strongholds.

Lewis, during this period, was cultivating Herbert Hoover, Secretary of Commerce, whom he referred to as "an eminent mining engineer." Hoover had called the coal industry "one of the worst functioning industries in the United States," advocating a voluntary reorganization, with a long-term wage contract the first step in such a program. He found his man in John L. Lewis, whose economic and political thinking was, if anything, to the right of Hoover's.

The United States Coal Commission produced, at a cost of $600,000, a report which was timid, platitudinous, and empty. Its one sound proposal was to create a body which would collect and make available reliable information on the industry and its workings. Lewis denounced the extravagance of the Commission, but apparently agreed with it that nothing could be done—nature must take its course, no matter who suffered.

The national policy committee met in Jacksonville, Florida, in February, 1924. The national officers and representatives of the Central Competitive Field districts negotiated a contract, continuing the wage scales of the previous agreement until April 1, 1927—three, not four years. Lewis had the help of Hoover, behind the scenes, in influencing certain financial interests to accept the idea of a breathing spell. It was good to hold the wage line and prevent cuts, but it was stupid to pretend that no more than that was necessary. The union was too weak to get higher wages, but not too weak to mount a campaign for effective reorganization of the industry.

I returned from Jacksonville, to negotiate our district agreement, with grave doubts as to how much it would be worth. I heard that members of the scale committee returning from Jacksonville made the train rock with their chanting of: "We got a three-year contract—next time we'll make it five." I wish their glee had been justified.

At our district negotiations, in Altoona, B. M. Clark, president of the operators' association, argued that wages could not be maintained against intensified competition from the non-union fields, so the contract would not work. I pointed out that wage cuts would not help either. We signed up, finally, for the terms of the Jacksonville agreement, but as we left the meeting, Clark said to me, "Well, John, you've got your contract, but I don't think it will do you any good."

"What do you mean?" I asked.

"There's no market."

"I know," I said; "we went over that."

"It'll mean shutdowns, miners driven out of their jobs, and the operators' investments lost."

"That would happen, even with wage cuts, as long as the southern fields are unorganized. And only the union can change that."

He made it clear, without actually saying so, that the operators themselves were against the agreement and had been pushed into it by pressure from financial interests and some political figures. This was no basis for a union contract, and we soon saw the consequences of such a maneuver. The contract was hardly signed before the operators began their attack on it. For the first year, they confined themselves to propaganda for wage cuts, circulated through their Chambers of Commerce, service clubs, trade associations, and the press, to the effect that the "high" wages of the workers made it impossible to compete with non-union coal, therefore unemployment was the unemployed's fault. No mention was made, of course, of unemployment in non-union areas.

Before long, operators began to break the contract by cutting wages. The worst case in my district was that of the Buffalo, Rochester, and Pittsburgh Coal Company. B. M. Clark, head of the operators' association, was also president of this concern. The company leased certain of its mines to dummy operators, who introduced wage cuts averaging 30 per cent. This was a legal, but dishonest, way of abrogating the contract with the union. This company paid a dividend of 103 per cent in January of 1923.

Dozens of other concerns jumped their contracts, in our district as in all the others. We protested, of course, but there was not much else we could do. If we tried to strike, the operators simply shut down. The difference between part-time operation and none was not enough to bother them. In September, 1925, I sent Lewis, at his request, a complete list of contract violations, by companies. The list included about one hundred mines. Many of these had closed even after the wage cuts; the strong medicine advocated by the bosses had not saved them. Yet the pressure for wage cuts continued. Instead of the three years of peace promised by Lewis, we were subjected to three years of guerrilla warfare, and the union was bleeding from a thousand wounds.

Lewis said he wanted information on contract violations "to transmit to the federal authorities who are now giving the matter every consideration. I am making every possible effort to secure some action by the government designed to change this situation." Nothing came of his efforts. The free enterprise system was not working for Lewis, Hoover, or the miners.

On one occasion I went to see him, bringing a report of contract violations. He said he would try to get government pressure on the violators, and in the meantime we had to tighten our belts and wait for better days. When I said this was not enough, he turned on me with a growl, and asked, "What's your answer?"

I said, "We ought to use this chance to demand unification of the industry, or at least some effective government regulation."

"John, you know there is no chance," he replied, "of getting Congress to regulate coal, as things stand now."

"That may be true," I said, "but that doesn't absolve us from the duty to agitate. If they don't accept our method, which is nationalization, let them propose something else. But we have to demand. Strikes don't work any more. Mining is a hopeless occupation, and it is the best men who are leaving the mines for other jobs. Pretty soon the union will be too weak to raise its voice. We can't just wait."

Lewis dismissed this with a grunt. He couldn't attack the record of my district, which had been one of the first hit by contract violations, and had fought as hard as anyone against them. In spite of all we could do, the district membership dwindled to almost a third of what it had been. I was not content, like Lewis, to try to hold a hopelessly broken line and wait for better days. I kept up a persistent campaign for my program: nationalization, organizing the unorganized, a labor party, democracy in the union, labor education.

At every point, this program ran counter to Lewis's ideas. In 1924, for example, I was an elector in Pennsylvania for the La Follette-Wheeler ticket, while Lewis, out of gratitude to his good friend Hoover, supported Coolidge. I had attended a Farmer-Labor Party convention in Chicago in 1923, but soon recognized that the Communists had control, and joined with John Fitzpatrick of the Chicago Federation of Labor in walking out. When the Conference for Progressive Political Action, with strong labor support, launched the La Follette movement, I had great hopes for it. We got nearly five million votes, which I thought was good, but many labor men had expected miracles and were disappointed, so the movement petered out.

I welcomed every opportunity to advocate nationalization, though I now had to do it as an individual. Albert Coyle, editor of the Locomotive Engineers' *Journal*, published an article of mine in his paper, and from time to time I wrote for the Socialist *New Leader* and the *New Republic*. Oscar Ameringer, editor of the *Illinois Miner*, was hospitable to my contributions, and items appeared in other labor papers from time to time. The trouble was that I did not occupy a public position of great visibility from which to address the people generally, and the rank and file, even the limited number I could reach, were too demoralized by worry about making a living to enlist in the struggle against the UMW leadership for a long-term program.

My problem, throughout the years of my conflict with Lewis, was that I was the only person prominent in the Miners' Union who was both more interested in policy than in personal conflicts, and uncommitted to one of the radical parties. The Illinois people—Farrington and his group—and men like Alex Howat, of the Kansas district, were anti-Lewis for purely local or personal reasons. They would listen to my talk about a program and agree, for lack of any ideas of their own, but it was hatred of Lewis, not program, which moved them to fight him. The Communists worked hard, but for their own purposes, and could not be trusted from one day to the next. Besides, I had no use for their program, any more than they had for mine. They would "support" me, to injure Lewis, and to get a chance to talk to miners who would otherwise ignore them, but they would cut my throat on a moment's notice if the "line" called for it.

My conviction that growth and development of the labor movement, not just the miners but all labor, required a continuous program of education led to my connection with the Workers' Education Bureau and Brookwood Labor College. Both of these came out of a conference at the New School for Social Research in New York, March 31–April 2, 1921. I attended in response to an invitation from Jim Maurer, and found myself scheduled to make a speech on the last day. I talked about the "Miners' Program," our district educational program, and the need for classes, pamphlets on many subjects, and other educational work. We set up an executive committee of the Workers' Education Bureau, of which I was a member. Maurer was chairman, and others were Fannia Cohn, of the Ladies' Garment Workers, J. B. S. Hardman, of the Amalgamated Clothing Workers, several liberal intellectuals, and some others connected with labor schools or local labor bodies. Spencer Miller, who had some background in labor education and didn't require a salary, was the first director of the Bureau.

At first, the AFL was skeptical. The old-line leaders were suspicious of intellectuals and not much interested in adult education, which seemed to them a frill. There was not much money coming in, and Maurer and I and some others went to Washington to talk to Gompers about support from the AFL. We found it surprisingly easy to talk to Gompers, who agreed to endorse the WEB, to urge affiliated unions to support it, and to name people to represent the AFL on the committee. One of those he named was Matthew Woll, a very stiff person with very little understanding of social problems, reluctant to do anything that hadn't been AFL policy since the first convention of the Federation in 1881.

Brookwood Labor College was a different enterprise, though it developed out of the same 1921 conference. The Workers' Education Bureau was soon controlled by the AFL, and followed AFL policies closely at all times. Pretty much the same people were involved in starting Brookwood, but the AFL left it strictly alone, so that the more radical elements in the labor movement had a larger role in Brookwood. William Fincke gave a parcel of land and a building in Katonah, New York, as a campus for the new college. The Garland Fund supplied money to start operations, and supplementary gifts annually for a number of years. Union support usually took the form of scholarships for young unionists. District 2 was one of a dozen or more unions, mostly in the garment trades, which sent students to Brookwood.

We had set aside a fund of $15,000 in 1922, for support of workers' education. Some money from this fund was used to send students to Brookwood. Of the first two we sent, one was not a success, but the other, Mike Demchak, of Osceola Mills, Pennsylvania, was an active and devoted member of the union. I continued to serve on the Labor Cooperating Committee of Brookwood until shortly before the college's dissolution in the thirties.

We maintained an educational department in District 2, directed by Paul Fuller, and using the services of many members of the staff for classes in labor history, public speaking, parliamentary law, and similar subjects. The most popular classes studied the economics of the coal industry, combining lectures and discussion groups to give the miners an understanding of the disorderly industry in which they worked and of the need for a long-range program to cure its ills.

Out of these classes grew the idea of labor Chautauquas. We would select one of the larger mining towns, and with the help of local unions in the area would plan a week-long program of entertainment and discussion of public issues. Local people with musical or other talents contributed the entertainment. District officers gave lectures, and we tried to have at least one speaker from the outside in each program. People like Harry Laidler of the League for Industrial Democracy and Clinton Golden of Brookwood generously came into the district for no more than expenses. The programs were helpful in supporting the workers' morale and in contributing to their understanding of the problems we were all facing. For two years, Fuller, a young minister with liberal views, kept up a busy schedule of educational work on a slim budget.

By the beginning of 1926, there was little room for argument that the policy behind the Jacksonville agreement had been a disastrous failure. Unemployment and short time were still chronic, even though tens of thousands of men had left the mines for jobs in other industries. The decline in union membership continued, and the men lost were too often the best and most vigorous individuals, who refused to sit around and rot while the "law of supply and demand" worked its ruthless way with them. Without the anthracite membership, which, while also declining, was more stable than that in bituminous districts, the union would have been dead. The international organizers ceased to function as anything more than an internal political machine. Most of them never pretended to "organize" anything but the union miners—for the benefit of John L. Lewis. Lewis had relied on his skills as a conniver with politicians and operators to hold the union line. Whatever this policy achieved for him, it did not protect the miners. The swing of the economic pendulum, which he relied on so heavily in his book, published during these years,* did not occur. Instead, things got worse as demand for coal declined still further, and the irrationality of the industry grew worse. Miners and many smaller operators were squeezed out, as he had hoped, at a terrible cost in human suffering, but the result was not order, but chaos.

In order to hold his power against the discontent of the miners, Lewis became increasingly ruthless in crushing union democracy. "Provisionalism" became the rule. Lewis had the power to impose a "provisional" government on any district, if it got into financial trouble, or if its leadership was troublesome to him. Provisional administrations became permanent, so that Lewis could use them to dominate the international board and perpetuate himself in power. Fortunately, District 2 was one of the best managed and most solvent in the union, so he could not use that particular weapon against me.

Slowly but inexorably, I was driven to the conclusion that Lewis's power had to be challenged by a candidate for the presidency of the UMW who would offer a constructive program for rebuilding the union. Lewis's opposition in the past had arisen out of personal ambitions. Some individuals, like Thomas Kennedy, were reconciled to Lewis and integrated into his machine. Some (like Farrington of Illinois in 1926) were crushed and driven out. Some (like Fishwick of Illinois and Howat) held onto district strongholds for a while and conducted guerrilla warfare against Lewis. I hoped that I might be able to unite the pockets of anti-Lewisism-for-its-own-sake and add to them enough votes from miners interested in a constructive program to upset his machine. It was a slim gamble, I knew, because the Lewis machine had demonstrated more than once its skill in winning elections by shady methods, but at least my campaign would have educational value, by dramatizing the issues. The strongest argument against my making the attempt was the fact that I was worn out by years of frustrating struggle, and that I would be subjecting myself to an even

---

* *The Miners' Fight for American Standards* (New York, 1925).

worse ordeal. I knew the methods of the Lewis gang. I would have to face storms of slander. I would have to pit my puny financial resources and my tenuous links with individuals here and there against the Lewis machine, with all the funds of the international union at its disposal, with political agents masquerading as organizers spotted in every center, and with its well-oiled machinery for producing votes even where no votes existed.

I talked to my associates in District 2 and wrote to people in other parts of the country, asking their views on my candidacy. The local leaders, with few exceptions, were dubious or unwilling to back me, though they gave me soft answers. Most of them finally decided that Lewis had the power and would not risk their positions by opposing him. Though I had strong rank-and-file support and could have been re-elected to the district presidency (and the faint hearts would have gone along with me on that), coming out and challenging Lewis was another matter, and they had no stomach for such a fight. Most of the assurances of support that I received from around the country came from rank-and-filers or local officials. I knew that Illinois would vote for me, as it always did for anyone opposing Lewis, and Alex Howat's small Kansas District would do the same. The insurgency that had appeared from time to time in the anthracite districts had been tamed, so I could expect little from there.

I put together a ticket for the three top offices. William Stevenson, of Bay City, Michigan, a national board member whom I had known during my stay there years before, ran for vice-president, and William J. Brennan, of Scranton, a former president of District 1, for secretary-treasurer. Neither was a "personality," able to deliver large blocks of votes, but both were able men and fully qualified.

In August, 1926, I announced my candidacy, pledging myself to organization of the unorganized fields, advocacy of nationalization of the mines, and support for a labor party. Local unions sent in enough nominations to ensure that my fellow candidates and I would appear on the ballot. I then issued an open letter to the membership, printed in a four-page leaflet under the caption, *Save the Union.* I pointed out that entire districts—West Virginia, Maryland, Tennessee, Alabama, Colorado—had been destroyed, and others were crumbling away because of the do-nothing policy of the international administration. Local and district strikes, effective twenty years before, were no longer effective, because of the increasing prevalence of large corporations controlling many mines in many districts. The cause of the union's decline was the shortsighted policy of allowing operators to sign up for part of their holdings. Our desertion of the non-union fields in 1922 had cost us 100,000 members, and more were being lost every year. The policy of trying only to hold onto what we already had meant that we would soon be unable to hold onto anything. Aggressive and active field organizers, armed with a hopeful and constructive program, could still bring the non-union fields into the union fold. Nothing could be done by a gang of political gumshoers, miscalled organizers, who sat around hotel lobbies waiting for something to happen.

I rejected flatly all proposals for wage reductions—this would change nothing in the industry, except to drive the miners' standard of living to even more intolerable levels. Wage cuts were taking place everywhere, however, and could not be stopped by futile proclamations about "no backward step." If we failed to push forward, we must inevitably fall back. Nationalization would give us a concrete and practical alternative to the anarchy and futility of private operation. It would be a threat we could use to get better government controls over wasteful practices, even before we could win our full program. A labor party was necessary to cut the union loose from dependence on reactionary politicians like Hoover and Coolidge, and to get justice for labor in the courts and legislatures.

Throughout the campaign, I stressed the necessity of restoring democracy to the union by the reinstatement of Alex Howat (who had been expelled by Lewis on flimsy charges), by the curbing of provisionalism, and by the conduct of honest elections. I disavowed any personal grudges, but asked only that there be a full and fair discussion of the real problems of the union.

I need hardly say that I got nothing of the sort out of Lewis. He made no effort to discuss my platform, or even to refute my charges as to his failure. I was charged with dualism, disruption, trafficking with outsiders of various kinds, from Communists to capitalists, and lots more. My effort to get the administration and membership to face the facts of the decline in union strength was pictured as undermining the union and an attempt to destroy morale. Lewis and company radiated optimism, while I was denounced as a "prophet of doom and gloom," if I may borrow that phrase from a later, but similar, situation.

I had two or three hundred dollars to spend on printing and postage, most of which went to mail out copies of my open letter. My campaign committee consisted, for the most part, of Powers Hapgood, Anita, and me, sitting around a table sending out the open letter. Copies were sent to all local unions, but since I did not know anybody in most of them, I had to send the material to the local secretaries, many of whom were Lewis men and who no doubt loyally consigned my letters to the wastebasket.

I had to keep my work as president of the district going, so, with that and the lack of money for train fare, I was unable to get around much to speak to local unions, though there were some, even outside the district, where I might have gotten a hearing. Powers and one or two others—Mike Demchak, for instance—did try visiting some places, but they had no great success and in some places were chased out of town by Lewis's goons. Howat and Frank Feeney, of West Virginia, stumped the anthracite region for our ticket.

I remember making one trip to Hazleton, Pennsylvania. It was a bitterly cold night, and the turnout, though friendly, was extremely small. I had no support from any major leaders in the anthracite region. Thomas Kennedy had made his peace with Lewis, and he had also affected a reconciliation between Lewis and Chris Golden.

There were people in some of the districts who believed in my program and did what they could to make it known. But there is no question that most of my support came from people who opposed Lewis for reasons of their own and found in my candidacy an opportunity to vent their hostility. These people ranged from conservatives to radicals, and from idealists to union politicians hardly preferable to Lewis. I did what I could to make it clear that I stood on my own platform and nobody else's, but I could not escape some identification with oppositionists with whom I had fundamental differences.

One of these was Frank Farrington, president of the Illinois District; my biggest bloc of votes came from that state. In September, Lewis made public a contract of employment which Farrington had secretly signed with the Peabody Coal Company, in July, while still president of the district. He was to be paid $25,000 a year for three years as a "labor consultant," which was five times his union salary. Nobody ever found out, so far as I know, how Lewis got his information, though there was speculation, even in the newspapers, that Peabody leaked it to him deliberately. This would make sense: the company could thereby drive Farrington out of the labor movement, while at the same time putting Lewis under obligation, for future purposes.

When the news broke, Farrington was in Europe as a fraternal delegate of the AFL to the British Trades Union Congress. His defense, when he returned, was that he had a right to change jobs when he felt like it. In his new job, he would support pay cuts to "set the industry on its feet." He was one of many who have shifted from the labor to the employer side, and an illustration of the corruption inherent in opportunism unfettered by principles. Although I had never been a friend of Farrington's, and had fought him more than once, his connection with District 12 was used to picture me as a friend of corruptionists and pay-cutters.

Another fake "issue" was created over a letter which Albert Coyle, editor of the Locomotive Engineers' *Journal,* was alleged to have sent to Powers Hapgood, about plans for a labor paper and about pushing my candidacy. This was used to insinuate that "outside influences," probably sinister, were backing me, though the letter, if it ever existed, never reached Powers, and neither he nor I knew anything about it until Lewis made it public.

Lewis outdid himself in a speech at the AFL convention in October, in which he charged that my campaign was part of a "Bolshevik plot" to take over American labor, and pictured himself as Horatius at the bridge, valiantly fighting off alien hordes. I denounced this display as a smokescreen, raised to hide Lewis's unwillingness to debate issues. Lewis's charge got more publicity than my answer; a sensational lie is better "news" than anything so humdrum as truth.[*]

In December, the tellers in the international office announced that Lewis had won, by a vote of about 170,000 to 60,000. Nobody was surprised by the outcome, but I was a little surprised that they had admitted to that large a vote for me.

The constitution provided that the tellers' report be published, with figures for each local union. At the international convention in February, 1927, I demanded that this be done, but it was May before I received the accounting. Reading the report, I could see the reason for the delay: it would take time to cook the figures that thoroughly. For example, in anthracite District 1, out of a reported membership of 9,262, 8,466 votes were counted for Lewis and 232 for me. District 7, also anthracite, gave Lewis 3,483 votes out of 3,704, and I got 9. More fantastic was the vote in District 20, Eastern Kentucky. The district paid per capita on one member for the first six months of 1926, and

---

[*] See *New York Times,* October 13, 1926, p. 1; October 16, 1926, p. 7.

on none at all for the last six months, during which the vote was taken. But sixteen locals, with an alleged membership of 2,686½, cast 2,686½ for Lewis and none for Brophy, indicating a membership not only of impressive unanimity, but also of such good health and intensity of interest that not one man failed to come out to cast his ballot.

I was able to check the actual vote sent in to the national office from five locals in District 5 and compare it with the national report. The actual vote was: Lewis, 487, Brophy, 635. The reported vote was: Lewis, 1,473; Brophy, 158. Thus in only five locals, Lewis was given 986 stolen votes and I was robbed of 477. I secured affidavits from officers of these locals, but evidence had no effect on the international board, which rubber-stamped the report of Lewis's tellers.

Nobody can ever prove who won the election of 1926, because the evidence can never be secured. Those reports that were not falsified in the locals were taken care of by agents of the international office. But the vote-stealing is so obvious and flagrant in the official report itself that the inference that Lewis would not have won without stealing votes is a defensible one.

I took the position that my running mates and I had been elected, and sent a letter to the international board, pointing out the prima facie evidence of fraud in the report and demanding an impartial investigation. The board refused to act; for them the election was over. I sent copies of my letter out to the local unions, but very few of them had energy or interest enough to back up my appeal. There was no Honest Ballot Association, or anything of the sort that could have been called in. And it was contrary to union custom to take such a matter into the courts, which I could not have afforded to do anyway.

My protest got publicity in some of the radical and labor papers not under Lewis's spell, such as the *Illinois Miner* and some members of Federated Press. A few newspapers in coal towns printed something about the matter, but it was no time for "rocking the boat." Lewis had built up a reputation as a "conservative labor statesman," and, if anything, the general press gave him the benefit of the doubt.

All I could do was to try to keep alive the "Save the Union" program, even though I now held no official post in the union, and was soon to lose even my membership, as Lewis moved to eliminate me altogether.

!!!

16

MAKING A LIVING AND

MAINTAINING A PROGRAM

Loss of the election meant that I was out of a job. District and national elections were held at the same time, and under the constitution no man could run for two jobs. James Mark succeeded me as district president. He and most of the district officers had decided that there was a better future for them in playing ball with Lewis than in loyalty to me or my ideas, so there was no chance of my getting a job with the union. Mark and his friends preferred to get me out of the district. I was a threat to their positions as long as I was around.

I thought of returning to the mines, but not for long. Unemployment was universal; even where a job existed, my name and reputation were such that any boss would put me at the top of his list of undesirables. I had experience only as a miner and as a union official. Neither experience was marketable in any other line. Thus, at forty-three, I was out of work with no prospects, and a wife and two small children dependent on me.

We had some money in the bank, but that would not last long. The first thing was to cut expenses, by moving to Pittsburgh. My wife's family had a large house, with space for us in addition to a variety of Ansteads. Besides a married sister and her grown son, there were two

219

single sisters and Anita's mother, to whom we added our four. Mary Anstead, Anita's sister, was tired of their old house, though it was a good one of its kind. She wanted something more modern and decided to build a new place for us all, on the assumption that we could get along well together.

Mary still had her stenographic and mimeographing shop, in which Anita worked. Anita's pay was our most reliable income in Pittsburgh. Powers Hapgood suggested that I go to Indianapolis and take a job in the Hapgood family business, the Columbia Conserve Company, but we felt some obligation to stand by Mary and at first turned the proposal down. I worked for a while as a laborer on a new building that was being erected. And when Anita's brother opened a real estate office in 1928, I tried working for him as a salesman. I sold one house and rented one, which, while pretty good for unskilled help, hardly marked me as a hot-shot salesman. By the end of 1929, after the stock market crash, the business was in trouble. Powers renewed his suggestion that we go to Indianapolis. By then we felt that we were more of a burden than a help to Mary, so we made the move in November, 1929.

I had not lost my interest in the labor movement, and did all I could to keep in touch and to contribute to the labor cause. During the summer of 1927, Jim Maurer suggested that I join with him and some other labor men in a trip to Russia. A delegation of British trade unionists had visited Russia previously, and the chairman of the Trades Union Congress, A. A. Purcell, during a visit to America as a fraternal delegate to the AFL convention, urged that Americans also try to establish friendly relations with the Soviet unions. Money was raised, largely from the Garland Fund, to pay expenses of the trip, and we were guests of the Soviet unions while in Russia. Certain of the delegates were able to pay part or all of their own expenses.

Naturally, I was interested. Nobody in this country knew much about Russia in 1927, much less about the Soviet unions. If we could find some basis for understanding between Anglo-American and Russian labor, we might make a contribution to peace. The example of the British delegation gave us hope of accomplishing something. Our group included, besides Maurer and me, Frank L. Palmer of the Typographical Union of Denver, Colorado; James W. Fitzpatrick, president of the Actors' Union; and Albert F. Coyle, editor of the Brotherhood of

Locomotive Engineers' *Journal*. We were accompanied by a technical and advisory staff. The AFL refused us its official blessing.

In Paris, the British delegation to the International Federation of Trade Unions, which had just concluded a meeting when we arrived, gave a dinner in our honor, at which we met people from many lands. We visited labor centers in Britain, France, Belgium, Holland, Germany, and Poland on the way to Russia, finding some people, especially Leon Jouhaux of France, less convinced than the British of the value of our enterprise. From the Russian border to Moscow, there were welcoming delegations at various towns. In Moscow, we were housed in the Grand Hotel, which had been grand indeed in pre-revolutionary days, but was badly deteriorated by the time we got there.

Our contacts with Russian labor left some puzzling impressions—puzzling to both sides, I'm sure. For example, at a convention of workers on river and inland lake boats, Silas Axtell, an attorney for the AFL Seamen's Union, gave a speech about the Seamen's Act; I doubt that anyone in his Russian audience had enough knowledge of American conditions to get much out of his talk.

Everywhere, we were questioned about the Sacco-Vanzetti case; it was impossible to clear up that question, even if we had known the right answers. Sacco and Vanzetti were executed while we were there. For three or four days all the towns we visited were hung with mourning for the victims of "American capitalism."

Toward the end of our visit, we split up for visits to different places. Jim Maurer, Paul Douglas (a University of Chicago economist, now U.S. Senator from Illinois), and I went to the Ukraine, to visit steel mills and other factories. In Kharkov, we spent an evening with some American engineers whose company had a contract to modernize coal mines in the Don basin. We went down into some of the mines, old diggings predating the Revolution, in which machinery was being installed and new workings opened up. The mining towns were raw and depressing, like mining towns anywhere, but there was a boom spirit prevailing, which we could sense. The miners we interviewed through interpreters said working conditions were very good, but what I could see gave me grounds for some doubt. This was just before the first five-year plan, which might explain the backwardness of the mining development. Douglas and I went on to visit a farm machinery plant and some agricultural collectives and co-operatives. Paul was deeply interested in these things, and wore out the interpreters and managers with persistent and searching questioning. The landscape and the soil of the Ukraine reminded me of the prairies of our Midwest, though even I, with my vast ignorance of farming, could see that the farms were neither as well cultivated nor as prosperous as their American counterparts.

The entire delegation had interviews with Trotsky, Stalin, Tchicherin, the Commissar for Foreign Affairs, and others. Tchicherin explained Soviet repudiation of the Czarist debt, then still a sore point in international relations, and told us the Soviet Union wanted peace while it was engaged in the great work of building up its economy. We assured him, with good conscience, that the Americans were for peace too. This conversation was entirely in English.

Trotsky had just been demoted to the post of Commissar of Foreign Concessions. He used the interview to present his position in his dispute with Stalin, addressing us in Russian through an interpreter, though he appeared to understand English when we asked questions. Perhaps because Trotsky's session with us was reported in the newspapers, Stalin agreed to meet us toward the end of our stay. There was a great contrast between the two men. Trotsky was an intellectual, who lectured us with great vigor and assurance, speaking rapidly and with complete control of his knowledge of Communist theory. We submitted a series of questions to Stalin in advance, each of which led to a lengthy speech, delivered in a heavy, dogmatic fashion. He asked us some questions about American labor, through his interpreter, which were so phrased as to suggest that American labor was very backward and should learn from the Russians. He was not looking for enlightenment; he knew the right answers, to his way of thinking, no matter what we said. Afterward we realized that in his speeches he was talking over our heads to the newspapers, in answer to Trotsky. Unlike Trotsky, he met us in a military uniform, and maintained a formal atmosphere, though we were served tea and cookies during the long interview.

One or two people in our own group understood Russian, so we could check on the interpreters. Most of the people we talked to knew very little about the Western world, and not much more about their own country outside their neighborhood.

On our return, we published a pamphlet as a report,* though we all felt there was much more we would like to know. It seemed to us that

---

* *Russia After Ten Years* (New York: International Publishers, 1927).

Russia was developing rapidly, and could be expected to become a major industrial power. We found no evidence that unions functioned freely, like those we belonged to, but the Russians all insisted that there was no possibility of conflict between the unions and the "workers' government." Our one concrete recommendation was that the United States recognize the Soviet Union, because the Soviet government was firmly established and therefore had the right to expect that we would deal with it, according to international law. Our conclusions were by no means world-shaking, and I had to reassess some impressions in the light of later events.

During our first two winters in Pittsburgh, I was able to make use of my knowledge of unionism in running a little labor school. Three professors at the University of Pittsburgh participated in this work: Colston Warne, now at Amherst; William L. Nunn, now at the University of Minnesota; and W. E. Chalmers, now at the University of Illinois. These three men were shocked by violations of civil liberties during the 1928 coal strike in the Pittsburgh district, and worked hard, through the American Civil Liberties Union, in defense of the miners. This activity got them into conflict with the chancellor of the university so intense that they left for better jobs elsewhere and the University of Pittsburgh was left with a black mark it took years to overcome.

Warne negotiated the free use of some rooms in the North Continuation School at Eighth Street and Duquesne Way. We got endorsements from the Central Labor Union and the Workers' Education Bureau. Some prominent men, including Father James Cox, pastor of St. Patrick's Church, Dr. William Davidson, superintendent of the Pittsburgh public schools, Bishop Francis J. McConnell, of the Methodist Episcopal Church, and Dr. Percy Kammerer, rector of Trinity Church, also endorsed the school. We offered courses in public speaking, economics, current events, and labor problems. The three professors and I were the principal instructors, though we drew in other men from the university at times. Classes, recruited from the local unions, numbered about twenty people, on the average. Some unions were well represented, others were indifferent. As I recall, there were a number of men from the Flint Glass Workers, a few railroad workers, and odds and ends from other groups. The miners were not represented; there were no mines in Pittsburgh itself. The Garland Fund supplied a small sum to enable me to act as secretary of the school. After I left Pittsburgh, the school died. I derived a great deal of satisfaction from this work, though it was no substitute for a job.

When we finally gave up the struggle to make a living in Pittsburgh and moved to Indianapolis, we spent about six weeks settling in, while I worked in the plant getting acquainted with the business and the unusual setup of its management.

The Columbia Conserve Company manufactured canned soups and other food products which it sold to jobbers and wholesalers under their labels, putting out very little under its own label. The concern had been a family enterprise of the Hapgoods, but they had turned over a large share of ownership and control to the workers in the plant. It was not a complete co-operative, but there was a great deal of sharing between the workers and the Hapgoods. William Hapgood, Powers' father, was the head of the concern. He knew more about the business than anyone else, and ordinarily the Council, made up of all the workers, went along with his policies, largely because he was usually right, but also because he was who he was and they knew he really believed in the idea.

I went out as a salesman, traveling through the Midwest and East, from New England to Missouri, and from Minnesota to southern Illinois. I went by train to the towns where I met jobbers, and then their salesmen took me around to stores where I made my sales talk for our products. Selling was not much fun for me, except when I got a chance to talk about the company's social experiment. Then I put real enthusiasm into my talk, and I found that often helped surprisingly to make a good sale. I was helped by genuine confidence in the quality of the goods I was selling. The drawback of the job was that I was away from home for long stretches of time. I would divert myself by investigating the town I was in, learning all I could about it. I would talk with other salesmen who, like me, had time on their hands and no desire to spend it in their hotel rooms. Anita got long letters from me regularly; it did me good to tell her all about the experiences of the day. In the coal-mining regions, I had a special interest in talking to miners and finding out what was going on in their minds. On weekends, the salesmen for Columbia would rendezvous somewhere, to swap experiences and talk over news from Indianapolis.

As the depression went on, the company began to feel the pressure. We were all paid pretty good salaries (mine was $37 a week) for the canning industry, which was not then well paid, and still is not. Everybody was on a regular salary; we had the guaranteed annual wage long before the idea was taken up by CIO. And there were what would now be called fringe benefits. Everybody owned a few shares of stock and we had a good medical care program and other things of that sort. By the end of my first year, as the depression deepened, William Hapgood began arguing that the company could survive only by cutting wages. He was right that expenses had to be trimmed, but a few of us—mostly salesmen—began asking questions at Council meetings about other ways of saving, such as reducing administrative expenses, and before long there was a real fight going on. Unhappily, Bill Hapgood took our questions as evidence of doubts about him, which was not the case, and became very angry about the controversy. With my long experience at speech-making, I soon found myself occupying center stage, whether I wanted it or not. Bill Hapgood decided that I was a troublemaker, though I thought I was simply following out the principle on which the co-operative experiment was based—the right of the workers to know what was going on and to decide for themselves whether it was good or bad. Finally, he insisted that either I had to go or he would quit. He put the demand that I be fired before the Council, which had to act on my discharge. The Council didn't want to discharge me, but neither did they want to repudiate Hapgood. There were meetings at which some of the women were reduced to tears. Poor Powers was terribly torn, having to choose between his friend and his father, and able to see some right on both sides. I soon realized that my presence was complicating the situation unbearably. Hapgood could not be expected to back down, and I could not keep quiet, in good conscience. And if dissension continued, the whole enterprise might be endangered, including the little jobs these people had to protect themselves against the depression. So I resigned, and decided to return to Pittsburgh.

During all these years, I tried to keep up my ties to the United Mine Workers. It was not easy to do, because I had not only lost my union job, but even my membership. This can best be explained by going back to the beginning of 1927.

I was elected a delegate to the 1927 international convention by my old local in Nanty Glo. At the convention, I tried to make my protest about the national election, and to push for my program. At first, Lewis intended to keep me from getting the floor, but there was so much protest from some of the delegates that he finally conceded me some time. His people kept the convention in an uproar while I was speaking, which Lewis made no effort to quell. I demanded publication of the tellers' report on the election. Lewis interrupted to ask which election I meant. I told him the last two, neither of which had been published up to that point. He made no comment.

Even without the published results, I could point out that the number of votes reported far exceeded the usual proportion cast, and probably exceeded the true paid-up membership of the union. There had to be a large proportion of phantom votes, and even of phantom districts, existing only in books kept especially for the purpose by some of Lewis's henchmen. Some idea of the atmosphere in which I was making my plea can be gotten from the fact that Powers Hapgood was set upon on the convention floor, and later brutally beaten in his hotel room by administration strong-arm men.

I've been asked, recently, why I was never beaten up, in spite of all the tough situations I've been through. My answer was that whenever I saw that violence was imminent, I "wrapped myself in the cloak of my innocence and quietly walked away." The answer was as good as any; I have always avoided the scene and occasion of violence. Powers ran into trouble a couple of times by trying to argue with Lewis men in barrooms; I kept out of such places because I've never had much interest in drinking and because brawls were too likely to occur. Beyond that kind of caution, I guess the explanation may be just good luck.

In my district, the situation was not much better. My term of office expired on the last day of March, 1927. A convention was scheduled before that date, at which I would present my final report. Lewis advised the district board that the convention should be postponed, because there were delays in getting the Central Competitive Field contract negotiated, and he might have to call the international Policy Committee together to pass on it. Then a meeting of the Policy Committee was held, and the way was clear to call the convention. Even so, the board delayed until protests began to come in from local unions, with threats to force a convention by action of the locals, which was constitutionally possible. The convention was finally called for May 3, 1927, by which time I was out of office and no longer entitled to preside. I began to think I would be shut out altogether, so I wrote up my report and had it printed in pamphlet form and sent around to the locals. A local union elected me its delegate and I went to Du Bois, prepared to do battle.

The first move of the new officers was to disqualify me as a delegate, on the grounds that I had moved out of the district. The vote on seating me had to be taken several times, but was finally declared to be 53 for and 58 against. James Mark conceded me the right to speak on my report when that was presented, but my not being a delegate deprived me of the right to speak on other matters.

In my report, I showed that District 2 had fought as hard as any, and harder than most, to maintain the Jacksonville agreement against the attacks of the operators and the disintegration of the industry. We had sent the international nearly $550,000 in tax and assessments during the past three years, in return for which we had received a donation of $7,000 for the victims of two mine explosions and a $20,000 loan. By reason of shut-down mines and the movement of men out of the industry, our membership had declined to scarcely more than a third of what it had been, a decline comparable to that in the strongest districts and in the national union. Lewis's pretense that the union was in good condition was built on the assumption that exonerated (unemployed) members counted for as much as dues-paying employed members. Many districts had hardly a dues-paying member left, but existed only on paper. These were just the shadows of unions, and would continue to be until we developed a policy to revive the organization by giving it a live purpose. I cited figures reported by the international secretary-treasurer on dues-paying membership. District 2 had, from 1923 to 1926, declined from 39,933 to 17,042; District 5 from 39,025 to 18,780; District 6 from 40,967 to 20,926; the West Virginia districts from 24,655 to 1,311; and District 21 from 6,187 to 1,307. These were larger districts; some of the smaller ones had practically disappeared.

I reviewed the fiasco of 1922 and showed how the divisive policy adopted then had cut away centers of union strength and would continue to do so, and concluded with an appeal for adoption of my program.

After my report, the convention voted to invite Lewis to attend the convention "to explain certain statements against the National Administration contained in John Brophy's report." Lewis was unable to attend, but sent Phil Murray to represent him.

Murray followed the administration line, though he took the tone of speaking more in sorrow than in anger to his "old friend, John Brophy." He called the membership figures I had cited lies, and said whoever had given me the figures was a "darned, dirty liar." District 5 (his old district) he said had 45,000 members, even if not one man in it was working. He had been in some of the other districts mentioned, which I had not been, and their membership was larger than ever before. This was no time to "sit around in a condition of abject laziness and criticize the policies of those who are working and fighting." He praised the international for winning higher wages for the miners, and predicted that the current strike in the Pittsburgh area would be won (it was lost). He called my speech "untimely," "divisive," and a "mire of pessimism." He called on the members to unite solidly behind Lewis, "a man whom I love, and a man whom countless thousands of miners and their wives and children love, respect, and admire." The combination of Pollyanna optimism and a call to arms against the employers was a hard one to penetrate, but I made the effort, though it took me from the fourth of May to the ninth to get the floor, by which time Murray had left.

I pointed out that the "darn, dirty liar" referred to by Murray was none other than the international secretary-treasurer of the United Mine Workers, in his report to the members, available to anybody who wanted it. And I pointed out that Murray had glossed over the problems of the union, instead of trying to discuss them fully and frankly. The dispute was not created by my feelings against Lewis or Murray or anyone else, but by hard facts. We were up against problems which would not be solved by unity in the pretense that they did not exist. President James Mark then congratulated himself for having given me the floor and made a speech to the effect that there was nothing to be gained by rehashing the past, that we must turn our attention to the future. "This is a business organization and we must confine ourselves to the things we can do. Theories are good at times but generally they are way ahead of the times. . . ." *

I returned to Pittsburgh to do what I could to keep my program alive. I was invited to speak to meetings sponsored by local unions in Pennsylvania, Ohio, and Illinois, invitations I accepted whenever possible. In spite of efforts of the Lewis supporters to prevent or to break

* *Minutes of the Proceedings of Thirtieth Consecutive and Seventh Biennial Convention of the UMWA, District 2. 1927.* 2 Vols. Murray's speech, I: 71–88; my reply, II: 281–301.

up such meetings, they were well attended and gave me a friendly
hearing.

Much has been made, by my friends and my foes alike, of the "Save
the Union Committee." The name was taken from the headline on my
1926 pamphlet. But the Save the Union Committee was not an organization. It never held a convention. I was called the chairman because
I was the most prominent spokesman for the platform, which was,
after all, my platform. I had neither the time, the money, nor the energy to create the kind of political machine, or dual union, I was
charged with creating. There was nothing to prevent anybody from
printing a paper, or making a statement, or holding a meeting, in the
name of the Committee. The Communists saw in this situation their
opportunity, and worked hard to identify themselves with the name. I
would guess that much, if not most, of the public outcry in the name
of the Committee was the work of the little, but incredibly hard working, faction of Communists who were trying to build themselves a base
in the miners' union. This judgment is based on hindsight; I had very
little experience with Communists at that time. There were none, to my
knowledge, in District 2. I knew that my friend Maurer detested them,
but not much else. I had had dealings with Socialists, but Socialists did
not conceal their identity or their purposes. And, more important, men
like Jim Maurer were immovable in their devotion to democracy, while
the Communists would accept anything they could use for their purposes.

The only meeting I addressed during this period that was broken up
was in Renton, a little town near Pittsburgh. The meeting was held in
the headquarters of the local union, and was well attended. I spoke for
some time, and was followed by Pat Toohy, who had also been invited
by the local. He was organizer of the Pittsburgh section of the Communist Party, and he departed quickly from the concerns of the miners
to talk about other things the party line required. He got as far as a
demand that the Marines "get the hell out of Nicaragua," when he was
interrupted by a corporal of the State Police, who pushed his way to
the platform, and tried to knock Toohy down. The policeman was a
former Marine, who objected to what he considered a slur on the
sacred Corps. Toohy and I were arrested on the charge of rioting and
inciting to riot. The Civil Liberties Union sent Clarence Darrow and
Arthur Garfield Hayes to defend us. Perhaps impressed by the size of
the uproar created, the prosecutor, when our case came to trial, moved

to dismiss the charges, admitting that the only rioting had been the work of the state policeman. Hayes announced that the Civil Liberties Union would file suit, in behalf of Toohy and me, for damages for false arrest and malicious prosecution, but nothing came of that. Hayes and Darrow were the stars of a meeting in YMHA hall, after the chancellor of the University of Pittsburgh had refused to allow them to speak on the campus. The whole case was such a mess that even the Pittsburgh newspapers condemned the arrests and the fact that the prosecutor had kept us under indictment for five months before discovering that there was no riot.

In September of 1928, the Communists gave up their effort to bore from within the miners' union and called a convention which formed the dual National Miners' Union. Even before then I had become disturbed by the way things were going and "resigned" my unofficial title of chairman of the Save the Union Committee in April, giving ill health as my reason, in order not to discourage the genuine advocates of a progressive program for the UMW. The ill health was genuine enough to justify the move anyway. I was worn out from overwork and worry.

Powers Hapgood and a few other non-Communists went to the NMU convention, but soon withdrew. I refused to have anything to do with it, on the ground that dual unionism played into the hands of the operators. The United Mine Workers was in the field already, and what organized miners there were belonged to it. Our duty was to build that union and to make it a better one, not to divide the workers.

I held to that position in spite of the fact that I had been expelled from the union by the international executive board, without notice and without trial, early in May, on the ground that the Save the Union Committee was a dual movement. My local in Nanty Glo was instructed by the district officers to kick me out. The local secretary sent me a copy of their letter and an invitation to appear before the local to answer the charges. I was unable to do so, but it would have made no difference if I had, because the local could not stand against the illegal assumption of power by the international. I wrote to the Nanty Glo local explaining that I was unwilling to expose them to Lewis's wrath, that he intended to stamp out every trace of independence in the organization and that I could only hope that a revival of the rank and file would some day change things for the better. It took courage for them even to invite me, under the circumstances, and I was touched by their loyalty.

The coal strike of 1928, centered in western Pennsylvania, dragged dismally to failure. In June, the executive board of the Illinois District asked the international Policy Committee for permission to negotiate the best contract it could get. The Policy Committee meeting was perfunctory; there were mild protests from here and there, but nobody had any better idea to propose, so permission was granted, not only to Illinois but to all districts, to negotiate contracts "mutually satisfactory." This was a euphemism for wage cuts. The end product of Lewis's booming talk about "no backward step" was the disintegration of the whole collective bargaining position of the miners, won by a generation of struggles. The shrunken Illinois and Indiana districts and a few small areas in the West were able to get contracts, on the operators' terms, but Ohio, Pennsylvania, and the southern districts could not secure even this much. There was no difference between the Farrington forces in Illinois and Lewis at this point; both were out to salvage what they could and let the rest go. The membership was demoralized, deserted by the union, subject to ever sharper attacks by the operators, and feeling that the coal-mining industry was on its last legs. They could hardly be blamed if they also decided that the best thing to do was to save themselves and forget about the union. Many men left for other jobs; the rest suffered through, hoping for something to turn up.

Even Lewis was moved by the course of events. His good friend, Herbert Hoover, was elected to the Presidency in 1928, and Lewis turned to the government in hope of getting some help. He asked that a joint conference of operators and miners be called by the government, but Hoover refused to act. Lewis began to give active support to the idea of federal legislation to control the industry, but even the feeble bills he could get his Republican friends to introduce into Congress were not passed. The Kelly-Davis Bill of 1930, for example, would help operators by setting minimum prices, but because it also had some clauses that might help workers organize and bargain collectively, the operators never let it get out of committee.

Lewis started a campaign to take over the Illinois District by a "provisional" government in 1929. The district balked him by securing an injunction forbidding him to interfere, but he was determined to wipe out this center of disaffection. I urged everyone to stand behind Illinois, in letters and articles in the *New Leader, New Republic,* and *Illinois Miner.* Then Lewis gave the Illinois people an opening by calling off the biennial convention of 1929 required by the constitution.

The Illinois people took the position that by this act he had terminated the union, because the constitution specified that it was in effect only until the date of the next regular convention. It was a fine legal point, but there was no doubt that Lewis had violated the constitution, which gave some reason to hope that a reorganization convention, held in Springfield, Illinois, on March 10, 1930, might win recognition as the legal union and end Lewis's dictatorship. I attended the convention, eager to help create a strong clean union of the miners.

My hopes did not last long. The credentials committee reported the name of Frank Farrington as a delegate from some local. I took the floor and insisted that he be barred from the convention. We could not possibly go before the miners carrying the burden of this discredited man. The District 12 leaders, who were his men, fought to keep Farrington. I had been told beforehand that he would not be there, and I was shocked at this duplicity. The vote was 225 for Farrington and 145 against. Since there were few delegates from outside Illinois, it was clear that the district leaders had put heavy pressure on their delegates in his behalf.

I announced that this was the end for me. I might not have much but my name to offer, but what I had I would give only if I could fight for the new union with a clear conscience. Accepting Farrington as an ally would foredoom us to failure among the miners, no matter what the courts decided. I was told that he would not hold any office—this was just a little gesture in view of his past services—but it seemed to me the wrong kind of gesture to make in the midst of a fight, and I pulled out.

The Springfield union was a failure. Alex Howat was president, and while he had his qualities, stability was not one of them. They had the Illinois District and its treasury, but little else. They made gestures toward organizing elsewhere, but nothing came of them. The AFL recognized the Lewis organization as the legitimate union. Lewis hastily called a convention in Indianapolis, to patch up the constitutional hole, and when the matter came into the courts, he was upheld. The Springfield union fell apart, some of Illinois drifted back to the Lewis union, and the remnant finally set up a dual union called the Progressive Miners of America, which had a disorderly and brief career.

In April, 1931, a "rank and file" convention to clean house and start over again was called to meet in St. Louis. I knew nothing about it until I received the convention call, signed with 180 names, among them mine. Nobody had consulted me about using my name, so I did not attend. This affair, unimportant in itself, illustrates the disorganized state of the anti-Lewis elements in the union. Anybody could call a meeting, or even a national convention, and lots of people did. It was usually hard to tell who was behind any particular move.

By then there was nothing left of the union but the feeble remnants in the United Mine Workers, and scattered independent locals, mostly in Illinois, living precariously on old grudges. Coal mining was practically an open-shop industry. Lewis could maintain himself and his shadow organization on the treasury accumulated through the years, but the industry was completely out of his hands.

||||||||||||||||||||||||||||||||||||||

17

RETURN TO THE

UNITED MINE WORKERS

The fortunes of the miners, like those of the country, were about as low as they could get by 1932. In January of that year, delegates to the UMW convention in Indianapolis listened to reports of disaster after disaster, all couched in language of the cheeriest optimism.

Insofar as problems were admitted, they were blamed on reactionary business interests. Lewis, long a devotee of laissez faire economics, was now demanding government action. His remedy was the Kelly-Davis Bill, for which he expressed great hope, now that the AFL had endorsed it.

Losses suffered by the union were glossed over, but could not be concealed. The anthracite districts, though weakened, were keeping the union alive. Bituminous membership was at its lowest since 1878, and most districts consisted only of a paper organization and a few unemployed members in scattered locals. Many had not even that, but only a few officials drawing salaries from what was left of the treasury. Wages were as low as $2.50 a day; contracts, where they existed, were unenforceable; mining towns were abodes of misery and despair.

Lewis's report denounced dual unionism, but made no reference to my "Save the Union" program, though he appropriated the phrase for his own policy. The Illinois rebels, in the Progressive Miners' Union, were worse off than the UMW, retaining only a few feeble locals in southern Illinois. The operators had achieved the goal they had so long desired, the smashing of the union. This had not improved anything, and they had no other ideas to offer beyond cut-throat competition as usual.

Like almost everybody else in the labor movement, I had no trouble in making up my mind about the election of 1932. Whatever might be said against Franklin Roosevelt and the Democrats was negligible compared to the inadequacies of the Hoover administration. Our judgment on Hoover may have been unduly harsh—I leave that debate to the historians—but it was inescapable. Lewis was one of the few who stood out against the tide and supported Hoover. The miners ignored his political advice, as they were to do later in an equally dramatic election, and supported Roosevelt. Why did Lewis take this stand? He had always been a Republican and always remained a Republican, even through his brief honeymoon with Roosevelt; he probably felt it was his duty to deliver votes to Hoover in order to get the Kelly-Davis Bill through Congress. I have no explanation of why a man ordinarily so shrewd in politics misjudged Hoover's chances so badly. But there are no sure things in politics; I remember that some people were actually concerned lest Landon be elected in 1936.

I had a special reason for feeling hopeful about Roosevelt, based on a personal impression of the man in my one previous contact with him.

Sometime in 1925 or 1926, I was invited to serve as chairman of a meeting of the Foreign Policy Association in New York. The Association had invited Lord Thompson, of the British Labor Party, to address a meeting at Cooper Union on the foreign policy of the Labor government. He was a general who had been given a title by Ramsay MacDonald, to provide a spokesman for Labor in the House of Lords. I accepted the invitation, partly because I was curious to get a good look at a Laborite lord.

Lord Thompson turned out to be a very formal and rather pedantic man. His Cooper Union audience was not much interested in foreign policy, but was intent on abolishing the British Empire. In the question period, Irish Nationalists and a multitude of other Empire-baiters peppered him with questions until the poor man was at his wits' end. I did my best to control the situation, having had experience with hecklers at miners' meetings, but it was too much. The meeting was by no means a success.

About a week before the scheduled date, Mrs. Franklin Roosevelt had invited me to have dinner at her home, with Lord Thompson, before the meeting. I was almost as curious to get a close look at a Roosevelt, so I accepted. Being a country boy, accustomed to an early supper, I arrived at the Roosevelt home by six o'clock, nearly two hours early. Mrs. Roosevelt must have been frantic, trying to think what to do with me. She finally put me in with Franklin, in his study. So he and I had time for a long talk.

He told me about Al Smith asking him to make the nominating speech for Smith at the 1924 Democratic convention. Roosevelt questioned him on the League of Nations, and got his assurance that he was for America's joining. Knowing Smith was sound on domestic issues, Roosevelt agreed to nominate him.

Then we turned to talk about the labor movement. Roosevelt asked me about my experiences and ideas. He said his law firm had done some work for the Vinton Colliery Company, one of the worst non-union concerns in my district, and had been paid in stock, which he said he had gotten rid of. He knew about our troubles with that company in 1922. Though it did not appear that he knew a great deal about the labor movement, I was impressed with the intelligence and versatility of the man, and felt that he was genuinely concerned about social problems and the needs of the people.

My impression was fully borne out by the impact of the National Industrial Recovery Act, which, in the spring of 1933, transformed everything for the miners and their union. The miners, relying on the government's promise to protect their right to organize, flooded into the union. Within ninety days, the industry was organized. There was no need to campaign; an organizer had only to see that he had a good supply of application blanks and a place to file them, and the rank and file did the rest.

The union and the operators met to draft a code of fair competition, as required by the Act. There was division among the operators over the code, and especially over meeting with the union on any basis whatever, but this was worked out and a code adopted in September. Wages were set at $4.60 a day in the North and $4.20 in the South, and grievance procedures agreed upon.

These terms were incorporated into the first Appalachian Wage Conference agreement, covering the bituminous districts of Pennsylvania, southern Ohio, West Virginia, Maryland, Virginia, and Kentucky, a larger tonnage than the old Central Competitive Field, and serving as a new basis for agreements in the rest of the country. Shortly afterward, miners in the coke region of Pennsylvania, working in captive mines of the great steel companies, walked out on strike. The President intervened, on the ground that the strike would impede recovery, and an agreement was reached that the men would return to work and an election be held. The union won a contract on the terms mentioned above, the first contract in that field in over forty years.

While these changes were going on, I returned to Nanty Glo, where I had held my union membership for many years, and plunged into the work of reorganization. I rejoined my old local and was welcomed by the Nanty Glo miners. But not everybody was glad to see me. I wrote to James Mark that I had returned and intended to get work in the mines and do what I could in behalf of the union. I had addressed a mass meeting of the local, and had devoted my entire talk to the necessity of taking advantage of the opportunity to achieve complete organization. The tone of my letter was as friendly as I could make it, to indicate that I felt the time had come to bury old grudges. A month passed before I received a frosty reply. Mark said he had "no objections to the letter written by you, as it seems to be friendly," but it was his duty to inform me that since I had been expelled from the union, I could not rejoin until I had applied to the international executive board and gotten its permission. Mark informed the local that I could not be a member. The local courageously invited Mark to appear before it and discuss the charges against me, thus giving me the trial that had been denied me when I was expelled. Mark ignored the invitation, and threatened to take away the local charter if his orders were not complied with. To avoid trouble for my friends, I withdrew my application, but declared my intention of fighting for the right to membership.

Mark had good reason to be worried over my return. My prestige was high in the district, and he probably expected that I would try to make a political comeback. I cannot say what the outcome would have been if I had tried, but I had had my fill of the headaches of office and wanted only a chance to make a living and build the union.

Probably the most frightening thing to Mark was the reception I got from the Johnstown newspapers. I had a pleasant talk with the editor of the Johnstown *Democrat,* who suggested that I write some articles for the paper on the NRA and the miners. I sent him five, of which he published all but the last. I argued that the idea of NRA could succeed only if both operators and workers were fully organized and could work out mutually satisfactory ways of dealing with the industry's problems and each other. Then I discussed the procedures under NRA and the conditions for successful collective bargaining. I tried to avoid old controversies and emphasize hopeful prospects of the future. I know that the miners of the district read my contributions with interest and discussed them. Dispassionate and realistic discussion was something they wanted and needed, in order to understand the new situation. Mark could hardly be blamed for finding it disturbing that the man he had succeeded in 1926 had turned up again and was being accepted, more widely than Mark had ever been, as a spokesman for the miners.

Sometime in the fall I received a message that Philip Murray wanted me to call him. When I returned his call, he asked me to come right over. We spent some time in general talk about how things were going, in a friendly and relaxed atmosphere. Then he asked me what my plans were.

I said, "Well, I think you understand. I'm back in Pennsylvania to re-establish myself in the industry and in the union. Mark wants to keep me out, but I intend to fight for my right of employment and of membership. Now that the major problem on which I based so much of my agitation in the past—organization of the unorganized—has been resolved, I am anxious to co-operate in the union's forward drive. The officers of the union have no right to blacklist me. I will discuss issues, whether I am a member or not, but the primary issue will be restoration of my rights in the union."

Murray said, "I understand that, John. And I'm not unfriendly to your purposes. I'd like you to come back again tomorrow afternoon."

I returned the next day. "John," he said, "I've thought over our talk, and I've been in touch with Lewis, who is at the AFL convention in Washington. He wants to see you. Will you go there?"

"For what purpose?" I asked. "If he wants me to repudiate my views, it would be a waste of time."

"No," he said, "just go there and meet him. I think you'll find he's changed. There's been a lot of changes lately."

"Well, what about my situation in District 2?" I asked.

"You can understand their concern over your appearance."

"Sure, but it has no justification."

"Very well, but will you go to Washington? And when you return, regardless of what happens, will you come to see me?"

I promised, and went to Washington the next day. I called Lewis early in the morning, from the lobby of his hotel. He said he was tied up for the moment, but would send down his brother, Denny. By the time Denny appeared, I had encountered Christopher Golden, who was secretary of the Anthracite Joint Commission, and the three of us had a very lively talk until word came that Lewis could see me.

Lewis was very cordial, said he had talked with Murray about me, and was glad we could get together. Finally he asked me what I was doing.

"My chief activity right now," I said, "is making a living. As to the rest, you know as much about it as I do, I'm sure."

He smiled, "Yes, I know, John. But you know the situation has changed for all of us. We are busy re-establishing the organization and collective bargaining, now that the organization of the unorganized, which you used to make such a point of, is done. I've seen copies of your newspaper articles, and they seem all right."

"They are an indication of willingness to co-operate under the new order of things," I said, "and to tackle new problems which will appear as we go along."

He said he understood that, and we went on to talk for an hour or so about some of the difficulties of operating under the NRA codes. Then he said he had to go to the AFL convention, but he was glad to have had the chance to talk to me; Phil Murray had expressed a great confidence in me; Lewis wanted to think things over and talk to Murray. When I got back to Pittsburgh, I should see Murray, who would have more to say to me. And if I had time, he would suggest that I visit the AFL convention; I might meet some friends there. We shook hands and I left, not quite sure what to think. There had been no raking up of the past, no attempt to get any pledges out of me. Of course he knew my position, and he knew me. His only real comment on our past relations was that he supposed our differences were ones of timing. I let that understatement pass.

I went over to the convention and sat through the morning session. I left a few minutes before adjournment, and found myself sharing the elevator with Sidney Hillman, whom I had known before, and whose union had just been admitted to the AFL, largely through Lewis's influence. He said Lewis had told him of meeting with me, and that Lewis thought there was a place for me in the new situation. "John," he continued, "I want you to avail yourself of any opportunity to get back into activity. Lewis is not hostile to you; he has changed. I've been working closely with him lately, and I've seen something of this new side of him."

I returned to Pittsburgh and paid my promised visit to Murray. He said he had been authorized by Lewis to offer me a commission to work for the union. I asked about my membership, and he said he would work that out.

"All right," I said, "now, what is the assignment?"

"We want you to go to Illinois and study the factional fight there— the Progressive Miners. Take plenty of time, look into things thoroughly and report."

"To whom?"

"To Lewis."

"Does that include recommendations?"

"Yes."

"Well, you know that if you expect any skullduggery, there's nothing doing."

"No, John," he said, "what we want is an independent appraisal of the situation. Take your time."

He explained that I would not be required to get in touch with the district officials, unless I wanted to. Their position was known, and so was the opposition's. What he and Lewis wanted to know was the true state of things, and what could be done about it. How I found out, and what conclusions I drew, would be my affair. "John," he said, "this is just the beginning. Believe me, there's no intention of putting you in any invidious position. This is the start of an opportunity for you to do useful work in the miners' movement. We need everybody, instead of being all at sixes and sevens. I want you to trust me."

I said, "All right, Phil, I'll go."

This was in October of 1933. I spent a month traveling about Illinois, talking with people wherever I could, with special attention to the rank and file. I found that the Progressive Miners were in poor condition. They had not been able to take advantage of NRA, being pocketed in a limited area of Illinois. In other fields, miners went to the UMW, instead of turning to a feeble independent union. There was dissension and loss of morale in the PMA over this failure. Undoubtedly, the organization was doomed, in the long run. But it would be a very long run, because there were so many whose bitterness against the UMW would keep them out long after any hope of victory was lost. There were men who said to me, and meant it, that they would scab before joining the Lewis union, or that they preferred defeat with the Progressives to victory with the United Mine Workers.

Many men who knew my past record would talk to me, but were suspicious that I had sold out. My answer was always the same: that the miners were in the UMW and I felt my place was with them; I was not an apologist for Lewis, but neither did I intend to rehash the fights of the past. There had been very violent struggles in Illinois, and the bloody shirt was waved. I had to insist on facing the present situation, because nobody could live on the memory of past wrongs. There had been plenty of wrongs, but the Progressives had not been able to get anywhere on that basis, nor would they in the future. When the discussion got too emotional, and I was asked personal questions as to whether I was on Lewis's payroll, I answered, "Yes, I am. And I'll tell you what I'm getting. It's six dollars a day. But that's not the point. The point is, what are *you* getting out of keeping this feud alive?"

After awhile, the PMA paper denounced me bitterly, and I found that I was not getting any new information, but only a repetition of increasingly angry arguments. So I returned to Pittsburgh and sent in my report.

I told Lewis that the PMA was declining, but would take a long time to die. The war of attrition could go on for years. On the other hand, the proposal of a generous peace could wipe out the trouble in ninety days. I suggested that the members of PMA be invited to return to the United Mine Workers with full privileges, and that a district convention be held with all parties represented, to adopt a constitution and hold a free election of officers. If the leaders of the independent union turned this down, their rank and file would walk out on them, with few exceptions. And we could afford to be generous, because of our overwhelming success in all other fields. Even if men who had been identified with the dual union were elected to office in the new district organization, they would be bound by UMW policy, and as long as the union continued to function successfully they would have no basis for renewing the quarrel. If, on the other hand, the Lewis faction turned out to be the true majority, there would be no danger for the ex-Progressives in a free and democratic union.

Lewis and Murray each acknowledged my report with thanks and praise for its thoroughness, but my proposal was not acted upon. Instead, Lewis allowed the fight to continue until the Progressives were destroyed, at great cost to the miners. The thing that Lewis balked at in my report, I think, was that I was proposing to restore district autonomy in Illinois. For his purposes, the districts had to be administrative units of the national organization, rather than autonomous organizations. Autonomy for Illinois would create a demand for autonomy in other districts, imperiling the Lewis machine. I had found the right answer to the problem, but not the right answer for Lewis. He probably just digested the parts in which I predicted the decline of the PMA, and let the rest go. If time would give him what he wanted, why should he bother?

The restoration of my membership in the United Mine Workers was handled expeditiously, though not very graciously. I had to write to the international executive board asking that the ban against me be lifted. Lewis replied in a couple of weeks that permission had been granted me to rejoin on probation, with the understanding that I would not be eligible for any elective office until my full rights had been restored by action of the board. I promptly rejoined my old local, 1386, in Nanty Glo, paying the initiation fee as a new member. I would not have been eligible for elective office for three years, anyway, so the officers of District 2 could relax.

My next assignment also came through Murray. He suggested that I look into the by-product coke industry, which had been growing rapidly. Coke was displacing anthracite for domestic heating at a rate which gave concern for the future of anthracite. The workers in the coke industry were unorganized, though many were ex-miners. New methods of coke-making were creating new industrial products, utilizing gas and tar which had formerly been wasted. Much of the new coke industry was connected with the big steel companies, which processed bituminous coal in their own coke ovens right beside the mills in which the coke was used. Organization of these workers would be possible only in connection with organization of the solidly non-union steel industry.

On the other hand, there were stirrings of unionism in plants in the Boston metropolitan area. Soft coal was shipped up the coast to New England, where it was processed and the coke and gas sold to local distributors. Chemical industries which used the by-product tars were also developing. About a dozen small federal locals, affiliated directly to the AFL, were scattered in towns around Boston. The leaders of this movement wanted to organize on an industrial basis, one union to a plant, instead of being broken up along the jurisdictional lines of craft unions which laid claim to them. If we could organize the coke by-product workers, they could be useful allies in the coming struggle with the steel companies over the captive plants. We needed to know more about the industry in general, and the newly organizing workers in particular. Murray proposed that I go to Boston, look the situation over, and see what could be done.

I got in touch with a young man named James Nelson, who was the leader of an unofficial council of federal locals in the New England industry. His group was eager to get some arrangement which would enable it to launch an organizing drive throughout the industry. The AFL tolerated the council and paid Nelson a salary as an AFL representative, but showed no signs of chartering a national union with an industrial jurisdiction. Nelson and others appeared before the AFL executive council several times to plead their case, but were told only that their problems would be given careful consideration. The AFL leadership was unwilling to concede their demands, but the unity and determination of the coke workers prevented any move to break up the federal locals.

I had no hesitation in approving the demand for an industrial union, which suited my ideas exactly and fitted with the long experience of the United Mine Workers. The coke workers' council invited President William Green of the AFL to come to Boston and speak at a conference, hoping to demonstrate that they had the strength to maintain their own union. Green approved the calling of the conference, but sent a representative, William Collins, in his place. This was a letdown for the workers. I advised them to get on the long-distance telephone and call Green directly, to tell him that Collins was no substitute for the president of the AFL. The convention had been called to meet Green, who could take a night train and be in Boston for the second day. They followed my advice and got Green to show up. He made a generalized speech on the aims and purposes of the labor movement, but did not commit himself to any more than toleration of the council and continuation of Nelson's employment. He had nothing to say about expanding the organization. The delegates were by no means satisfied.

I kept in touch with this situation through 1934 and 1935, meeting frequently with Nelson, and visiting plants in the Middle West and elsewhere, to see what could be done about organizing them. Wages were extremely low—as little as thirty-five cents an hour—and organizations that had mushroomed in the early days of NRA had dwindled from neglect and isolation.

In August of 1934, the New England group held a convention in Pelham, New Hampshire. They were disheartened by the inaction of the AFL, and instructed their officers to consult with John L. Lewis about affiliation with the United Mine Workers. I had recommended to Lewis a plan for a new national district of the UMW with jurisdiction over gas, coke, and chemical workers. After the San Francisco convention of the AFL in October, 1934, this plan was carried out, and the coke workers became the nucleus of District 50, which now includes a majority of the membership of the UMW. I might claim to be the father of District 50, except that Lewis did not permit the district autonomy which I had taken for granted or confine the jurisdiction to gas and coke workers.

The San Francisco convention of the AFL illustrated how rapidly conditions were changing in the labor movement and how great was the need for new methods of handling new problems. Lewis took the lead in a drive to change the Federation's policies. For nearly half a century, the UMW had been the biggest exception to the domination of the craft union idea in the American labor movement. We had jurisdiction over everybody who worked in and around the mines. This jurisdiction was easy to defend because most mining towns were small and isolated—there were not enough people of any craft to maintain separate locals, so the craft unions left us alone. The Brewery Workers, on the other hand, located in large cities, were constantly harassed by the Teamsters and others.

The demand of a large industrial union minority at San Francisco in 1934 for a policy which would welcome into the labor movement new millions whose work in mass production industries had no relation to traditional crafts produced a compromise resolution, largely the work of Charles P. Howard, president of the Typographical Union. The resolution instructed the executive council to issue charters for new unions in the automotive, cement, aluminum, and other mass production and miscellaneous industries, and to launch an organizing campaign in the iron and steel industry.

I sent Lewis an enthusiastic letter, congratulating him on his part in achieving this much. It turned out to be less than it appeared. For example, an auto union was chartered, but the AFL imposed its own choice of officers on the union, over the protests of the founding convention. These officers were routine AFL organizers, more skillful at counting per capita than in organizing. As a result, Communists, Coughlinites, and others got their fingers into the pie, and before long there were several unions fighting among themselves and dissipating the energies of the workers. This waste of opportunity by sheer inaction was also the rule in other industries crying for organization, especially steel.

Lewis sent me out from time to time to meet with groups, like the coke unions, who wanted industrial organization, but I spent most of 1935 in Washington, working in behalf of the Guffey-Snyder Coal Bill. I worked closely with Henry Warrum, chief counsel of the UMW and principal author of the act. He had a rather stiff and formal manner, but we soon became warm friends. Warrum considered the Guffey bill inadequate, but if it could be passed and could get by the test of constitutionality, it would be an important step toward regulating the coal industry.

The Supreme Court's ruling that NRA was unconstitutional threw all of our activities into confusion, but we hoped that the Guffey act would cover the coal industry for the time being. However, it too fell under the Court's disapproval, and the Guffey-Vinson Act of 1937 was a feeble substitute. Fortunately, the Wagner-Connery Labor Relations Act, passed shortly after the outlawing of NRA, preserved the essential factor, the right to organize.

At the San Francisco convention of the AFL, A. Philip Randolph of the Pullman Porters' Union had presented a resolution calling for action to eliminate anti-Negro membership clauses in the laws of unions affiliated with the Federation. Randolph was a thorn in the side of officialdom on this subject, and was usually brushed aside with a toothless resolution approving the principle of equal treatment for all, but recognizing the autonomy of affiliates. On this occasion, William Hutcheson of the Carpenters' Union offered a motion that a commission be appointed by President Green to look into the matter and report. Hutcheson's proposal was probably intended to be just another way of brushing the subject off. It was passed, and shortly after I heard from Lewis that Green had asked him to suggest a man for the committee. Lewis asked if I would serve, which I agreed to do.

The committee was organized with John Rooney, of the Plasterers, as chairman, and me as secretary. We met with Green first, and agreed to write to affiliated unions, inviting them to send us information about admission of Negroes, and to send representatives to speak for them at hearings in Washington. Randolph and a few Negro organizations testified at the hearings for two days on discriminatory practices, but none of the unions which practiced discrimination appeared. A few sent letters answering our questions, specifying constitutional or ritual clauses which barred Negroes. We put this together into a report, and asked Randolph what he would suggest as a next step. He proposed that we go out to other cities and hold hearings as to what was going on there. The committee went into executive session to discuss this proposal. I was the only one strongly in favor; the others were afraid we would be exceeding our commission, unless Green approved. Green did not approve, so that ended that. We submitted a report, which was not unanimous, favoring further study and action on the matter, but it was buried at the Atlantic City convention by the device of having a member of the Executive Council prepare a "supplementary report," evading the whole problem. Randolph fought to get our report approved, but was voted down by the convention.

Though I found my work in Washington interesting and rewarding, my heart was really in the organizing field. As time went on, it became clearer and clearer that some way had to be found to cut through the doubts and delays standing in the way of effective organization. The most exciting period of my life was during these years, as a number of us tried to work out the strategy which would release the energies of the unorganized workers and enable them to take their place in the labor movement.

!!

18

T

BEGINNINGS OF CIO

he 1934 wage contract won the miners the seven-hour day and a daily wage of $5.00 in the North and $4.60 in the South. The union was firmly established in all coal fields, and built up its treasury at a rapid rate. Lewis was therefore free to turn his attention to long-range problems, especially to organizing steel and other mass production industries. He had never believed that the AFL meant to do anything about the 1934 convention resolution on the subject. Or it might be more accurate to say he was sure anything they might do would be inadequate. The events of the next year bore out his view.

The first evidence of trouble came from one of the long-established industrial unions, the Mine, Mill, and Smelter Workers. This union of metal miners had jurisdictional trouble with some craft unions of the AFL Metal Trades Department during a strike in Butte, Montana, in 1934. Its president, Thomas Brown, came to Washington in February, 1935, to protest to the AFL Executive Council against the raid on his membership. He came to Lewis, as the one member of the Council he could expect to be sympathetic, for advice and help. Lewis asked me to help Brown prepare for his appearance before the Council, using the miners' term, "John, hold Tom a light; he needs it."

I checked the AFL records and found that Mine, Mill had been chartered in 1911, under UMW sponsorship, with the same jurisdiction in its industry as the coal miners had in theirs: the right to organize all who worked in and around the mines. Brown and I appeared before the Council with this evidence of the rights of Mine, Mill. But Lewis's was the sole voice raised in our support. The majority voted that there had been no infringement of the metal miners' jurisdiction. Mine, Mill appealed the decision to the AFL convention, where the question was debated for two days before the Council was upheld by a vote of 18,464 to 10,897.

By the early part of 1935, the auto workers' union membership had declined from 100,000 to about 20,000, according to reports we received, chiefly because the speeches of the appointed president, Dillon, were no substitute for an autonomous union with a vigorous organizing program backed by adequate funds. The workers would flock to a union which fought for their demands, but not to a weary, do-nothing bureaucracy. There were several conferences of local union leaders, to try to get free of the AFL-imposed "leadership," and spontaneous strikes broke out here and there, which nobody seemed to know what to do about. Individuals and delegations from auto, and from rubber, the electrical industry, cement, and other industrial groups, turned up in Washington from time to time, like lost sheep, wondering who would give them guidance, or even freedom to develop in their own way.

The most striking evidence of the futility of AFL methods was provided by some steel workers who came to see Lewis in June, 1935. The AFL had left organization of this great industry in the hands of the Amalgamated Association of Iron, Steel, and Tin Workers, a small union of certain skilled workers in a few plants, which had been content for years to cultivate its little garden of dues-payers without worrying about the masses outside its fold. Even if the leaders of this union had wanted to organize steel, they had no resources for the job. The president, Mike Tighe, was pushing eighty, and wanted only to be left alone to enjoy his salary. New members who joined after NRA wanted action. When they did not get it, they raised a row, and found themselves expelled. They felt, with reason, that their expulsion was not because of any real misconduct but because of the union leaders' fear that their activity might disturb peaceful relations with the steel companies and jeopardize the old membership's slightly privileged status.

Lewis advised them to tell their story to the Executive Council—to argue that they only wanted to carry out the 1934 decision to organize steel. They did get to talk to Green, but were not permitted to appear before the Council. Lewis was indignant because it seemed obvious that these were exactly the men most needed for the big job to which the AFL had pledged itself, and turning them away was tantamount to admitting that the steel-organizing campaign was a bluff. The Council's delicate regard for the "jurisdiction" of the Amalgamated was absurd; it was a union only in name, and if steel was to be organized there had to be a big effort by all of organized labor, with hundreds of thousands of dollars and a small army of men committed to the task. The important block to launching a steel campaign was the fact that a number of craft unions would not allow any move to transform the Amalgamated into an industrial union, but would co-operate only if they could snip off certain members for themselves from each steel local union. Since this would have resulted in dividing the workers in a single plant into twenty or more different unions, only one of them predominantly made up of steel workers, it is not hard to see why AFL approaches to the steel problem never got anywhere.

Tighe took the position that the industrial union approach was the only one that could work. He had had the experience of trying to work through a co-operative effort of craft unions in the disastrous 1919 steel drive, and knew there was no future in that. Lewis kept in close touch with him, as well as with the insurgent lodges of his union, ready to use either or both to advance the organization of steel. Steel was the key to understanding Lewis's policy; the mine workers would never be safe until steel was unionized, which he was determined to do at any cost. Organization of the other mass-production industries was a by-product of steel. Thus Lewis and the UMW, intent on steel, were driven to create the CIO, because there was no other way to get the job in steel done. There would have been no CIO without Lewis and the miners; the maturity of the American labor movement would have had to await another generation. Under AFL policy, the most that could have been hoped for was a small increase in membership, which would soon have been frittered away, as the pre-CIO experience in auto and rubber demonstrated.

Numerous delegations from federal locals in rubber, radio, and other industries passed through Lewis's office in 1935, all telling the same story, of restricted jurisdictions, arbitrary control of such international unions as the AFL chartered, lack of support, sniping from the craft unions, and menacing competition from company unions. There was great danger that the employers would be able to divert the energies of the workers into the dead end of company unionism, simply for lack of any competition from organized labor. Instance after instance was reported of men, ordered to leave federal locals and join "appropriate" craft unions, who just quit altogether or were induced to take leading roles in company unions. Some craft unions charged initiation fees and dues two to fifty times as large as the federal locals; factory workers could not possibly consider such terms. But the insuperable problem was the fact that collective bargaining between the great industrial giants and odds and ends of their employees organized in craft unions was impossible.

Lewis invited several of us to have breakfast with him one Sunday morning in the summer of 1935 to talk over the situation. Murray, Warrum, and one or two others connected with the UMW were present. Lewis told us that he had no confidence whatever in the ability or willingness of the AFL to organize the workers who were giving such dramatic evidence of readiness for industrial unionism. The question was, what to do next? We agreed that a determined fight must be made at the coming Atlantic City convention to force the AFL to carry out the San Francisco mandate, and to broaden and strengthen that commitment. If we could not get a majority of the resolutions committee to accept a clear-cut industrial union position, we must offer a minority report and make every effort to line up support for it. None of us had any illusions that the fight would be easy, or that we were likely to win. But we agreed that we must convince everyone that we meant business and were ready to fight all the way. Nothing was said about the next step; that would appear later. Our opponents could not surrender, and neither would we. By making our determination clear, we would guarantee that some kind of explosion would take place. We could then decide what to do about it.

This breakfast meeting set in motion the whole series of events which split the American labor movement temporarily, multiplied its membership five times or more, and transformed it from a feeble minority on the fringes of the working population to a mass movement which represents a high proportion of America's workers.

The seedbed of the CIO was the great depression, which destroyed any illusion in the minds of the workers that the employers and the government would take care of them. The inadequacy of all efforts to deal with unemployment during these years is too well known for me to rehearse it. Even the AFL, however, bound by an outworn tradition of "voluntarism," fought such things as unemployment insurance until as late as 1932, using arguments which echoed the most reactionary employers. While this stand was belatedly, and reluctantly, changed by the depression, even more fundamental changes, this time in the labor movement itself, were stoutly resisted by the older leadership. Lewis was somewhat in advance of the others on the question of using the powers of government for the benefit of the workers, because of the special problems of the mining industry, which he had in part recognized by supporting the Guffey bills. And it was easier for him to recognize the relevance of industrial unionism to the new prob- lems, because the miners' union had always been industrial in form. As AFL membership dwindled to scarcely more than two million, the craft union leaders merely tightened their defenses, so that when NRA came along and the great opportunity for labor was created, surprisingly few of the craft unions made any substantial gains in membership. Company unions in the mass production industries probably had more members than the entire Federation in 1934.

NRA code authorities were, in too many cases, dominated by anti- labor employers in the absence of strong unions. Many employers learned to exploit the famous Section 7A by creating company unions. Some craft union leaders merely shrugged this off, saying that in- dustrial workers were unorganizable anyway, and the real unions would be better off without them. The compromise decision of the AFL, granting charters to federal locals in the unorganized industries but not allowing these locals to grow into self-governing internationals, left them suspended, to be cut up at leisure by the craft unions.

We came to the Atlantic City convention of the AFL prepared to make a good fight. We planned two preliminary skirmishes designed to undermine the authority of opposition leaders. One plan was to offer a resolution forbidding officers of the AFL to be members or officers of the National Civic Federation, an organization which ostensibly brought together employers and labor leaders in the interest of har- monious relations, but which progressives had long considered a device to blunt the fighting spirit of labor. The United Mine Workers, years before, had required John Mitchell to resign from the NCF in order to hold his union membership. Matthew Woll, an outstanding con- servative among the AFL leadership, was acting president of the NCF. If he could be forced to resign, his attacks on industrial unionism would carry less weight. One of my jobs was to study the history of the NCF and provide facts for the attack on it.

Our second preliminary move would forbid the editor of the *Federationist,* the monthly organ of the AFL, to accept any more advertising from anti-union employers. Our resolutions were both adopted, though Woll blunted the effect of the one on the Civic Federation by resigning his post during the convention, just before the vote was taken.

The resolutions committee divided nine to six on industrial unionism. The majority report said that the industrial unionists had misunderstood the action at San Francisco. That decision protected the rights of craft unions in members working in industrial plants. It was only intended that "mass production employees" be organized into industrial unions; any other course would destroy the craft unions. Woll and John P. Frey made the most extended defense of the majority position, both basing their arguments on the historic rights of the craft unions and paying little attention to the problem of organizing the big industries.

Charles P. Howard, president of the Typographical Union, presented the minority report. As the head of a major craft union, one of the oldest and strongest in the Federation, he could not be accused of any ulterior interest in the question, though some craft unionists were bitter against him as a "traitor" to their cause. He argued, in a quiet, scholarly way, that failure to organize at this time would create a threat to the entire labor movement, by driving potential recruits into company unions. He called the workers in mass industry "composite mechanics, specialized and engaged upon classes of work which do not fully qualify them for craft union membership." Such members could only be classified intelligently into industrial unions, in which they had a right to complete autonomy.

Lewis's speech in support of the minority was as vehement and explosive as Howard's had been quiet. Lewis was in his best form, turning out quotable phrases. He declared that he was now convinced that the Council had no intention of issuing any industrial charters, that the San Francisco declaration was a fraud. He accused the majority of a breach of faith; organization during the past year had been an utter failure, and failure would continue until we accepted the changes necessary to fit the times. The debate rolled on for nearly eight hours, getting hotter and hotter. But it is doubtful that it changed many votes. The final vote came on acceptance of the minority report, which had been offered as a substitute for the majority. It went against us by 18,024 to 10,933, much as had been expected. It is worth noting that the federal locals, the nearest thing to representation of the industrial workers in the convention, voted overwhelmingly for the minority report. Their votes did not count for much at that time, but theirs was the prophetic voice of many millions who would soon find a place in the labor movement.

We of the minority did not feel cast down. On the contrary, most of us were pleased with what we had accomplished, both in the debate and in the vote, because we were so sure that the future was ours.

The question of industrial unionism kept coming up in connection with other matters, as the convention went on with its business. During debate on enlarging the jurisdiction of the rubber workers to include all who worked in and around the factories, William Hutcheson, president of the Carpenters' Union, made a point of order that a rubber workers' delegate was trying to reopen the industrial union question. Lewis shouted that it was "pretty small potatoes" to call a point of order on a delegate from a small union who was fighting for his organization's existence. Lewis and Hutcheson exchanged some compliments, which have been variously reported, and finally locked in a scuffle which turned over some chairs and landed Hutcheson on the floor. I had a fair view of the battle from where I sat with the miners' delegation. Both men were carrying a lot of weight, so it was not much of a fight, but the newspapers made much of it, and it is always referred to in any account of Atlantic City, so I suppose I must record my view of it. Its significance is only to show how much tempers had been roused, and how much personal feelings came to be identified with one side or the other, forcing us toward a breach.

The one man who might have been able to bring a workable compromise out of this mess was William Green, but he made no move. If he had chosen to throw the prestige of his office behind a compromise, he would have had support from many who were not willing to accept the total virtue of either set of arguments. There were such people, as later events demonstrated, on both sides, people who considered the unity of the movement worth some sacrifices. But Green was the captive of a mechanical interpretation of majority rule, the notion that he was merely the servant of the side with the most votes. I think Gompers would have made himself a factor in the situation, and would have tried to keep things from being pushed too far.

I was not a delegate to the convention, though I sat on the floor, and took part in the caucus of the industrial union delegates on the day after adjournment of the convention. We had about fifty people, mostly from the federal unions, though leaders of many of the larger unions were also present. Lewis reviewed what had been accomplished, and proposed that we continue to push the industrial union program. The group agreed that he should call together a committee to continue the work. The personnel of the committee was left to his discretion. This decision did not spell out any detailed plan; it simply registered the verdict of all present that the fight was not to be dropped.

A few days later, Phil Murray told me that Lewis had decided to issue invitations to seven presidents of national unions to meet with him in Washington and consider next steps. The committee would reaffirm our commitment to industrial unionism, but anything beyond that would depend on circumstances. Murray also said that Lewis was thinking of making me director of the work.

The meeting was held at the UMW offices on November 9, 1935. The union presidents in attendance were: Lewis, of the Mine Workers; Charles P. Howard, Typographical Union; David Dubinsky, Ladies' Garment Workers; Sidney Hillman, Amalgamated Clothing Workers; Thomas F. McMahon, Textile Workers; Harvey C. Fremming, Oil Field, Gas Well, and Refinery Workers; Max Zaritsky, Cap and Millinery Department, United Hatters, Cap and Millinery Workers; and Thomas H. Brown of Mine, Mill. Lewis invited Philip Murray and me to attend. The presidents constituted themselves the Committee for Industrial Organization, to "work in accordance with the principles and policies enunciated by these organizations at the Atlantic City Convention of the American Federation of Labor," according to the press release Howard and I prepared after the meeting. The release continued, "It is the purpose of the Committee to encourage and promote organization of the workers in the mass production and unorganized industries of the Nation and affiliation with the American Federation of Labor. Its functions will be educational and advisory and the Committe and its representatives will cooperate for the recognition and acceptance of modern collective bargaining in such industries. Other organizations interested in advancing organization work along the lines of industrial unionism will be invited to participate in the activities of the Committee and name representatives to join in its work."

Lewis was chosen chairman of the Committee, and Charles Howard was secretary. On Lewis's motion, I was named director, "to supervise the work of administration."

There has been some talk about who thought up the name. Personally, I would say that it didn't have to be thought up—it just happened. Our purpose was industrial organization and we were a committee. That's all.

What we intended to do was accurately stated in the release. We knew we would face opposition within the AFL. We could not predict how far that would go, but we knew we had to put what resources we could command into organizing the unorganized, and we were ready to face the consequences when they happened. I am sure that no two men at that meeting would have forecast the future in exactly the same way. But all would have agreed that there was a job to be done and that they intended to do it. Above all, they did not intend to split the labor movement, but rather to build it up to greater strength than it had ever known before. The realization that a split was developing came to each of us differently, at different times, and with different effects, but that possibility, and all the other possibilities, many of which never happened, we were willing to await and deal with as they came up. Our mood was one of optimism and of relief that at last we were going to get to work.

‖‖‖‖‖‖‖‖‖‖‖‖‖‖‖‖‖‖‖‖‖‖‖‖‖‖‖‖‖‖‖

19

CIO—YEARS OF GROWTH

With the announcement of the Committee for Industrial Organization, a storm of speculation swept across the country. Much of what came out in the newspapers was nonsense: dark mutterings about "power struggles," and the like. In the minds of the workers waiting for organization, we soon learned, there was only one question: did the Committee mean business, would it go all the way? I had no inside source of information as to the reactions of the AFL leadership, but I could guess.

Lewis had few illusions about how the Executive Council would take our move. He expected trouble. The greater our success, the greater the trouble. But he was ready for it, if he could organize the unorganized. In the first years of CIO, Lewis showed his best side: his readiness to see a fight through; his grim indifference to criticism from any source; his colossal self-confidence. He resigned his vice presidency of the AFL, to get free of legalistic tangles and efforts to get commitments from him on the basis of his membership in the Council.

Hillman and some of the others probably understood the situation as clearly as Lewis. Dubinsky and Zaritsky had closer ties to the AFL than did Lewis and Hillman, and I think they hoped the Council would not go nearly as far as it did in opposing us. But at the first there was no disagreement or hesitation among the Committee members. They were not accustomed to working out elaborate theoretical analyses of their policies in advance. In the tradition of American trade unionism, they took things as they came and worked out the best answers they could at each stage.

Lewis went on the radio shortly after CIO was formed, to explain the Committee's intentions. He described the growth in the numbers of industrial workers, the failure to organize them up to that time, the opportunity offered by new conditions, and the plans of CIO to broaden the labor movement by bringing these people in. The speech gave assurances that CIO would not fight the craft unions or the AFL, but would give all possible support to workers who wanted to organize in new or old industrial unions. A month later, on December 29, 1935, I followed with another broadcast, describing our plans and purposes for 1936. My chief point was that if the Executive Council would proceed with an organizing campaign in auto, steel, and other industries, we would give it every support; if the Council delayed, we would not hesitate to take the initiative.

Almost the first thing I had to do, as director of CIO, was to go to Detroit and meet with some of the leading men in the auto union. There, where the AFL way of handling the new unions had been most thoroughly tried out, I got the views of the men on the scene. I found them worried, frustrated, and resentful, almost as bitter against the AFL as against the employers. Membership was dwindling, the countermoves of the auto companies were endangering all that had been achieved, and the unions could not fight back. They needed money, they needed experienced help and advice, and most of all they needed enthusiasm. I assured them that Lewis and the Committee really would back them the whole way, and that they could plunge into the work of building their union with certainty of success. I decided that just as soon as I could get my office set up, I must take immediate action to give those men support and good counsel.

We hired some office space in the Rust Building, at 15th and K streets in Washington, and Lewis and I both brought people in to staff the office. I hired my niece, Bernice Welsh, as my personal secretary. Mrs. Katherine Ellickson, who had been a teacher at Brookwood Labor College and knew the labor movement, looked over incoming material, prepared information for me that she knew I would need, and helped draft communications. Lewis sent over a girl from the UMW to help with typing, and others were brought in later, as they were needed.

By February we had started a clip sheet, called the *Union News*

Service, to be sent out to labor papers and the press generally, with news items, some editorial comment, and even cartoons. We got good coverage from the press, because there was no doubt that we were news. I brought in Len DeCaux to handle this work. He was, at the time, Washington correspondent for the Federated Press. I had known him slightly at Brookwood, and when he worked for the *Illinois Miner*. He asked for a day to think the offer over; I now know enough about him to suspect that he wanted to consult with his friends in the Communist Party, which had not yet committed itself to support of the CIO. The party had about come to the end of its effort to create dual unions and was working out a new line. I had no idea then that DeCaux worked closely with the Communists, though this came out later. He took the job, and did it very well.

When Lewis heard of this, he had some reservations about DeCaux, but only because of his connection with the *Illinois Miner*. Lewis asked if I couldn't get somebody else, but finally approved my decision. DeCaux worked directly under me for the first year, but after that he operated mostly in relation to Lewis, partly on Lewis's initiative, partly on his own.

In the early days, the financial arrangements of CIO were complicated and informal. I remained on the payroll of the Mine Workers for two years, until CIO acquired its own per capita income. At first, all income was in the form of donations from member unions. The United Mine Workers provided between two-thirds and three-quarters of the money for CIO in the first year or two.* The Amalgamated Clothing Workers and the International Ladies' Garment Workers sent in substantial sums, but the other member unions did not have large resources, so their donations were smaller. If a need for money arose, I would call Lewis and he would send over a check. We did not make requests of the other unions, but let them send in what they wanted. Lewis was nearby, he had the biggest treasury of all, and he was willing to provide the funds. After a few years, as affiliates started to send in per capita tax, CIO became more self-supporting, though large gifts continued to be made for specific purposes, usually by Lewis, such as to help a new union which was developing at a rate faster than CIO could support. Lewis also had a large staff of experienced organizers

* For example, from November 28, 1935, to February 28, 1937, out of contributions by member unions of about $720,000, the Mine Workers contributed $535,-000, or 74 per cent. The percentage varied somewhat at different periods, ranging between 60 per cent and 80 per cent.

on his payroll, and since the miners were solidly organized, he found it easy to spare many of them for assignments in steel, auto, or elsewhere.

I was not the only one of his old opponents that he brought back into activity. The first organizer sent out by CIO was Adolph Germer of Illinois. He was originally a coal miner, had been an organizer for the UMW and other unions, had been vice-president of the Springfield UMW during its brief existence, and had been national secretary of the Socialist Party during World War I. Lewis suggested his name as the labor member of an NRA compliance board in the Midwest, and when CIO started, he approved of using Adolph as an organizer. I sent Adolph to Detroit to help the auto workers, beginning in December, 1935.

Powers Hapgood had spoken to me at the Atlantic City convention about getting into activity; he was rather at loose ends at that time. I told him to go to Lewis and tell him he was ready to collaborate in organizing the unorganized, which he did. A little later, Lewis asked me if I thought Powers could be used. I said he could, and he was put to work. He helped with the rubber workers and auto workers, then was made director of the New England region, and later put in charge of the United Shoe Workers. In all of this he did good work. It was a pity he died so young, of a heart attack at the age of forty-nine. As he had requested, I read the miners' burial service at his funeral in Indianapolis.

I occasionally suggested to Lewis the names of men for various posts; for example, I suggested that Gus Scholle, a leader of the Flat Glass Workers' local in Toledo, be put into the field. Gus is now president of the Michigan state AFL–CIO. I was not always enthusiastic about the men Lewis sent in from the UMW, but events moved so fast that even routine types found themselves working harder than they ever had before, and as the new unions grew, younger men from the ranks often pushed the others aside and established their own leadership. That is how men like Reuther and Carey rose to the top. Our perennial problem was finding enough competent men to do the work, and we often had to be content with second-best. Thus, it was easy for Communists to establish themselves in the new unions. They were energetic and self-sacrificing and would go into any situation. Some got on the CIO payroll, but they were not the ones who established Communist centers of power. That was done by men from the ranks, who became local leaders with a solid following based on their services to the unions. Later, when the party line required them to go contrary to the interests of the CIO and of their own rank and file, such men lost their power. But until that happened, many were able to go far. Lewis would say, "If the bosses hire them, I can't shut them out of the union," which was true enough, but I think he felt that they should be allowed to work as long as it helped the movement and that he could throw them out if they got out of line.

Lee Pressman was the principal advocate of the Communists in the CIO, and had much to do with persuading Lewis that they were all right. Lewis sent Pressman to see me early in 1936, telling me only that he wanted me to look Pressman over and report my impressions. Lee came to my office, accompanied by Jett Lauck, an economist who had served as a consultant for the UMW and other unions. Jett introduced us and we started to talk about the CIO. Pressman soon reduced the conversation to a monologue, arguing that CIO needed the specialized help of an attorney. I demurred, pointing out that our work at that stage was organizing, not negotiating contracts, that we had no legal problems so far, and that I thought we could handle our own organizing, publicity, and any negotiations that might become necessary. But he persisted in arguing, until I rather resented his manner of lecturing me for my own good.

A few days later, Lewis asked me about the interview, and I told him I didn't see that we needed a lawyer at that point; Pressman had a lot of drive and persistence, but I had no idea whether he was a good lawyer or not. Shortly after, Lee showed up at the CIO office. Lewis had hired him without any further word to me, and he moved in and started working. I had very little legal business with him. He preferred to deal with Lewis, anyway, which was all right with me.

Pressman made himself much more than a legal counsel. He was intelligent, energetic, and very adroit, and he made himself useful to Lewis in preparing papers and policy decisions. He was also willing to do detail work for Lewis, who was impatient with such things. John made the basic decisions, no question about that; he was no pushover for anybody. But Pressman became a sort of grand vizier, efficiently serving the man with power. I never saw any evidence of his proselytizing for Communism; I don't know, of my own knowledge, whether he was a party member or not. But I do know that he threw his influence on the side of tolerating them, and seemed to be attuned to their shifts of line. This was not difficult for the first few years, because they were not fighting any basic CIO policy. Even when the Furriers came into the CIO, we had no hesitation about accepting them. Their president, Ben Gold, was universally known as a Communist, both when he was in the AFL and in the CIO. But we could see no reason to exclude him at the time.

The lines of authority and responsibility were not clearly defined, because Lewis did not operate that way. My work was pretty much what I was able to make of it, so long as I kept in regular touch with the real center of power, which was Lewis. We got along well for years, because we were both working for the same ends, and had only to discuss ways and means. If I thought money or manpower was needed somewhere or that a statement should be issued, or anything of that sort, I got in touch with Lewis and he usually agreed, with a minimum of discussion. I made reports from time to time of things that came to my attention, either from correspondence or from my frequent trips into the field. They might be written or oral reports, depending on the subject. Lewis's way of giving an assignment was to tell me to look into something, and either give him a report, or get some result he wanted, or even to do what I thought needed to be done. As long as I handled the situation, he was not concerned with details. I knew Lewis too well to let my guard down entirely, however, and his old habits showed up in keeping tabs on me.

He installed his brother-in-law, Raymond Bell, in my office as controller, to handle income and disbursements. I still made direct contact with Lewis when money was needed, but Bell handled the money. Then after a while, Walter Smethurst showed up. I came in one morning and found Walter sitting at a desk. He said Lewis had hired him and sent him over to make himself useful. He was on the UMW payroll, and under Lewis's direction, as far as I could find out. Well, he was useful, but it was clear to me that Lewis was dividing authority in the CIO headquarters. Smethurst was a very decent man, and I think he was embarrassed by his peculiar position. Ralph Hetzel was another Lewis assistant in the CIO office, who spent most of his time writing reports and press releases for Lewis. He was a very mild, quiet young man, who worked very hard.

When we began to set up regional offices, Lewis and I consulted about appointing regional directors. I attended a conference of local unions in New England in December, 1936, which was held primarily to give some of the newer unions in textiles, shoes, and other industries a feeling of belonging to a great movement. It was a successful meeting, and one outgrowth of it was the appointment of Powers Hapgood as director for that area, with which he was familiar. When Lewis had a candidate of his own for a particular post, he would consult with me, go over a list of possibilities and indicate the one he preferred.

Lewis selected Allan Haywood as regional director in the very important New York area. Adolph Germer had been there, but Adolph was very outspokenly anti-Communist, not at all bothered about who heard his views on the subject, so there were complaints about him. New York then was a stronghold of the Communists, especially in the new small unions. A real fight between the Communist and anti-Communist factions in New York would have wrecked the movement there, so Lewis looked for a more pliant and accommodating man to replace Adolph. Adolph was given some story about his being a Westerner and therefore more effective in a western post. Allan Haywood proved able to get along with all factions and to adapt himself to Lewis's wishes.

Haywood, like Germer, came out of the Illinois mines. He was one of those who accepted Lewis's victory over District 12, in 1932, and returned to the United Mine Workers. Haywood's home town was so vehemently anti-Lewis that he had to move his family out to get away from the neighbors, who considered him a traitor. Lewis assigned him to the Rubber Workers, then to the Auto Workers. The New York appointment was something of a promotion for Allan, and since he did not suffer from Germer's rigidity of principle, he was successful in that post. Haywood's strong suit was an easy-going, friendly manner to everybody, which he never allowed to be upset by disagreements. He had an almost automatic adjustment to Lewis's wishes during these years, which brought him safely through the hazards of factionalism in New York and in the national organization.

I spent far more time on the road than in the Washington office. Sometimes I went out alone, to consult with people in the various unions. On a few occasions, Lewis and I went together. One such occasion was our visit to Akron and Cleveland, in January of 1936. The rubber workers in Akron and auto workers in Cleveland needed assurance that CIO would stand behind them all the way, and there seemed no better way of giving that assurance than to have Lewis offer it in person. We had a very successful mass meeting on a cold, snowy Sunday afternoon in Akron. Lewis was in his best form, stirring the crowd to wild enthusiasm. The meeting that evening in Cleveland, with the storm even worse, was also fairly well attended. There Lewis was tied to the script of a prepared speech, and therefore not as effective as in Akron, but we were well satisfied with the results. We conferred with men from the vicinity, who wanted most of all a personal guarantee that the fight would be pushed through to victory. These meetings had value for us as a demonstration that the workers would respond to bold leadership.

The walkout in the Goodyear rubber factory in Akron, February 17, 1936, launched the first great CIO strike. The Goodyear local got its AFL charter in 1934, starting off with great enthusiasm, but two years of inaction dissipated the enthusiasm until the local was reduced to a handful. Pay cuts in November, 1935, and January, 1936, provoked sitdown strikes in some departments. The Akron mass meeting, followed by layoffs in the factory, revived the union. The strike was spontaneous and practically unanimous. Very few of the thousands who walked out of the Goodyear plant were union members, but many had had union experience, including numerous ex–coal-miners. The company moved aggressively to break the strike, with injunctions, police and deputy sheriffs thrown in to break up picket lines, a barrage of publicity in the newspapers and over the radio, and the enlistment of supervisors and the office force in a company union to provide meaningless statistics of the numbers still at work. We sent everybody we could muster to Akron—organizers, publicity men, and experienced negotiators. We sent Germer and Powers Hapgood, who were followed by Rose Pesotta, of the ILGWU (her book, *Bread upon the Waters*, contains a wonderful narrative of the strike), Leo Krzycki, of the Amalgamated Clothing Workers, and Ben Schafer, of the Oil Workers. Of course, there was a howl about outside agitators making trouble, but our people found that one of their most demanding jobs was to restrain the local talent on both sides from converting the strike into open warfare. A former mayor, who had been defeated for re-election, started a so-called "Law and Order League," which, like most such outfits, was a thin disguise for vigilantes. And many of the strikers, recent arrivals in the city from the rural South, were used to carrying weapons and would have had no hesitation about using them against any provocation. I encountered a chilling indication of the explosiveness of the situation shortly after my arrival in Akron, a couple of weeks after the strike began. I was taken on a tour of the many posts along the picket line around the struck plant. As I got into the car for the trip, I saw a big gun drop out of the hip pocket of the man next to me.

"What's that for?" I asked.

"Just a precaution," he said, "if any of those fellows try to pull anything on us, we'll meet them with the same thing."

I asked, "Do they know this?"

"Sure," he answered. "We've passed the word to the police that we'll give them as good as they send. And they know we mean it."

The police and the strikers, being of the same breed, understood each other. Fortunately, public pressure averted open violence against the strikers, except for a few minor scraps. Shortly before an agreement was reached, the vigilantes threatened to open the plant by an all-out attack. To warn the strikers in the event of a vigilante attack, the union bought time on the local radio station for the entire night, certainly the most fantastic broadcast in the history of radio. All night long, local musical talent of every conceivable sort was used, and McAlister Coleman, a fine labor journalist, turned out copy as fast as his typewriter could sputter—news, skits, talks—anything and everything. Coleman was a veteran of the *Illinois Miner* and other labor papers, as well as of regular newspaper work. His book, *Men and Coal,* is well worth reading for its understanding picture of the life and the problems of the coal miners.

The agreement which came out of this strike was a significant victory for the workers in the new unions.

We had campaigns going in a number of industries simultaneously, so that it is impossible to follow a chronological order in discussing my work with the various unions, or even to include reference to all the unions I did help at one time or another. I shall confine myself to some account of those I consider most important and interesting, with a few minor examples which will give a rounded picture of the kind of work I had to do.

Before we could do much about steel, we had to establish whether the AFL intended to obey the mandate of the Atlantic City Convention to organize that industry. The Amalgamated Association of Iron, Steel, and Tin Workers (which I shall refer to hereafter as "the Amalgamated," not to be confused with the Amalgamated Clothing Workers) presented a plan of organization to the AFL Executive Council in January, 1936, which was rejected as impractical because it called for one union in the industry. William Green then submitted a plan to affiliated unions, asking for a fund of $750,000 and the loan of organizers for a campaign under AFL direction, which would respect and safeguard the jurisdictional claims of all affiliated unions. Many unions did not even bother to reply; those that did pledged about $8,000 and a handful of organizers. The craft unions would cheerfully accept members from steel if somebody else would be so kind as to do the work of organizing for them.

The CIO submitted its proposal to Green on February 21. We called for a fund of $1,500,000, of which we offered to give $500,000 immediately. We stipulated that the campaign should be placed under the direction of a "responsible, energetic person, with a genuine understanding of the steel workers' problems, who will work in conjunction with an advisory committee representative of the unions supporting the drive," and that action should be taken quickly, since too much time had already been lost. Our offer was turned down, because of the conditions attached to it. In April we submitted our offer directly to the Amalgamated, which promised to take the matter up at its forthcoming convention.

I was scheduled to speak for the CIO at the convention of the Pennsylvania Federation of Labor in Uniontown, which met simultaneously with the Amalgamated convention at Canonsburg, a few miles away. Following my speech at the Uniontown convention, Lewis Hines, representing the AFL, made a lengthy attack on me and on the CIO, but the convention passed resolutions favoring industrial unionism, nevertheless. I went directly from there to Canonsburg, where I presented the CIO proposal. The papers published stories about me at this time which made it appear that I was running around with a check for half a million dollars in my pocket. It was a small convention, about a hundred delegates representing the eight to ten thousand members of the Amalgamated. There had never been anything this exciting at any of their previous conventions. The delegates instructed their officers to negotiate an agreement with us. The officers were very slow-moving; it took some time for us to prod them into coming to Washington. When they came, President Tighe was not well enough to attend, but he sent several board members. Lewis, Murray, and I met with them. David McDonald, Murray's secretary, was also present. We drew up an agreement, providing for the creation of the Steel Workers' Organizing Committee (SWOC), representing the Amalgamated and CIO. Philip Murray was to be the chairman. CIO agreed to provide money and manpower for a major drive. The Amalgamated would issue charters to new locals, and receive the charter fees. Dues payments, when they began, would come to SWOC. Eventually, the Amalgamated was swallowed up in SWOC, which became the United Steelworkers of America. By then Tighe was dead. The agreement was important mostly for the legal framework it provided for the steel campaign. We were staying as much within the legal niceties of the AFL organization as we could. Even so, we were denounced for fostering "dualism." We could not see then, and I cannot see now, anything "dualistic" about providing aid from one union to another for organizing campaigns. As for the charge of infringing upon the jurisdictions of craft unions, we could not work up any great concern for jurisdictions which had never been exercised and which were meaningless in the industry we were organizing. The argument that a man operating a machine that cuts wood is a carpenter, while the man operating a similar machine that cuts metal is a machinist or sheet metal worker involved distinctions much too metaphysical for men as busy organizing workers as we were.

Murray rented offices in the Grant Building in Pittsburgh (on whose construction I had worked as a laborer a decade before), and began to set up his staff. He consulted me about regional directors for the drive, which would be too big an enterprise to be directed entirely from a central office. He asked me if I would serve as one of the three directors, but I told him I felt an obligation to CIO to stay where I was. I would have been spared some bitter days if I had accepted his offer. He had thought of Van Bittner, at that time provisional president of UMW District 17 in West Virginia, for the Chicago center, and William Mitch, head of the UMW district in Alabama, who had been associated with me years before in the Nationalization Research Committee, for the Southern office in Birmingham. I proposed for Murray's assistant in the Pittsburgh area Clinton S. Golden, then Pittsburgh regional director of the National Labor Relations Board. These appointments were made, and Murray started hiring men to work in the field. Over two hundred organizers were sent out in the steel drive. Many were drawn from the UMW, some from other unions, but the largest number were men from the steel mills who showed aptitude and enthusiasm in the early days of the organization. We had no trouble finding work for the men; our problem was always finding men for the work.

I spoke at the first mass meeting of the campaign, held in the open air in New Kensington, near Pittsburgh. We brought our own crowd, by mustering all the coal miners for miles around, to bolster the spirits of the few steel workers daring enough to run the gauntlet of company spies. Enough men from the mills showed up to carry our message back, and thanks to the miners, we had an impressive demonstration.

The drive was a phenomenal success. One striking feature of it was the frequency with which whole company unions rebelled against company control and joined SWOC in a body. We had the same experience in the rubber, electrical and radio, and other industries. We did not have to go after the company unions. Leading men came to us for advice. We told them to present the workers' real demands to the company and when the demands were rejected to use the experience to show the members the need for a real union. The companies never failed to play into our hands; there was no profit in supporting a company union if it was going to act like a real union. The steel companies spent a fortune on newspaper advertising bearing down on the "outside agitators" theme. Traditional weapons—company police, spies, saboteurs, and agents provocateur—no longer had much effect. Even small pay increases failed to diminish the workers' enthusiasm for a union. The companies had previously denied that they could afford any raises; the workers knew perfectly well what had changed their minds.

My part in all this was limited. I was a member of the Organizing Committee and attended its meetings regularly. But Murray was running a successful campaign, and did not require my help, as other unions did.

I had more to do with the early fortunes of the United Auto Workers. I have already mentioned that one of my first trips, after CIO was organized, was to Detroit. On that trip, I met with Matthew Smith, the president of a small organization of skilled men in the auto industry called the Mechanics' Educational Society, to get him to affiliate with the AFL and CIO. He was an Englishman with socialistic ideas, who was strongly anti-AFL. But he was content with the small success he had had with his skilled men, and not much interested in the rest of the auto workers. We were ready to back his organization, as well as the UAW, in a co-operative drive to organize the industry. If Smith had been able to see the possibilities of the situation, he could have taken the real leadership in the auto workers, because his small organization was quite secure and the UAW had not yet developed its own leaders. But Smith was unwilling to move. His organization later affiliated with CIO, but by then the UAW was well established.

In November, 1936, the UAW and CIO agreed to launch a new organizing drive, centered in Detroit. The organizers and leaders of the local unions were brought together for a luncheon meeting, which was addressed by Phil Murray and me. The two of us then spent several days going to mass meetings at factory gates during the day, and in halls scattered all over the city in the evenings. Most of the indoor meetings were poorly attended; I remember an enormous high school auditorium on the West Side where hardly a baker's dozen turned up —this in an area with tens of thousands of auto workers. There was still fear of company spies. Murray and I paid no attention to the smallness of the turnout, but went ahead with our speeches as though we were addressing thousands, as indeed we were, for the grapevine passed along our promises of support.

Although the auto union made gains at plants in Cleveland, Toledo, and elsewhere, the critical fight which won the all-important Michigan area was made in Flint. There, the sitdowns started in November, a wave of strikes which swept through General Motors plants everywhere. Though the sitdown was not a new invention, its use on such a widespread scale was startling. The sitdown implied that the workers had a right in the plants equal to the property right of the owners. Though few workers thought this out, their dependence on a job for existence made them take this action—they had a right to defend their jobs, and what better place to do it than right where the jobs were? I went to Flint and entered the struck plants to advise and encourage the workers. The strike spread to Cleveland and Detroit. I was in and out several times, meeting with local leaders. During this period I got to know most of the important leaders in auto, including many young men who appeared from the ranks, like the three remarkable Reuther brothers. The least satisfactory of the new leaders was, unfortunately, the president, Homer Martin. He had been a hot-gospel preacher, and his strongest point was the ability to give long, emotional speeches very much like what I imagine his sermons had been. His style went over well with many of the boys from the South, but it was not enough of a talent for the job he had to do. He was flighty; I would make an agreement with him on some point of policy and he would reverse himself within a day. If I called him on it, he would agree with me again, but then reverse himself again. He had little knowledge of the industry, and no interest in the work of negotiating, which is at the very heart of a union president's job. He flitted in and out of wage conferences, leaving most of the job to subordinates, while he rushed off to make a speech somewhere. People like Germer and Krzycki were soon as exasperated with Martin as I was.

General Motors refused to negotiate until the strikers left the plants. We had no confidence in the company's vague promises to confer after this was done, and refused to act without a written promise. GM demanded that Governor Murphy have the sitdowners driven from the plants, which he refused to do. Instead, he tried to bring the two parties together. I took the train to Lansing with Wyndham Mortimer, a vice president of the UAW. We met the governor on the train and had breakfast with him in the diner, carefully keeping the conversation on safe topics. At the Capitol, the governer installed us in one office and Knudsen and some other high officers of General Motors in another. They had refused to sit down at the same table with us, so the governor was forced to go from one group to the other, like a messenger boy. Fortunately, he was able to put his duty to the people of his state above pride, conceding this ridiculous condition demanded by management in the interest of getting an agreement. It took a whole day, with the governor running back and forth, to reach an agreement that we would pull the sitdowners out of the plants, and then the company, within fifteen days, would enter negotiations with the United Auto Workers for all plants that were on strike. We insisted that an organization called the Flint Alliance, which had been created as a combination of company union and vigilante outfit, must not enter into the negotiations in any way. The company gave a vague promise but refused to put anything in writing. I was not satisfied. There had been too much of this go-between business; the company made too much of the "concession" involved in even talking to us. I advised against accepting the proposal. If we pulled out the sitdowners without any comparable concession from the company, we would be giving General Motors a chance to reverse itself and leave us stranded. But the UAW people were wobbly, especially Martin, who had shown up late in the day. I telephoned Lewis, taking Martin with me, and asked him to see if he could get Martin to understand what had to be done. He demurred at first, but finally agreed. Martin yessed Lewis on everything, but five minutes later was up in the air again. So we finally had to accept the promise to negotiate later as the best we could get.

Our meeting with General Motors ended on Saturday morning. We were to pull out the sitdown strikers on Monday. Early Sunday morning I got a call from Bill Lawrence, a newspaperman I knew. He said he had interviewed Knudsen, who said he intended to negotiate with both the union and the Flint Alliance. I phoned Martin and asked if he had heard about it. He had, but had no idea what to do.

I exploded. "Homer," I said, "this is a doublecross, one of the worst I've ever heard of. We've got to countermand the orders to the sitdowners, tell them to stay put tomorrow morning. We've got to see the governor, and we've got to tell the newspapers that it's all off until GM comes to its senses." I told him to come to my hotel—we were back in Detroit by this time—and we went to the governor's apartment. Murphy was very much upset by this development. He understood what it meant, even if Martin didn't. He phoned Knudsen, who confirmed the story. Murphy said this was not his, or the union's, understanding of the agreement. I repeated to the governor that we would not order the strikers out, and he relayed that message to Knudsen. Martin sent word to the sitdowners to stay put. I stuck to him like a brother, talking constantly about "doublecross, doublecross." I figured that he could at least remember the word if I repeated it often enough. We had a big mass meeting in Detroit that Sunday afternoon, which was well attended because word of the hitch in plans had gotten around. I was right at Martin's side until he stepped forward to make his speech. He got the lesson; he gave a fighting speech, to which the audience responded enthusiastically.

Knudsen's move was really a break for us. It gave us a chance to increase the pressure on the company, to spread the strike to more plants, and to get rid of the absurd "preliminary agreement."

Governor Murphy stood fast against using police or troops to drive the strikers out of the factory. He was a humane, sensitive, and highly courageous man, who was horrified by the idea of setting off violence which could be averted by a reasonable willingness to negotiate.

There were other maneuvers by the company, such as its application for an injunction to a judge who held a large block of General Motors stock. We exposed the connection, and the injunction was ignored by everyone, including the county sheriff.

The union was not slow to counter the attacks of the company. In

Flint, there were two Chevrolet plants which had not been interfered with by the union. One, the Chevy 4 plant, was very important; the other, Chevy 9, was small. The problem was to get a sitdown in Chevy 4 with a minimum of disturbance, which would be hard to do now that company guards were concentrated at the key points. Bob Travis, the UAW leader in Flint, Walter Reuther, and Powers Hapgood cooked up a scheme. They got the strike committee to approve calling a sitdown at Chevy 9, though most of them could see very little point in bothering about it. Then Travis and Reuther got together a small "spy-proof" committee, who were entrusted with the real plan. Roy Reuther and Hapgood went with a sound truck to Chevy 9 at the change of shifts and raised a great hubbub. All the company guards were rushed there and thrown into a struggle with the men, clearing them out of the plant. In the meantime, Chevy 4 was occupied by some four hundred strikers, who had only to order out a few supervisors to get complete control. As soon as word was sent to Hapgood that this was done, he ordered the men at Chevy 9 to disperse, and they all marched to the union headquarters in triumph.

I arrived in town the next day, and was told that a military guard had been posted around Chevy 4 and was refusing to let any food or supplies go into the plant. I phoned the governor and indignantly berated him for issuing such an order.

He said, "Wait a minute, John, I understand there are some people in that plant who don't belong there." I offered to go into the plant and bring out any who had no right there, if he would cancel his order. He agreed to phone the colonel in charge to let me through.

I was escorted to the plant gates by two National Guard officers and admitted by the union gate guards. Inside I found Roy and Walter Reuther, Powers, and one other man who was not an employee of GM. I told them they would have to come out with me, made a speech to the strikers urging them to hold fast and promising that supplies would be coming in, and then made a tour of inspection, as I had promised Murphy I would do.

Two hours after I had entered, the five us of us went out to climb the high wire fence. When I got to the top I saw a man in civilian clothes approaching with two guardsmen. He said he was the superintendent of the plant and he intended to inspect it; he was the representative of the governor. I said, "You're not going in. I am the governor's representative. I have inspected the plant, and everything's all right. There are a lot of people in there who don't like you; you stay out here where you are safe."

The strikers enjoyed this immensely, especially when they saw him turn and trudge away. I rather enjoyed it, too. I called the governor, assured him all was well, and he ordered the military to let food be sent in. We picked up our sound truck, and with the loudspeakers playing "Solidarity Forever" we returned to the union hall with all the honors of victory.

Lewis negotiated the settlement with General Motors which secured recognition of the union, the first major breakthrough against the auto industry's resistance to unionism. Wages and other terms of the contract were left to be negotiated by three-man committees from each side. Wyndham Mortimer and Ed Hall, of the UAW, and I represented the union. We labored for four weeks with Charles Wilson and two others from the company. Much of the delay was caused by Wilson's habit of coming back the day after we had agreed on an item and saying that he had been talking to some of his plant managers and they thought it ought to be changed slightly. After awhile I got fed up and told him this had to stop, because it was holding us up. His reply was that we had had a lot of experience with this sort of thing, but it was new to his boys. We would have to be patient with them until they had learned how to do it.

On the last day, we had the agreement typed up, and I said, "Now we are through, and all that's needed is to make a final copy and have it signed. Is that agreed?" Everybody agreed, but the next morning Wilson was back with "just a little point" which he thought would really be of some advantage to us. I said, "Charlie, you promised me last night that this would be final. I don't want the advantage; I want to wind this up." The other two union representatives agreed to go along with whatever I said.

Knudsen was there, completely in a fog about the issue. Wilson tried to explain it to him, and Knudsen turned to me and said, "Why not?"

I replied, "Because I said no, no, no."

Knudsen sighed, "Oh, yes. I remember you over at Lansing. Every time we brought anything in you said no, no, no."

"Well, I say, no, no, no, now," I said. The agreement was signed and presented to the General Motors Conference of the union, at which a lot of complaints were raised. I was tired out, and worried lest it be turned down, because I considered it an important step forward which should not be jeopardized. I remember that Walter Reuther came over and sat down beside me. I suppose my concern must have shown in my face, because Walter leaned over and said, "Don't worry, John, they'll approve this as soon as they get some of their feelings worked off." He was right, as it turned out. Martin, incidentally, was still out on the road making speeches through all of this.

Very few of the unions I worked with drew me into such dramatic incidents as auto and rubber. In most cases, it was an undramatic routine of meetings, letters, and occasional personal contacts, with me in the role of adviser—arguing, persuading, or just giving encouragement to the men in the field. I had too many calls on my time to stay with any one union for long. Thus, when the electrical and radio workers set up a council of federal locals and tried to get an international charter from the AFL, I was in fairly regular contact with their leaders, particularly with James Carey. I encouraged them to keep up their campaign for a charter and wrote to William Green, giving the support of CIO to their application. They were turned down, and the Executive Council voted to give the Brotherhood of Electrical Workers jurisdiction. This meant second-class citizenship in the Brotherhood, which the federal locals would not accept. I encouraged them in their stand, and in the decision to hold a convention, organize an international union, drawing in several large independent unions, and then invite the AFL to charter them. This was done, but the AFL refused even to consider the application, on the grounds that the new organization had not been authorized, that it included people outside the AFL, and that the whole problem had already been disposed of anyway. One might think the AFL would be pleased that the federal locals had persuaded the independents to give up their objection to affiliation with the Federation, thus bringing tens of thousands of new members in, but this was not the case.

The only leader of this union that I got to know well in its beginning was Jim Carey, who would drop in on me frequently to talk things over. He seemed to me a very intelligent and forceful man, and I enjoyed talking to him about his union's problems and his problems with the union. I remember once lecturing him not to make Homer Martin's mistake in letting contract negotiations slip into other hands. And later, when he was locked in a hard fight with the Communists for control of the union, I talked to him several times about how to build support against them. He had a real battle on his hands, because his opponents were able men with a solid base in the union. This was one of the new unions, in which any man who was willing to work from the beginning could establish himself. Men rose fast, though some fell equally fast when they failed the tests of responsible leadership.

Shortly after the General Motors settlement, in late spring of 1937, Lewis asked me to go in his place to a convention of the Maritime Federation of the Pacific. At that time CIO had almost nothing on the West Coast but a few locals of the Mine Workers and the Ladies' Garment Workers and some odds and ends which did not add up to a sufficient base of operations. We badly needed somebody backed by a strong local organization to take the lead in organizing. Lewis had had some talks with Harry Bridges, of the Longshoremen, and he wanted me to get Bridges into CIO, along with the other unions in the Maritime Federation and anything else I could get. Lewis did not tell me that he had an understanding with Bridges, and that Bridges was committed to joining up. One reason for this was that Lewis had also talked to Harry Lundberg, of the Sailors' Union of the Pacific, who had made it clear that he would not affiliate unless he had full protection against Bridges. The two men had worked together for a while in the past, but had become bitter enemies for both personal and political reasons. Lundberg was a product of the IWW, and still had some Wobbly ideas, including an intense and bitter hatred of the Communists. Whether or not Bridges was a member of the Communist Party, his union was following the Communist Party line, as were the maritime and some land-based unions in the West. Lundberg's following included ex-Wobblies, Trotskyites, and other non-Stalinite radicals, but his only secure base was the Sailors' Union, while Bridges controlled, directly or indirectly, a much larger movement. It was typical of Lewis that, knowing all this, he just told me to go out there and try to get both Bridges and Lundberg, but to take either one if it had to be a choice. The Communist line had finally swung over to "support" of the CIO. Bridges was ready to come in but he expected special consideration for his affiliation (I don't know whether Lewis had promised to put him in charge of the West Coast or not, though Bridges would certainly have expected it). Thus, my real job was the almost impossible one of persuading Lundberg to come along with us and take his chances under Bridges.

I talked to Bridges before the convention and got his views. At the convention, I spoke for an hour, urging the delegates to join the CIO, and then answered questions—there must have been two hundred of them, from formal matters, such as the constitution of CIO, to very intricate questions about the autonomy of affiliated unions, our attitude toward war, rank-and-file control, etc. These men had been through the union wars, they had studied the problems of organized labor, and many had been steeped in the radical press for years. They missed very little. The questioning went on through the morning and afternoon, though they gave me a chair in the afternoon so that I could at least sit down.

I had two long talks with Lundberg, whose organization was in favor of affiliation, as attested by a referendum vote just concluded, and who was himself in favor of CIO. In spite of all I could do to assure him that his union would be safe from Bridges if both joined up, he stuck to it that he would not join if Bridges did. So I had to return to Washington and tell Lewis we had the Maritime Federation, but not the Sailors.

Before I left Portland, Bridges tried to find out from me what he could expect from Lewis, perhaps double-checking on what Lewis had already told him, whatever that was. I simply held to the general line that aid would be forthcoming to any union that affiliated and showed it could use such aid. He brought up the question of a director for the West Coast. I said I knew nothing about that; it would be decided by Lewis when the time came. So Bridges didn't get anything from me beyond what he had heard from Lewis or from Lee Pressman. When I talked to Lewis I told him what he already knew, that there was no choice on the Coast. The UMW representatives there were nonentities. The garment workers and others were weak and not capable of providing leadership. So the choice was between Lundberg and Bridges. Bridges represented much the larger organization, and was ready to come in. Rejecting Bridges in order to get Lundberg would leave us with a much smaller base than we needed.

I don't believe Lewis was ever happy about Bridges, who was not one to be captured or used, but had his own ideas and ambitions. And he was very tough, just as tough as Lewis. Later on, after Bridges had been in charge of the West Coast for some time, Lewis divided the job and put another man in charge of the Los Angeles area. But Bridges represented real power, which Lewis respected, so there was no break between the two men.

Questions about unions outside the AFL kept coming up all through the early years of CIO. I've referred to some of the independents in auto, radio, and maritime. They were products of NRA and the slowness of the AFL to accept industrial unionism. Bridges' West Coast Longshoremen were in conflict with the corrupt leadership of the AFL union in that field, which was concentrated on the East Coast. Affiliation with CIO meant a break with the AFL.

We kept getting appeals from small independent unions in the shoe industry, and I met with representatives of four or five of these in December of 1936. The Boot and Shoe Workers, the AFL affiliate, was weak and had survived largely because it could give a union label to manufacturers of men's shoes. There had been dual unions for forty years, none very strong, but the current crop had some promise if they could be persuaded to merge. There was a lot of jealousy among the independents—some represented only a single city—so I had to find a man among them who could give leadership for unity. Fortunately, I found such a man, James Mitchell, known as "Scotty." He was not colorful, but he was solid, and everybody trusted him. With his help, I persuaded all but one of the independents to accept provisional unity, and sent Powers Hapgood to direct the work of organization, especially in New England. I had three or four meetings with people from these unions, some lasting for hours, and I had to use all the skills of a diplomat to get them to bury past differences and work together. The merger was successful and built the biggest shoe union ever. My reason for describing this development is not so much the importance of that particular union, which was only one of a number of smaller unions I worked with, as to illustrate the nature of so much of my work: meeting with people, talking over their problems, trying to get them to agree on programs of action which would lead to organization, and then when it seemed they could handle things, passing on to the next problem, knowing well that I might have to come back later and do it all over again.

I had little to do with the long-drawn-out wrangle with the AFL. That was in the hands of Lewis and Howard, in consultation with the other union presidents. The subject has been covered thoroughly in several books, to which I have little to add.

I do know that Lewis was not at all anxious to patch things up with the AFL. He considered the split a far lesser evil than the danger of interference with successful organizing campaigns. When committees representing the two organizations met in October, 1937, the CIO proposal was intended to provide such secure safeguards for the new unions that the AFL committee would not be able to accept. They did not accept, but their counter-proposals included some concessions, enough to worry Lewis. At a meeting I attended with Murray and the other members of his committee, Lewis for the first time said plainly that he was opposed to unity. Murray had not realized this, and was embarrassed by the position he was put into by Lewis's change of tone. I don't think anybody but Dubinsky really disagreed with Lewis at this stage. Dubinsky felt strongly about unity, partly because a large faction in his own union had been reluctant to go along with CIO from the start. At this point, Dubinsky began to distrust Lewis.

Murray was instructed to insist upon the original CIO position, which thus became an ultimatum, and the talks failed. Lewis, I think, believed that if we pushed ahead with our campaigns the CIO would outstrip the AFL in membership and we then could dictate our own terms. The craft unions proved to be more adaptable than he expected. Some, like the Carpenters, Electrical Workers, Machinists, and Boiler-makers, developed their own campaigns and became partly industrial, partly craft unions. By the time unity was achieved, jurisdictions were more scrambled than ever before. In the meantime, I agreed with Lewis on the general principle that the prerequisites for unity were recognition of the gains made by CIO and guarantees that organization of the unorganized would continue.

||||||||||||||||||||||||||||||||||||||

20

CIO MATURES

John L. Lewis's exit from CIO was a complicated process. The immediate occasion for his disowning his own child was the controversy over a third term for Franklin Roosevelt in 1940. This had its roots in the disputes between Lewis and Roosevelt over the Little Steel strike and the international situation. There may have been even more to it. The story that Lewis wanted a place on the Democratic ticket in 1940 may or may not be true; he did not confide in me. But I do know that Lewis was dissatisfied for several years before then.

The Little Steel strike was CIO's first major defeat. Lewis was bitter about it, as were we all. When Roosevelt called down a plague on both houses, Lewis was provoked to a stinging and often-quoted retort: "It ill behooves one who has supped at labor's table and who has been sheltered in labor's house to curse with equal fervor and fine impartiality both labor and its adversaries when they become locked in deadly embrace." I thought Lewis was making it a little strong, but it is usually wise not to let any administration take labor for granted, and I expected the storm to blow over.

The next morning, I encountered Lee Pressman in the lobby of the Carlton Hotel, and was chatting with him when Hillman came in, very upset. He thought Lewis's statement was far too extreme and said to me, "You ought to take care that things like this don't happen."

I pointed out that I had just returned to town and was not present when Lewis made his statement. Hillman then turned on Pressman and said that Lee should see that Lewis did not go off on such a tangent. Lee laughed and said, "What can I do with Lewis? What can anyone do with Lewis?" Although most of the top CIO people agreed with me in thinking the storm would blow over, Hillman's fears turned out to be justified. Lewis drew farther and farther away from Roosevelt, creating friction within the CIO leadership. It was as though, having failed to dominate the President by the use of his power in CIO, Lewis was driven to gamble even his CIO position in a desperate effort to retrieve his losses, thereby losing everything.

Lewis, Hillman, and George Berry of the AFL Printing Pressmen's Union had been the prime movers in organizing Labor's Non-Partisan League (LNPL) to support Roosevelt in 1936, but Lewis treated the organization as his private possession. He expected a return on his "investment" in Roosevelt's re-election, and when it became clear he would not get everything he wanted, he soured on the administration. His report to the 1938 convention of CIO contained no word of good will toward the President. By the 1939 CIO convention in San Francisco, Lewis had succeeded Berry as chairman of LNPL. Roosevelt sent a long friendly message to the convention, which Lewis curtly dismissed, saying the secretary would reply to communications. The convention endorsed the policy of neutrality toward the struggle in Europe. There were no resolutions adopted against Fascism. Lewis declared flatly that he would not continue in the presidency of CIO unless he was free to oppose involvement in European quarrels. The other leaders bowed to his ultimatum, and Hillman nominated him for re-election.

Lewis launched his campaign against Roosevelt at first through the Mine Workers and such men in other CIO unions as he could directly control, ordering them to throw their weight against a third term for Roosevelt.

He convinced himself that a mass movement of discontent with the administration was building up, because of unemployment and fear of involvement in the European war. When he found that staff people in LNPL did not agree with him, he started a purge, forcing Eli Oliver, the executive vice-president of the League, to resign. Oliver had been Hillman's choice for the post, so his departure marked a break between Lewis and Hillman on the political front. Other staff members of LNPL also resigned, and before long the organization was reduced to a shadow of John L. Lewis. During 1940, Lewis made speeches before the Youth Congress, the National Negro Congress, and the Townsendites, as well as some CIO unions. He expected to build up a great alliance of many forces in support of his vendetta with Roosevelt. The first two organizations mentioned were Communist-front groups. The Communists, at that point, were denouncing the war as an imperialist slaughter, and thanks to the Nazi-Soviet Pact, considered the anti-Fascist alliance even worse than the Nazis, so they cheered Lewis enthusiastically. He mistook their cheers for the voice of the people. He tried first to put over the isolationist Senator Burton K. Wheeler for the Democratic nomination; when that failed, he turned to the Republican candidate, Wendell Willkie.

These political shifts contributed to worsening relations between Lewis and me, because I, like most of the labor movement, could not accept Lewis's political views, and made no secret of that fact. However, Lewis was concerned about me even before 1940.

Probably the thing that ruined my standing with Lewis was the aftermath of Charles Howard's death in July, 1938. Howard's position as secretary of CIO had started as a more or less honorary post. His union was not affiliated, so he did not represent any organized force. But his name was useful to us, because of his high prestige in the labor movement as president of the Typographical Workers, so he was given the title of secretary, which required no more than attaching his signature to certain letters. He did not even keep minutes of the Committee meetings, because Lewis did not want minutes kept. I brought Kitty Ellickson to some of the meetings and had her take rough stenographic notes for my own information, the nearest thing to minutes we ever had. With the establishment of the Congress of Industrial Organizations, in 1938, the secretaryship became potentially an important post. In my capacity as Director, I had long been doing much of what a secretary would normally do. From July to November, 1938, when the convention met, I was acting secretary; my name was signed to the convention call with that title. It was widely assumed, both among the leadership and throughout the country, that I would be elected secretary. Even James Carey, who was actually elected, has said many times that he went to Pittsburgh intending to vote for me, and was astonished to find himself elected instead.

Although Lewis dropped hints that putting my name on the convention call was not without significance, something happened to change him. I am sure that one factor in that process was the procession of people who went to him to urge that I be named. I know that people like Hillman and Murray spoke to him on the subject, and he told me himself that almost every delegation he saw included an endorsement of me among the things they had to say. He told me to stop the delegations from bothering him on the subject, but I could do nothing about it because I was not informed of their intentions. The evidence that accumulated before him of support for me probably was the worst thing that could have happened. He wanted no equal, especially not a man he had had on his payroll, one notoriously subject to the vice of thinking for himself. It was not so much that I would be a rival to Lewis, but that I would become independent of him and with the prestige of election on my own merits, would be listened to when I disagreed with him.

The other factor in Lewis's change of attitude I heard about from Phil Murray. During the week before the convention, Murray told me, he and Hillman had lunch with Lewis, who proposed to make his daughter, Kathryn, secretary, and asked their advice. Hillman immediately replied that he thought it would be a mistake, and would injure the movement. Murray said nothing until Lewis asked him directly what he thought, then agreed with Hillman.

Lewis said, "Well, what am I going to do?"

Murray replied, "Why not John? After all, he's been doing the work for quite some time."

Lewis looked at Hillman, who nodded agreement.

"No," said Lewis, "with you and Sidney as vice presidents and me as president, that would be too many miners, three out of four top officers."

"Why not leave me out?" said Murray. "There are plenty of others who can serve, and I've plenty to do without that. I think you ought to get John." Lewis gave no answer, but sat and glowered at them.

I don't know where the idea of putting in Kathryn Lewis came from, but I do know that Lewis was strong for his family, and always backed them to the limit. It was obvious that Kathryn could not be put over, but he was determined not to take a chance on me. Whether Kathryn suggested Carey as a substitute or whether it was Lewis's own idea, I don't know. Whoever thought of it, it was a good choice, because it gave recognition to the younger generation and to the newly formed unions, and Jimmy has done good work for the labor movement. There were some who wanted to put my name in nomination anyway, but I refused to allow it, because if I could not have the support of my own union, I would not accept. And I had no desire to be a storm center, especially when no issue of principle was involved. I could spare CIO a controversy over personalities, and go on doing my best in the job I already had.

But I was not allowed to hold even that for long. The following year, Lewis sprang a surprise on the Executive Board at its meeting following the 1939 San Francisco convention. This was just a week after the session at which he forced them to draft him for the presidency on his own terms. Without offering any criticism of me or of my work, he proposed to dispense with the post of National Director. He said that I would be given "a place of distinction," without specifying what it would be. He appointed Allan Haywood Director of Organization, which was practically the post I had held, and I was made Director of Local Industrial Unions. That was much nearer a post of extinction than distinction. But Lewis, knowing I was well liked, would not try to wipe me out with one blow. He just set my feet on an escalator headed downward.

I no doubt helped bring on my demotion by asserting my views on the international situation. It seemed to me shocking that we should ignore the abominations being practiced against the people of Europe and the Far East by the Axis powers, and desert the labor movement which was being wiped out in country after country. On Labor Day of 1939, Lewis made a radio speech arguing that the war was none of our concern, and we should confine ourselves to taking care of our needs at home. I spoke in Des Moines on the same day, taking the opposite line. On the way back to Washington, I changed planes in Chicago and met Lee Pressman on his way back from speaking in Duluth. I expressed my shock at Lewis's line, and Pressman and I got into a heated argument. I not only condemned the Nazis, but also the Soviet Union for its agreement with Hitler, opening Poland to invasion. He defended the Pact, and finally said to me. "Your position is not Lewis's."

"I know that," I said. "Lewis is wrong; we can't be neutral." Nobody was as intimate with Lewis at that time as Pressman, so Lewis undoubtedly learned about that exchange the minute they got together.

In December I was invited to address the convention of the Retail and Wholesale Clerks in Detroit. I told Lewis I was going, and asked if he had a message to send. He said something about giving them his greetings, which I promised to do.

I talked first about the organizing gains being made by CIO, then wove in a reference to the "greetings from President Lewis, with whom I talked before coming to Detroit," just to soften them up for the next part of my speech, which was a blistering attack on the Nazi-Soviet Pact and on the devastation of the European labor movement by the Fascist-Communist combination, ending with a warning that we could not be neutral because our turn was coming. This convention was swarming with Communists, who were floored by my speech, especially because it sounded so official. Even Allan Haywood was puzzled, trying to figure what I was up to. Archie Robinson, at that time a reporter for a Detroit paper, and an old friend of mine, came to see me after the meeting and remarked, "Well, John, you certainly built a fire under the Comrades today." I knew perfectly well that I was playing with fire, in more senses than one, but I have never been notorious for my ability to keep my mouth shut when I think it should be opened.

I attended the convention of the United Mine Workers, in January, 1940, as a delegate from my old local in Nanty Glo, and heard Lewis declare that Roosevelt could not and should not be re-elected. Lewis brought in his candidate, Senator Wheeler, who got polite applause for his speech, but aroused no enthusiasm. A resolution was introduced at this convention expressing sympathy for Finland in the war with the Soviet Union. The resolutions committee reported against it, whereupon I took the floor to speak. I attacked Russian aggression against Finland vigorously. The issue did not mean much to most of the delegates, so there was only a mild response. Lewis was not attacking the Soviet Union at that time. His followers, who had tried their best to create a demonstration for Wheeler, sat silently through my speech. The only signs of enthusiasm in the whole convention came when Lewis spoke on union matters and when references were made to Franklin Roosevelt.

In May, 1940, I went to the convention of the Pennsylvania State CIO Council. Tom Kennedy was there, and the Mine Workers' delegates dominated the convention. My speech was not controversial, but Emil Rieve, of the Textile Workers, almost upset Kennedy's plan to prevent an endorsement of Roosevelt for a third term. Rieve came out strongly for F. D. R., and the delegates, who had been apathetic up to that point, broke out in cheers. In conversations with miners at this convention I learned that there was no rank-and-file support for Lewis's political line; they were solidly for Roosevelt.

On my return to Washington, I went over to see Lewis. I told Kathryn Lewis that I had a message I thought her father would be interested in hearing. She went into his office and returned promptly to say, "He will see you now, Mr. Brophy." Kathryn was always very formal with me.

Lewis was sitting at his big desk, just about to light one of his Churchillian cigars. He started to offer me one, then said, "You don't smoke, as I recall, John."

I declined the cigar, and also declined the chair facing him by sitting in another which did not leave the desk between us. I said, "John, we haven't talked for some time, so I thought you ought to hear what happened at the Pennsylvania convention. As you know, most of the delegates were miners, and while they didn't formally endorse Roosevelt for a third term, there is no doubt that they, as well as the other delegates, were solidly for him. They proved it by cheering every mention of his name, no matter how it came up. I don't know what people have been telling you, but there is no doubt that labor is behind Roosevelt today, both on domestic and foreign questions. The workers are concerned about what is happening to labor abroad, and about Hitler's program of extermination of the Jews. They are not neutral."

When I first came in, he had been very affable, but as I went on, rubbing it in a little and enjoying it, he began to scowl. He growled, "Don't they understand that if Roosevelt is elected, it means war?"

"No," I said, "they don't understand it that way. They think the question of our involvement in the war will be settled by the Axis, not by Roosevelt. And they are for support of the Allies against Hitler. These are our people, the miners, John, and they have made up their minds."

He glowered at me and said something to the effect that anybody would be better than Roosevelt.

I replied, "Well, John, you can't beat somebody with nobody."

"That's right," he said; "I haven't got a candidate."

"Any candidate you find," I said, "will have to be more popular than Roosevelt. And despite his limitations, there is great feeling for him because of what he has done for labor, even though he has not gone as far as we would have liked."

Well, I had spoiled his day. And, as the bringer of bad news, I had not boosted my stock. But I did tell him the facts as to where his political adventuring was leading him. Even so, he continued to think he could swing the tide for Willkie, as he tried to do in his broadcast just before the election.

I had returned from the January UMW convention with a bad case of influenza, after which I did not recover my usual vigor. Thinking a little sun might help, I arranged for several weeks of work in the South, but was not helped by the change. When the summer heat in Washington became oppressive, after my return, I made a trip to Canada, still hoping for a complete recovery. The high point of that trip was a visit to St. Francis Xavier University, in Antigonish, Nova Scotia, where I saw the work of some of the priests in encouraging co-operatives among the farmers, fishermen, and miners of the region.

When I returned home, still unimproved, Anita insisted on calling in another doctor, who told me I had a heart condition that required absolute bed rest, perhaps for months. I reported this to Lewis, who told me to take as much time as I needed. Thus it happened that I took no part in the 1940 election campaign, during which Lewis declared that he would consider the election of Roosevelt a vote of no confidence in himself, as a consequence of which he would resign the presidency of CIO. The workers voted overwhelmingly for Roosevelt, and Lewis, forced to live up to his threat, offered his resignation. If he had hoped for another draft, none was forthcoming. By then CIO was well established, and there was complete agreement on the choice of Murray to succeed Lewis. Murray was head of the Steelworkers, a union as large as the Miners, if not larger. CIO could now get along without Lewis, and many were relieved to be free of his eccentricities.

One of the most remarkable things I encountered in the political tangle of 1940 was a visit from Harry Bridges, who insisted on seeing me although I was not supposed to have visitors. He told me he had been talking politics with Lewis. He agreed with Lewis and assured him of support in the fight against Roosevelt. I lost my temper, though I was supposed to be very quiet. I told him, "I'm ashamed of you. You're supposed to be a militant, but I can't see it. You'll take this lawyer for the power companies in preference to a man whose policy has made it possible for labor to make the gains it has. I'd have thought you'd be above such things."

"Well," he said, "Lewis——"

I interrupted, "Lewis is wrong, too. And you should know better than to encourage him." Harry tried to argue with me, but finally gave up. I have thought that Lewis may have suggested that he see me, to find out whether I might change my mind. If so, I convinced him that I was a hopeless case. This was a strange alliance, of the Republican and the president of a Communist-dominated union, but it was an alliance Lewis had created. He couldn't peddle his line to anyone else. Bridges, like the Communists, could change his line as easily as taking off his hat, but I was not built that way, nor were most people in the labor movement.

My physical condition continued to be bad, with complications delaying recovery from the heart condition. I was unable to attend the Atlantic City convention at which Lewis made his exit from CIO. He later returned to the AFL, but not being able to play the role there to which he aspired, broke away again after a few months. I suppose the Mine Workers will remain independent as long as Lewis lives, because he will never let go of actual control of the union. But his great days of service to labor ended with his departure from CIO, which he forced to reject him in spite of all his genuine contributions to the cause.

When I was finally ready to return to work, on the first of December, I found that my desk had been removed from the office, my secretary was gone, and there was nothing left to indicate that I was ever expected to return. Lewis had taken advantage of my illness to remove every trace of me from the Washington office. If events had not brought about his resignation at just that point, I would, no doubt, have been assigned to some outer-Siberian exile as punishment for "disloyalty."

!!!

21

SERVICE ON MANY FRONTS

As soon as Murray learned that Lewis had cleaned me out, he ordered that my desk, my secretary, and my office be restored to me. Not only that, he gave me a more important assignment, shifting me from the work with local industrial unions to the post of Director of Councils. This job grew in importance, as I will demonstrate shortly.

Lewis had not immediately withdrawn from CIO, evidently hoping to make a comeback. Unfortunately for his plans, history played him false. Hitler invaded Russia a few months later, and the Communists overnight became ardent partisans of American intervention to save the "Workers' Fatherland." By the end of 1941, we were forced into the war by the Japanese attack on Pearl Harbor. Lewis was left without any allies whatever and when he did finally pull the miners out of CIO, no other union followed his lead. Before Lewis's withdrawal, he and Murray clashed, because Murray insisted on co-operating with the government against the Fascist threat. Lewis demanded that Carey be removed as secretary because of the sharpness of his criticism of Lewis, but Murray refused to abandon Carey.

Early in 1942, Lewis used his position as chairman of a CIO unity committee he had himself appointed several years earlier to propose a plan of labor unity, bypassing Murray. Murray was furious at this attempt to go over his head, and was backed by the CIO executive board in rejecting the maneuver. He went ahead in his own way to prepare for unity by co-operating with the AFL in the combined Labor Victory Committee, and later in founding the International Confederation of Free Trade Unions (ICFTU). In May, SWOC was transformed into the United Steelworkers, with Murray as president. Lewis took this opportunity to remove Murray from the vice-presidency of the Miners, after a contrived and humiliating "trial" on the charge of holding two jobs.

Murray had been for many years the most important individual among Lewis's supporters. His great talent as a negotiator had been indispensable to Lewis. Both in dealings with coal operators and in the major settlements of the early CIO years, Murray often did the hard work of negotiation, with Lewis coming in at the end to make a speech and affix his signature to the agreement. Further, Murray was invaluable to Lewis in relations with people. He could soften the impact of Lewis's ultimatums and lead men to co-operate who might otherwise have been alienated by Lewis's driving. The two men were never friends in any real sense, and I know that Murray was often unhappy about his relation with Lewis, but he swallowed his resentment in the interest of the union. He had suffered from Lewis's habit of limiting the authority of subordinates. After the UMW headquarters was moved to Washington early in the thirties, Lewis brought in his brother, Denny Lewis, and had him handle matters which should have gone to Murray. Murray was annoyed by this undercutting of his constitutional position in the union, but there was nothing anybody could do when Lewis pushed forward a member of the family. I know Murray talked to Lewis abut it, but Lewis's response was, "Well, what does it matter, Phil? When there is real work to be done, you're still the man for it. This is just detail you should be glad to get rid of." It was true that Denny lacked the ability to handle important jobs, so Phil had to settle for that, but he was not happy about it. Several times, Murray and I drove together from Washington to Pittsburgh, and he let me see that he was dissatisfied with the way he was being treated. Fortunately for Phil, history was on his side. When the break came, he was able to maintain his position against Lewis's attacks.

I found it easier and pleasanter to work with Murray than with Lewis. The most important difference was that when Murray appointed me to a post he left it to me to do the best I could and backed me all the way. I was not expected to be able to read his mind, nor did

I have to check everything out with him before following accepted policy. In short, I could feel that I knew what I was doing and go ahead and do it.

For the first few months of Murray's presidency, the Communist Party line was still opposed to our involvement in the war, as evidenced by their efforts to prolong the strike at the North American Aviation Company. The dispute was referred to the National Defense Mediation Board, created in March, 1941. Murray and Thomas Kennedy represented CIO on the Board, and I was an alternate. Murray backed the decision of the Board, calling on the workers to return to work while the strike was being settled. For this he was roundly denounced by the Communists as a strikebreaker.

Communist sabotage of national defense was ended by the invasion of Russia, and for the rest of the war the chief problem with them was their excessive eagerness to abandon all efforts to improve or even to maintain labor's position. CIO had given, and kept, a no-strike pledge, but was not willing to yield the workers' rights, which would have suited the Communists as long as the Soviet Union was in danger. With the end of the war, the party line shifted again and the Communists went back to obstructionism.

Murray had never been happy about Lewis's indifference to the presence of Communists in important CIO posts. He had made sure that any Communists who showed up in SWOC were either silenced or quietly squeezed out. In CIO, he watched the situation carefully, biding his time until he was sure he could get rid of them with a minimum of damage to the movement. An open anti-Communist campaign during the war would have allowed the Communists to charge us with sabotaging unity and all-out production, and they might have won sympathy from people who did not understand them as well as Murray did. But with these false issues removed by the beginning of the cold war, Murray could move strongly against the Communists.

My work as Director of Councils frequently threw me into the fight with the Communists. When I took up the job, there were well over a hundred regional, state, and local Industrial Union Councils, set up as equivalents to the City Central bodies and State Federations of the AFL. They were designed to provide a means of mutual aid on the local level, to engage in legislative work, public relations, and many kinds of community activity. They did not possess the autonomy of affiliated national unions, but were required to conform to national

CIO policy. From the end of the war until the expulsion of the Communist-dominated unions, the Communists made every effort to pack certain councils and use them for propaganda. On such questions as the Marshall Plan and Henry Wallace's campaign for the presidency in 1948, the Communists came into head-on conflict with the CIO majority. Their agitation for immediate and complete demobilization at the end of the war led them to prolong and exacerbate strikes, in order to make the government appear anti-labor.

The Communists were well entrenched in the councils of New York, Detroit, Chicago, Milwaukee, and Los Angeles, among others. When the Los Angeles Council endorsed the Wallace third-party movement in 1948, after opposing the Marshall Plan and supporting nuisance strikes, the anti-Communist minority appealed to me. I laid down the law to the Council, and shortly after received a long-distance phone call from Harry Bridges, who argued that this was a violation of our pledge that autonomy of subordinate bodies in CIO would be respected. My answer, which I had to repeat again and again—Harry was not one to give up easily, no matter how high his phone bill went —was that affiliated national unions had autonomy, that individuals could campaign for anybody they pleased, but the councils were created by CIO and must not go counter to CIO. Harry was not satisfied, but I made my ruling stick, in that case and in others, so that neither the prestige nor the funds of the councils could be misused.

The fight with the Communists in the Milwaukee County and Wisconsin State councils was prolonged and complicated. The affiliation of the Brewery Workers in 1946 added enough new delegates to the Milwaukee Council to upset the left-wing majority. In order to keep control, the left-wingers proposed to delay seating the Brewers until after a Council election. I ruled that under the regulations laid down by CIO, the Brewers had to be seated. The left wing then charged that there were irregularities in the election, and Murray sent Haywood and me in to investigate. We found no evidence of irregularities and recommended the appointment of an administrator, Peter Markunas, to manage the affairs of the Council until the next election. When the election was held, the right wing won easily. Then, the right wing presented a slate against the leftist officers of the State Council. Again, the Communists tried to use a constitutional quibble to maintain a fictitious majority, and I went to Wausau to give my ruling on this question in person. The Communists attached themselves to me from the moment I arrived, arguing for their position. I refused to commit myself, insisting that I had to talk to the other side and would make my ruling only in the convention. They would not give up, but kept hammering at me to get a favorable commitment.

The next day, I ruled that the vote had to be taken in the way that would give the right wing a chance. The vote was taken as I prescribed, and it was soon clear that the right wing was winning. The outgoing secretary-treasurer came over to me as the votes were being counted and said, "John, I'm going to be defeated, and you're the cause of it." I told him it was his own fault, for letting himself be used. I don't think he was ever a party member, but he had been taken up on a high mountain and shown the kingdoms of this world, and he let himself be tempted. He was not the only good trade unionist who was trapped in that way in those days.

The decisive battle with the Communists was fought in Wisconsin in the Allis-Chalmers strike of 1947. This story requires some background history of the United Auto Workers. I've described the trouble we had with Homer Martin, which got worse and worse. He was incapable of exercising his authority as president, but he was determined to cut down anybody who threatened him by demonstrating either ability or a critical attitude. Thus he came into conflict with one after another of the new men who were rising to leadership in the locals, men like Wyndham Mortimer of Cleveland and Walter Reuther of the big West Side local in Detroit. Martin was constantly under attack from the Communists, but instead of organizing the anti-Communist majority to crush them, he tried the prima donna role and managed to alienate almost everybody. He expelled members of the executive board until there was scarcely anybody left.

Finally CIO had to intervene. Lewis called all the leaders, expelled or not, to meet with him and Murray and me in Washington. Lewis ruled that Murray and Hillman should supervise a special convention, with all factions represented, at which a compromise slate of officers would be elected. Martin at first accepted this proposal, but as always, changed his mind and later rejected it.

All the factions, except a negligible remnant which still followed Martin, met to reorganize the UAW. R. J. Thomas, who had managed to get along with Martin longer than anybody else, but who could be relied upon to carry out convention decisions, was elected president, as Lewis had proposed. Thomas was a very likeable man who had no strong enemies, so it was hoped that he would hold things together. At the time, I felt that the ablest man had been passed over—I refer to Walter Reuther—and I let my opinion be known. But Murray considered that Walter was too young, too brash and outspoken. This was a reflection of Lewis's views. Reuther had not impressed Lewis favorably, for the same reasons—he had even interrupted Lewis at one point and argued with him, which was not the way to treat the master.

In spite of all his qualities, Thomas did not hold his position for long, but was defeated by Reuther in a later election. When the Allis-Chalmers crisis came along, Thomas was a vice president of UAW trying to build support for a comeback. Reuther, with his Socialist background, knew the Communists like a book, and was the greatest threat to them for that reason, far more than the most rigidly right-wing Republican. So the Communists backed Thomas against Reuther. And Thomas, seeing the situation as just another distribution of factions in the union, accepted their support without committing himself to their objectives.

Reuther's whole future depended on winning his second election to the presidency. If he blundered in handling the Allis-Chalmers strike, which was attracting nationwide attention, he would wreck his career, yet if he let it go on without doing anything, the effect would be equally disastrous.

The company was willing to make a reasonable settlement, but the local union leaders rejected everything, presenting extreme demands just to provide the Communist Party with something to agitate about. The strike was doing labor great harm in Milwaukee, a good union town. Walter called Murray to tell him that a meeting had been set up with the Allis-Chalmers management, and he wanted somebody representing CIO to go into it with him. Murray at first proposed to send Haywood, but Reuther asked for me. We met with the management people and then went to Detroit to report to the UAW executive board. The board was about evenly split, and Thomas tried to argue that our meeting with management constituted an effort to undercut the strike. I backed Walter's position with a public statement which disposed of Thomas's objection.

In order to get a binding agreement, we had to whip the local leadership into line, so Walter went to Milwaukee. He had the help of a local Methodist minister, Reverend Ensworth Reisner, who had known Walter in Detroit and was well informed on the labor situation. Reisner had arranged the preliminary meetings between Reuther and me and Walter Geist, president, and Harold Story, counsel, of Allis-Chalmers. Then Mr. Reisner arranged for a further meeting at his own home. Some officers of the company were present, several leaders of the local union, Reuther, and Reisner. It was the dead of winter, a terribly cold and stormy day. Reporters had been dogging the negotiators' steps all the way, and were waiting outside in the cold, even with a newsreel truck. Reisner stage-managed things. He asked those present to join him in prayer, which threw the Communists off balance from the beginning.

The company representatives made it clear that they were ready to accept an agreement which seemed fair and reasonable. The Communists struggled to stay angry, while everybody else got along well. At one point, one of the Communists managed to provoke a heated exchange with one of the company men, and it looked as though the meeting might break up in a fight after all. Just then, the minister's puppy came in and made a mess on the floor. That broke up the argument. An agreement was finally reached by everybody but the local boys, who said they would have to consult. What that meant was that they wanted to check with Harold Christoffel, who was honorary president of the local and, as leader of the local Communists, the power behind the throne.

Christoffel issued a statement blasting the settlement. Nevertheless, Reuther took it back to the executive board in Detroit, and made a fight for it. Thomas was able to bring together a majority to reject it, and a statement was issued which was almost the same as Christoffel's. But this was not a victory for the Thomas forces; on the contrary, Reuther made this question a major issue in his campaign for the presidency of the UAW. The strikers started going back to work, and eventually the strike was broken. Reuther secured a good contract with the company after Communist control of the local was ended. This issue alone gave him enough of a weapon to smash the Communist opposition in the UAW.

About this time I had a long talk with Emil Mazey, who had been away on military service, but had been re-elected to the executive board on his return and was still feeling his way in the changed situation. He drove me to my hotel from a meeting of the board, and we sat in his car discussing what was going on. He was undecided between Reuther and Thomas and wanted the views of a veteran observer. I told him I thought Reuther had the power securely in his hands because he had the ability, he knew how to meet the responsibilities of the presidency, and none of his opponents could measure up to him. I drew parallels from my own experience, and I think Mazey was impressed. He is now secretary-treasurer of the UAW. Later, I did much the same thing in describing to Murray what had happened. Murray still had his doubts about Reuther, but I think he took my praise of Reuther's handling of the situation seriously. This particular fight helped convince Murray that the time was at hand for the campaign against the Communists, which he carried through successfully during the next two or three years.

My time as Director of Councils was by no means taken up entirely with holding the left wing in check. There were innumerable problems on which I had to advise the local bodies from time to time, having to do with types of legislation favored by CIO and similar matters. One activity that I was associated with in 1940 has been greatly expanded and developed, the idea of community-service work by the unions in the health and welfare fields. Irving Abramson, president of the New Jersey State CIO Council, and Ted Silvey, secretary-treasurer of the Ohio State CIO Council, were the prime movers, along with me, in setting up a CIO Committee for British and Allied War Relief, in the latter part of 1939 and early 1940. After a while, we got a very generous response from the workers. Abramson was chairman of the committee, Silvey was secretary, and I was treasurer. When the United States was drawn into the war, we changed the name to CIO War Relief Committee. Altogether we raised millions of dollars which were devoted primarily to helping trade unionists in the war-devastated countries, though it was not long before we were directing our funds through other organizations to all kinds of people who needed aid.

After the war, we had a record of accomplishment and thousands of people who had learned to organize and carry through a fund-raising drive, so we thought we should make use of that experience. We became the CIO Community Services Committee (now the AFL–CIO Community Service Activities). Leo Perlis, as director, has made this a very successful agency. The effort was now directed to encouraging trade unionists to contribute to community causes. Labor men served on the boards of Community Chests and welfare organizations. We organized training courses for our people, bringing in experts from the charitable and welfare organizations to explain their purposes and functioning. This work continued as long as CIO existed, and has carried over into the merged AFL–CIO. I continued my association with this work; my latter years of activity were devoted primarily to Community Services and voluntary health and welfare agencies; and I did not lose interest in this work after my retirement. It has been a very important means of drawing the labor movement into community life, and of fostering understanding between labor and other elements of the population.

Another activity we got under way was the National Resources Committee. I headed this Committee, manned by members drawn from the CIO State Councils. Its concern was with flood control of the Missouri and other rivers and water power development and irrigation, particularly in western areas of the country. For several years this Committee did a great deal of educational work among CIO members and the general public. This work continued up until the merger. The issue in one form or another still is a live subject before Congress.

During the war and afterward, I served on several government bodies. The history of my part in these activities is amply spread on the public record, and there is little I could add to that record, so I shall not attempt any elaborate account. I have mentioned my service as an alternate member of the National Defense Mediation Board. The Fair Employment Practices Committee was created by President Roosevelt, in June, 1941, to investigate complaints of discrimination against Negroes and other minorities in defense training programs and contracts. I was at first an alternate for Philip Murray, then later a full member of the Committee, serving throughout its life. The Committee was limited in the means at its disposal, but the public exposure of discriminatory practices, especially under wartime conditions, was surprisingly effective in opening work opportunities which had hitherto been closed. Once barriers had been lowered, it was harder to erect them again, so there were significant permanent results from this work.

I spent three years on the War Labor Board, either as an alternate or full member, from its inception in January, 1942. This was a full-time job in itself, though I continued as Director of Councils in the CIO, usually going to my office in the morning before attending the WLB. Most of the routine work in my CIO office could be handled by staff people, and fortunately, no major crises arose which would have created a conflict with my obligations to the WLB. In the work of the

Board there were very few sensational matters, though the rare instances of defiance of its decisions—like the troubles with John L. Lewis, on the labor side, and with Sewall Avery of Montgomery Ward and George P. McNear of the Toledo, Peoria, and Western Railroad, on the management side—got most of the public notice. The Board handled over 17,600 cases, of which fewer than 50 had to be referred to the President to secure compliance. The most troublesome issue was the effect of wage or price increases in creating a danger of destructive inflation. I was not always satisfied with rulings, especially in the Little Steel case, which I felt imposed a limit on wages despite increases in the cost of living caused by inadequately controlled profit-making.

Toward the end of 1942, our power to grant wage increases was curtailed by the appointment of James F. Byrnes as Director of Economic Stabilization, with the power to veto Board decisions. For the next two years, labor complained constantly, I think with good reason, that it was being made to bear almost the entire burden of the stabilization program. Van Bittner and I, as labor members of the Board, protested vehemently. However, it is interesting to see how the proliferation of what are now called "fringe benefits" developed out of this situation. This did much to overcome the dangerous effects of the President's mistake of judgment in giving Byrnes such powers.

The last government body on which I served was the Wage Stabilization Board, to which I was appointed a few months after its creation in May, 1951, serving until it was terminated in 1953. The purpose of the Board was to advise on wage increases so as to allow for increases in productivity and in the cost of living without permitting inflationary tendencies to get out of hand. It was a complex equation we had to evolve. The steel industry made a vigorous effort to overturn a decision of the Board in 1952. The industry had formidable support from the press, of course, and from many men in political office, who approved heartily of a large increase in the price of steel, but thought wage increases would be dangerous. Neither side got all it wanted in our recommendations, but the industry was determined to get revenge, by destroying the Board, for even partial frustration. The labor members were called before the House Committee on Education and Labor. There I was subjected, as were other members of the Board, to a long and irrelevant grilling which tried to establish, by the use of ancient and discredited slanders dug up by one Congressman Vail, that I was a Communist, or at least a fellow-traveler. Although nothing could be made of the mishmash Vail presented, he never had the grace to admit that he had been hoaxed, or that he was wrong in attacking me.

I found much pleasure and satisfaction in attendance at international conferences as a representative of CIO. But here again, there are very complicated stories involved, which have been covered by other accounts to which I can add little. For example, I attended the Paris Conference, in October, 1945, which established the World Federation of Trade Unions (WFTU). To exclude the CIO, the AFL had used a constitutional provision of the old International Federation of Trade Unions limiting representation to one labor center from each nation. Sir Walter Citrine, of the British Trades Union Congress (TUC), wanted an inclusive body which would bring in both CIO and the Soviet trade unions, largely because of his experience in the creation of a joint TUC–Soviet Trade Union Council as a measure of wartime co-operation. Citrine found it impossible to understand the AFL's refusal to accept CIO participation in the international movement, so he went ahead with arrangements for a world congress without the AFL. I have read statements that the AFL was right and CIO and the TUC wrong about the possibility of co-operating with the Soviet unions. That is the judgment revealed by events, but I think it gives the AFL too much credit for foresight, and misses entirely the point that its objection to CIO was as strong as to the Russians.

I was suspicious of Louis Saillant, of France, who was elected secretary of the WFTU. He sounded and acted like a Communist to me, or at least overly friendly to the Communist point of view. Therefore, when it was proposed that I become one of three assistant secretaries, I was reluctant to serve. I reported to Murray, on my return, that the constitutional safeguards against Communist domination of the Federation would be inadequate if Saillant worked with them. Murray wanted somebody who would restrain the Communists and who would keep him informed. I proposed that somebody else be named assistant secretary, and that I be sent to Paris as CIO European representative, acting as alternate for Sidney Hillman on the Bureau and Executive Committee. Hillman was ill, and could not attend regularly, so I would not be undercutting him. Murray proposed this to Hillman, but Hillman resented the idea for some reason, and turned it down. Murray renewed his pressure on me to accept the assistant secretaryship, even going so far as to send me a formal letter of appointment.

I stuck to my guns, saying again that I would go to Paris only on the

conditions I had named, and would not accept the assistant secretaryship. Murray was very much upset, and for a while our relations were
strained. He finally sent somebody else, whose experience was just
about what I had predicted. The later breakup of WFTU because of
Communist use of it for cold-war propaganda and opposition to the
Marshall Plan is too well known for me to relate.

While I was in Paris, in 1945, I also had the interesting experience of
serving as American labor consultant at a conference of the International Labor Organization. And from November, 1947, to March, 1948,
I attended the United Nations Conference on Trade and Employment
in Havana, as a labor consultant to the American State Department
mission. There I had my first contact with Latin American unions.
Cuban labor was threatened by a split at that time, because of Communist maneuvers, and I found it instructive to talk to representatives
of both sides.

In 1948, I represented CIO at the Inter-American Catholic Social
Action conference in Rio de Janeiro. There I learned much about the
problems of trade unionism in underdeveloped countries. I proposed at
the conference that the labor unions of the hemisphere prepare a comprehensive Hemisphere Plan for economic and social development, to
be presented to the various government. I like to think that if this suggestion had been followed up, we might have had something like the
Alliance for Progress a little sooner.

I have made other trips to foreign lands for the labor movement. I
was at the preliminary conference in Geneva for an international conference to set up the ICFTU. I also attended in Mexico the founding
conference of ORIT—the Inter-American Secretariat of the ICFTU—
for which I made some of the preliminary arrangements.

One of the most extensive trips I made was as a member of a trade
union delegation sent by the ICFTU to Southeast Asia in 1950 to study
labor conditions there, to meet union leaders, and to learn how the
ICFTU could assist them. Our party consisted of two Americans, an
Englishman, a Belgian, and an Indian. The party split, each unit at
times going to different countries. My unit visited Pakistan, India, Thai-
land, Hong Kong, Indonesia, Malaya, Singapore, Borneo, Formosa, the
Philippines, and Japan. We had interviews with Nehru, Chiang Kai-
Shek, MacArthur (in Tokyo), and other political and trade union
leaders in each country. Korea was on our itinerary, but that stop was
cancelled because the invasion from North Korea had begun. The trip

was fascinating and educational, and out of it came a plan of assistance to several of the struggling new unions in that part of the world. Our report and recommendation have been the basis for other missions to underdeveloped countries.

I was a member of a delegation to Israel for the dedication of a memorial to Philip Murray in the southern part of the Negev. Histadrut was our host and showed us much of Israel's remarkable progress.

All my experience, from the mine committees of my youth to international conferences, has fed my basic interest in developing a philosophy of the labor movement. As problems change with the times, we must learn to apply our basic principle—mutual aid for the common good—to the new problems.

In the 1930's the major problem confronting labor was the organization of mass production workers. Neglected or fumbled for a generation, because the crafts could not, or would not, see the need for industrial unionism, organization was substantially achieved in the late thirties and early forties, but we still have to finish the job in such industries as textiles, among migrant workers, and in many parts of better-organized industries, including the building trades.

The greatest challenge to labor today is to organize white-collar workers for co-operative action with blue-collar workers. We must recognize the vast shift from blue-collar to white-collar work. White-collar workers are, or soon will be, more than half the total labor force, and only a small fraction of them are at present organized. Labor cannot afford to postpone this job until some catastrophic depression, or to wait twenty-five years to wake up to the urgency of enrolling engineers, technicians, and similar workers in our ranks. If we fail to do the job in this decade, labor's influence will quickly dwindle.

In the 1930's, it was impossible to have a socially and economically effective movement without strong industrial unions in mass production industries. In the 1960's, it is becoming impossible for us to be effective if we fail to organize technical and clerical workers.

My early experience in the miners' union convinced me that the most efficient way to run an industry was through labor-management co-operation and planning. Experience with such committees in wartime deepened my conviction that such co-operation and planning paid off in higher production and wages, and in industrial peace.

During the last years of his life, Philip Murray came to a like opinion and developed the idea of Industry Councils, representing both management and labor, to administer long-range co-operative plans for the nation's industries. I early associated myself with this idea and spelled out in some detail the area of operation that industrial planning would cover. The framework of the scheme is based on national economic planning by boards in the various industries, which might be termed Industry Councils, made up of representatives of labor, management, and government. These councils would be tied together nationally by a National Planning Board, composed of representatives of labor, management, agriculture, and consumers, as well as government, thus assuring democratic participation in major policies affecting the economy.

The area in which democratic planning would operate would include investment, employment, and production levels; the rate and nature of mechanization and technological change; establishment of minimum wages and ceilings on the hours of labor; price ceilings established through the corporations, but subject to democratic control; questions of the nature and quality of goods produced; labor-management relations, public relations (meaning propaganda and advertising), and the foreign relations of the big corporations; policy in relation to natural resources and the location and size of industrial plants.

Legislation will be required to launch such a plan. The 1946 Employment Act will need to be amended to ensure the needed levels of employment, production, and consumer purchasing power, and to provide for the Industry Councils.

Repeatedly during the last twenty years, approximations of the plan have been proposed in response to crisis situations, but not until these first limited steps lead to the adoption of a well considered and administered plan will the crises be averted and our vast economy be freed to work for the good of all.

One of Philip Murray's greatest ambitions was to reunify the labor movement, but he died before achieving it. He felt as I did that the CIO had accomplished the work it set out to do, organizing the unorganized in the mass production industries. The zeal that CIO put into its organization campaign energized the AFL and thousands of workers flocked into the old AFL unions as well.

Walter Reuther took up where Phil left off, and he and George Meany did carry through plans for merger, which were approved by both organizations at a joint convention in 1955. It seemed to me then that the immediate objective of the united organization should be to bring non-union workers into the fold and to increase wages in keeping with the great productivity of America, including a guaranteed annual wage. There was opportunity to work for such gains as adequate retirement pensions and welfare provisions, for industrial planning as envisaged in Murray's Industrial Council plan, and for improvements in social service work.

These programs have not yet been fully realized, but the work must be done. The rapid displacement of labor because of automation and technological change makes this imperative. The Economic Council should be tripartite, with labor, management, and the public represented. It should have power to recommend to the President and Congress steps in planning basic industries and the total economy. Collective bargaining must be extended and improved.

Social objectives are equal in importance to high production. They must go hand in hand if distress among the displaced workers is to be avoided. If management refuses to co-operate, legislative powers must be secured to compel it. For the American people to achieve a balanced economy there must be democratic planning for the common good.

The labor movement today need not search for new ways and new purposes. Here is a program, basic to overcoming the imbalance of our economy; a program to bring about intelligent social planning, wide enough to embrace the problems of all our people. We must also remember that labor has a concern in the international field as well. We have had some success in assisting workers in new nations, but it is only a beginning.

The past thirty years have been glorious ones in the annals of the labor movement, but we cannot live in the past. We have met the challenge of other years, and forged ahead. Every generation must face the new problems which arise in a changing society. They must battle as we did, but with the advantage of starting from a higher level. The assignment to today's men and women of labor is to demand strong leadership of a united movement and go forth to challenge the assumption of the business and financial group that they have a vested interest and a privileged position in the operation and management of industry, which they call "free enterprise"; to extend our democracy to the economic field and to enhance the lives of the common people not only in America but throughout the world.

REFERENCE MATTER

!!!

T he most important source was John Brophy himself; the manner in which this material was secured has been described in the Introduction.

I have also had the benefit of interviews, some taped, some less formal, with Rev. Ensworth Reisner, Mrs. Regula Plowe, Adolph Germer, Harold Story, George Craig, James Carey, Michael Demchak, Allen Croyle, Irwin Klass, Frederick I. Olson, and Ted Silvey. F. J. Michel, George Hall, Colston Warne, and William P. Fidler sent me information in response to enquiries.

I have had the use of John Brophy's papers, which include some correspondence, almost all relating to union business; manuscripts of speeches, radio broadcasts, reports, press releases, magazine and newspaper articles, and some unfinished writings on the history of the coal miners; several scrapbooks; newspaper and magazine clippings; convention proceedings of District 2, United Mine Workers, of the International Union, United Mine Workers of America, and of the CIO; numerous copies of the UMW *Journal;* single numbers of various newspapers; many pamphlets and books; a complete file of the CIO *Union News Service;* a few minutes of meetings of the Committee for Industrial Organization; and a great many miscellaneous pictures and other memorabilia. All the notes and materials used in preparation of this book have been added to the Brophy collection, which has been deposited at The Catholic University of America.

Wherever possible, Brophy's account of his public activities has been checked against appropriate convention proceedings, union reports, newspaper accounts, transcripts of hearings and other government documents, books, and the recollections of other participants, all of which have demonstrated that his memory was excellent. The *New York Times,* and the Pittsburgh *Press, Dispatch,* and *Post-Gazette* have been used most extensively for this purpose; they are cited in footnotes only to indicate the source of quotations or of additional facts not included by Brophy.

It would serve no purpose to cite all books consulted. A list of those cited in footnotes or in the text (not including convention proceedings and reports of congressional hearings), plus a few others which have been particularly useful, follows:

Alinsky, Saul. *John L. Lewis, an Unauthorized Biography* (New York, 1949).

American Labor Year Book (New York, 1916–1932), 13 vols.

Blankenhorn, Heber. *Strike for Unionism* (New York, 1928).

Brooks, Robert R. R. *When Labor Organizes* (New Haven, 1937).

———. *Unions of Their Own Choosing* (New Haven, 1939).

Bruere, Robert. *The Coming of Coal* (New York, 1922).

Carnes, Cecil. *John L. Lewis* (New York, 1936).

Coleman, McAlister. *Men and Coal* (New York, 1943).

Cornell, Robert J. The *Anthracite Coal Strike of 1902* (Washington, 1957).

Dahlheimer, Harry. *History of the MESA in Detroit* (Detroit, 1951).

De Leon, Solon, ed. *The American Labor Who's Who* (New York, 1925).

Evans, Chris. *History of the United Mine Workers of America* (Columbus, n.d.).

Galenson, Walter. *The CIO Challenge to the AFL* (Cambridge, Mass., 1960).

Gluck, Elsie. *John Mitchell* (New York, 1929).

Goldberg, Arthur J. *AFL–CIO, Labor United* (New York, 1956).

Goodrich, Carter. *The Miners' Freedom* (Boston, 1925).

Hamilton, Walton H. and Helen R. Wright. *The Case of Bituminous Coal* (New York, 1926).

Harris, E. E. K. and F. J. Krebs. *From Humble Beginnings* (Charleston, W. Va., 1960).

Kampelman, Max. *The Communist Party Vs. the CIO* (New York, 1957).

Karson, Marc. *American Labor Unions and Politics, 1900–1918* (Carbondale, Ill., 1958).

Levinson, Edward. *Labor on the March* (New York, 1938; reprint, 1961).

Lewis, John L. *The Miners' Fight for American Standards* (Indianapolis, 1925).

McDonald, David J. and Edward A. Lynch. *Coal and Unionism* (Silver Spring, Md., 1939).

Morris, James O. *Conflict within the AFL* (Ithaca, N.Y., 1958).

Nelson, James. *The Mine Workers' District 50* (New York, 1955).

Parker, Glen L. *The Coal Industry* (n.p., 1940).

Pesotta, Rose. *Bread Upon the Waters* (New York, 1944).

Roy, Andrew. *History of the Coal Miners of the U.S.* (Columbus, n.d.).

Saposs, David J. *Left Wing Unionism* (New York, 1926).

Seidman, Joel. *American Labor from Defense to Reconversion* (Chicago, 1953).

Stolberg, Benjamin. *Story of the CIO* (New York, 1938).

Sulzberger, C. L. *Sit Down with John L. Lewis* (New York, 1938).

Taft, Philip. *The A.F. of L. in the Time of Gompers* (New York, 1957).

———. *The A.F. of L. from the Death of Gompers to the Merger* (New York, 1959).

Van Kleeck, Mary. *Mines and Management* (New York, 1935).

Vorse, Mary Heaton. *Labor's New Millions* (New York, 1938).

Walsh, J. Raymond. *CIO* (New York, 1937).

Wechsler, James. *Labor Baron* (New York, 1944).

Widick, B. J. and Irving Howe. *The UAW and Walter Reuther* (New York, 1949).

Wright, Helen S. *Coal's Worst Year* (Boston, 1924).

JOHN O. P. HALL

¡I¡I¡I¡I¡I¡I¡I¡I¡I¡I¡I¡I¡I¡I¡I¡I¡I¡I¡I¡I¡I¡I¡I¡I¡I¡I